"I found myself saying, 'Yes, yes, yes' as I read *Missional Spirituality*. So many books on spirituality are focused on self-improvement and private pietistic devotion, and they often leave me cold and uninspired. Roger Helland and Len Hjalmarson helpfully reconnect spirituality and mission, believing all truly Christian spiritual formation to be for the sake of the world. They take Jesus as their supreme example, the one who claimed that he was nourished by doing his Father's will and work. This book is a triumph."

MICHAEL FROST, author, *Exiles, ReJesus,* and, with Alan Hirsch, *The Shaping of Things to Come* and *The Faith of Leap*

"Roger and Len navigate a fresh perspective centered in Jesus, his creed for our lives, and the power that flows from his heart into ours and then out to the world. If you are tired of shallow outward techniques, and hungry for a deeper missional spirituality, then we highly recommend this book."

STEVE HOLT AND DANIEL ROLFE, Word & Spirit Network

"The spiritual life is lived in relationship on earth as it is in heaven. Roger and Len help us greatly by showing us how. Full of examples and ideas, *Missional Spirituality* challenges us to a more faithful and more fruitful Christian life."

KENTON C. ANDERSON, president, Northwest Baptist Seminary, and author, *Choosing to Preach*

"*Missional Spirituality* delivers on its title, reconnecting missional practice and the spirituality needed to sustain such practice. Written from the Pietist tradition but drawing on many sources, and set in the context of profound cultural transition, this book provides a theological foundation for a truly missional spirituality and a range of practices to earth this spirituality in daily life."

STUART MURRAY WILLIAMS, founder of Urban Expression

"*Missional Spirituality* is a call for the church to be committed to its spirituality by emphasizing the motivation for spiritual formation and being missional. I found myself wishing for this kind of stimulation when I began ministry forty years ago."

ARNELL MOTZ, president, Canadian Baptist Seminary

"Roger Helland and Len Hjalmarson offer us a guide to a spirituality that is deep and yet practical, mystical (in the best sense of the word) and yet missional. I recommend this book to all who do not want to escape the world, but rather want to engage and subvert the world from a life rooted and grounded in the trinitarian life of God."

PETER H. DAVIDS, Houston Baptist University

"After years of endless theoretical conversations about 'missional imagination,' Roger and Len take us to where we need to begin: a missional spirituality that creates the practices necessary for imagination and mission to emerge."

GARY NELSON, author, *Borderland Churches,* and president, Tyndale Seminary

"Doesn't spirituality end up in navel-gazing? Doesn't mission end up in spiritual burn out? No and no. Roger Helland and Len Hjalmarson show us that the biblical vision of Christianity is indeed a missional spirituality."

TODD HUNTER, author, *Christianity Beyond Belief,* bishop, Anglican Mission in the Americas

Roger Helland and
Leonard Hjalmarson

Foreword by Alan Hirsch

Missional
Spirituality

Embodying God´s Love
from the Inside Out

IVP Books

An imprint of InterVarsity Press
Downers Grove, Illinois

InterVarsity Press
P.O. Box 1400, Downers Grove, IL 60515-1426
World Wide Web: www.ivpress.com
E-mail: email@ivpress.com

InterVarsity Press® is the book-publishing division of InterVarsity Christian Fellowship/USA®, a movement of students and faculty active on campus at hundreds of universities, colleges and schools of nursing in the United States of America, and a member movement of the International Fellowship of Evangelical Students. For information about local and regional activities, write Public Relations Dept., InterVarsity Christian Fellowship/USA, 6400 Schroeder Rd., P.O. Box 7895, Madison, WI 53707-7895, or visit the IVCF website at <www.intervarsity.org>.

All Scripture quotations, unless otherwise indicated, are taken from the Holy Bible, New International Version®. NIV®. Copyright ©1973, 1978, 1984 by International Bible Society. Used by permission of Zondervan Publishing House. All rights reserved.

While all stories in this book are true, some names and identifying information in this book have been changed to protect the privacy of the individuals involved.

Lyrics to "Fall" by Peter Mayer (petermayer.net) reprinted by permission. All rights reserved.

Design: Cindy Kiple
Images: rural church: ©Helena Lovincic/iStockphoto
        trailer home on flatbed: Amy Eckert/Getty Images

ISBN 978-0-8308-3807-3

Printed in the United States of America ∞

Library of Congress Cataloging-in-Publication Data

Helland, Roger.
    Missional spirituality: embodying God's love from the inside out/
Roger Helland and Len Hjalmarson.
       p. cm.
    Includes bibliographical references (p.   ).
    ISBN 978-0-8308-3807-3 (pbk.: alk. paper)
    1. Spirituality. 2. Mission of the church. I. Hjalmarson, Len,
1960- II. Title.
    BV4501.3.H445 2011
    248'.5—dc23

2011023118

P	18	17	16	15	14	13	12	11	10	9	8	7	6	5	4	3	2	1
Y	26	25	24	23	22	21	20	19	18	17	16	15	14	13	12	11		

Contents

Foreword

Having written recently on the largely unexplored subject of missional discipleship in my book *Untamed*, I have become increasingly aware of how narrowly we tend to interpret what is known as Christian spirituality—the field of study of how God's people can engage and grow in him. Consult the standard reference books on the subject, whether popular or technical, and you will find an avalanche of good, articulate and even profound material. You will discover that when theology is not just a collection of heady ideas but is taken to heart, it feeds the soul. These writings will introduce you to a vast array of weird and wonderful people called "saints," who can intrigue you with their rather mystical and poetic wonderings of the spirit. Lastly, you will find veritable handbooks on spiritual disciplines: prayer, *lectio divina*, solitude, fasting, service and so on.

But seldom will you find books on what we can call a *missional spirituality*—a spirituality for the road, one that you can carry with you into the rough-and-tumble of everyday life. Most of our traditional spiritualities seem to require some form of dualistic disengagement from the world, a retreat into a religion of quiet moments and quiet places. While solitude and silence clearly are necessary, they are not the place or situation where most of us live

our lives—nor are we called to do so. And perhaps more important, most spiritualities are not specifically formulated to help us
become high-impact people in the various worlds in which we are
called to be Jesus' disciples and witnesses. We are left with the
impression that Christian spirituality is for the religious special-
ist, for the full-time Christian, for introverts, for people with too
much time on their hands.

I have always felt that this dualistic approach to life runs contrary to the kind of robust, loving, distinctly *embodied* form of
discipleship in our Scriptures. The Bible can become a sort of
crash course in what it means to pursue and hold on to God in the
context of the rough-and-tumble of a life well lived. It is played out
by fiery prophets, warrior-poets, crazed mystics, madcap activists,
fearless missionaries and an upside-down Messiah who engages
the unwashed masses not as some mystic who floats above the
earth but as a friend and Savior who enters our world as one of us.
Together they give us a picture of the ideal God-life altogether different from the somewhat sappy one idealized in the canons of
Western spirituality.

Missional Christianity, to my mind at least, offers a far more
biblical Christianity—partly because it rejects the incipient dualism that infests much of our thinking of God and spirituality, but
also because it takes life and context seriously. So *Missional Spirituality* will help us be empowered and embodied witnesses in the
very contexts in which we are each called to live. Roger Helland
and Len Hjalmarson have gifted us with a red-hot text, one appropriate to the red-hot life we are called to live. *Lechaim!* To life!

Alan Hirsch

Preface

You may ask, "There's so much out nowadays with the ambiguous label *missional*, so why even use the term?" In spite of its changing nuances, we continue to employ *missional* in the same way many continue to employ terms like *evangelical* or *liberal*. *Missional* has both ongoing context and ongoing currency, and this book is an attempt to enrich its meaning and application.[1]

The theological and practical connections between spirituality and mission with God will continue to be developed, because spirituality and mission are inseparable. Like the strands in DNA, they are a twinned pair. The Great Commandment and Great Commission are also twinned. When Jesus said, "My food . . . is to do the will of him who sent me and to finish his work" (John 4:34), he made a direct connection between his spiritual life *in* the Father and his mission *for* the Father.

We like to use the metaphor "coming home" to picture an integrated, not isolated, connection between being and serving in the Father's house of love. Richard Foster writes,

> It is not wrong for us to isolate some aspect of the spiritual walk for the sake of study, as long as we understand the artificiality of the isolation. Perhaps the technical sciences can

ignore the whole for the part, but in the spiritual walk it is ruinous. The life with God, hid in Christ, is a unity, a seamless robe.[2]

We hope to contribute to the missional conversation as we move through and beyond discussions of missional church and missional leadership to explore missional spirituality. The theological substance and structure for what we call *missional spirituality* is rooted in Mark 12:28-34. Journey with us as we explore together what it means to love the Lord our God from all our heart, soul, mind and strength, and our neighbor as ourselves.

Acknowledgments

In the winter of 2009, Roger sat at his home office desk in prayer and reflection. The notion that entered his mind was *Hmmm, seems like the time to write another book . . . but I wonder if Len would be interested in doing something together.* He tucked the thought away, possibly to return to it.

A week passed, and Roger received an email from Len, who mused, "Hey, been wondering if we should do a writing project together." Well, go figure! Long story short, we met for a couple of hours in Len's living room in Kelowna, British Columbia, agreed on our theme and then a title, later developed an outline and who would write what, and got to work early in 2010.

We knew we had a mutual passion to write on missional spirituality and to frame it within the theological contours of the Great Commandment. With Roger in Calgary, Alberta, and Len in Kelowna, hundreds of emails and edits back and forth kept us busy off and on for a year. As longtime friends and fellow workers, our hope is you'll hear our voices in stereo.

Special thanks to Dr. Peter Davids of Houston Baptist University, who read the entire first draft and offered scrupulous comments and suggestions. Also to our editor, David Zimmerman, and our external reader and copyeditor, whose combined keen input improved the style, structure and substance of the final draft considerably.

Roger acknowledges his debt of love to all the pastors and people in his Alberta district, some of whose stories here are examples of missional spirituality. Special appreciation also goes to his associate, Murray Jarman, whose ideas and leadership reflect a missional passion and purpose. Len acknowledges his debt of love to his band of brothers who met monthly together in Kelowna as a Theology Café. Affectionate acknowledgments go to our wives, Gail and Betty, who sacrificed their needs for our presence while we holed up with our computers for more hours than you can imagine. Finally, we bow before the Father, Son and Spirit who gave us a passion for our subject and an invitation to join them on mission together.

1

Exploring a
Missional Spirituality

*Every few hundred years in Western history, there occurs
a sharp transformation. Within a few short decades, society
rearranges itself—its worldview; its basic values; its social and
political structure; its arts; its key institutions. Fifty years
later, there is a new world. And the people born then cannot
imagine the world in which their grandparents lived and into
which their own parents were born. We are currently living
through just such a transformation.*

PETER DRUCKER, POST-CAPITALIST SOCIETY

What should we do when we are neither here nor there? One
April Sunday, Len's family visited a young church community in
their city. On the way to the meeting they noticed two very different restaurant signs. The first said, "Come in from the cold; warm
food and hot drinks." The second proclaimed, "Swing into spring.
Escape the heat with our smoothies and frappacinos." So, is it
winter or spring? Contradiction is an active element in times of
transition. When the seasons change, the old season hasn't quite
made its way to the new season. We don't know what brand of

weather to expect or whether to wear a jacket or a T-shirt. As we walk out the door, it could be chilly or warm. Or it might begin warm then shift to cold later.

Peter Drucker calls the changes happening in Western culture "transformation." We identify this as "liminality"—a threshold, an in-between place of ambiguity and uncertainty, disorientation and transition.[1] As Roger attended an Easter church service with his wife and kids, on the pulpit was a Bible, on the PowerPoint were the verses, and in his and his son's hands were their iPhones with Bible apps to fetch the same verses in any translation they chose. The "worship band" used a grand piano, an electric drum kit, a bass, acoustic and electric guitars, congas, video clips, hymns, psalms and contemporary songs. Grandmas, baby boomers, young adults, youth and children all sang and were "sermonized" together.

Anxiety is generated as we struggle to adapt to our bold new world. In *Bold New World*, futurist William Knoke argues that we are entering "the age of everything-everywhere" a "placeless society" where the difference between near and far is erased and where a resurgence of religion is likely to occur as people strive to cope with rapid change.[2] This is a great opportunity for the church to welcome these wanderers home. For those born in this new world, all seems normal, for that is all they know. Those born before tend to cling to "the good ol' days." While many grandmas don't use email, three-year-olds are as adept with their PCs as they are with their puzzles. T. S. Eliot wrote,

> In order to arrive at what you do not know
> You must go by a way which is the way of ignorance.
> In order to possess what you do not possess
> You must go by the way of dispossession.[3]

As we wander in liminality, God invites our attention. As we struggle to make things work as they once did, we are forced to discover new levels of dependence. Yet our inner resistance to change is profound. Walter Brueggemann wrote, "The dominant ideology of our culture is committed to continuity and success . . . and is also resistant to genuine newness and real surprise. It is curious but true, that *surprise* is as unwelcome as is *loss*. And our culture is organized to prevent the experience of both."[4] A missional spirituality is imperative during transformation. Only radical commitment to God's kingdom, as we walk in the ways of Jesus in the power of the Spirit will enable us to welcome newness and surprise as we join God on mission to reach lost people who also experience liminality.

In 2007, Roger and his wife, Gail, stepped out of their haven and ventured alone into an ocean of liminality where they questioned their own ability to verify God's leading. After pastoring for sixteen years and with a newly earned doctorate in hand, Roger thought God was leading him to return to full-time teaching in a seminary back east. Close, but no cigar! Instead, a denominational position in Alberta was in the cards. That summer, they gave away their daughter in marriage, left the home and community where they had lived for more than twenty years, and said goodbye to their friends and their two sons in Kelowna. Roger became the district executive coach for twenty-seven Baptist churches in Alberta in the areas of missional leadership, disciple making and church planting.

Eight months later, he learned that he had prostate cancer and then had surgery in August 2008.[5] Looking back, the couple realized that in the summer of 2007, in just a couple of weeks, they became empty nesters and changed jobs, churches, communities, provinces and homes. As they accepted God's next assignment, they also acquired a new and gnawing anxiety, uncertainty and grief over the loss of close contact with family and friends. They became strangers and uprooted resident aliens in a place not their home. How would they reach their neighbors when they knew few people now? How would they live a missional life? They needed to recalibrate their theology, ministry and spirituality. Complaining? No. Consternated? Yes.

In 2000, Len and his wife, Betty, ventured out of their haven of an organized faith community into their personal ocean of liminality. They left a secure place, where they knew the rules, for the uncharted waters of the future. That process launched them onto an emotional and spiritual voyage that they did not predict or expect and that they barely knew how to put into words. They began to do church in their home, mostly with unbelievers, and for three years had little connection to the broader church. Then suddenly in 2007 they became connected to Metro Community, a church plant in the core of Kelowna's downtown, among recovering addicts and street people. In 2009 both their daughters left home, and one married.

In late 2010 Len and Betty left the security and familiarity of Kelowna, where they had resided for twelve years. They moved clear across the country to Aylmer, Ontario, leaving furniture, friends and family behind to lead a church of five hundred into a multicongregational expression and church planting.

The author of Hebrews described Abraham as going but not knowing. And so it is with us. It's difficult to grasp what a mission-shaped spirituality is like while we live in a security-focused culture. When tomorrow looks the same as today, when our world is stable and predictable, we have little need for faith. Robertson Davies wrote, "The world is full of people whose notion of a satisfactory future is, in fact, a return to an idealized past."[6]

A more positive posture, and one that many organizations use to navigate the wide ocean of change, is to become constant learners and adaptive leaders who can change while standing on unshakable ground.[7] Missional leaders know the unshakable ground of God's covenant faithfulness, offered to us in biblical narratives—narratives that relate both sides of the story: adaptation and change, fear and denial. Narratives like the exodus—Israel leaves the comfort of Egypt and Joshua crosses the Jordan to enter the Promised Land—offer us both confidence to move ahead and correction for those who won't let go of the past and prefer a return to Egypt. As New York Yankees coach Yogi Berra mused, "The future ain't what it used to be!"

As we write, our world is very different than it was even a decade ago. The Y2K frenzy vanished like a mist; 9-11 forever introduced a new world of airport security and the ideology of terrorism.[8] Hurricane Katrina, Haiti's earthquake, Australia's floods, and Japan's earthquakes and tsunamis wrought unimaginable devastation. ADSL, avatars, Bing, Blackberries, blogs, digital cable, DVRs, flat-screen TVs and monitors, Facebook, Google, Google Earth, GPS, HDMI, iPhones, iPods, iPads, Kindle, reality TV, texting and sexting, Twitter, Wii, Wikipedia, Windows XP, Vista and Windows 7, YouTube—all appeared in the past decade. In 2009 alone, the United States inaugurated an African American president, recession ransacked the global economy, Michael Jackson died, Susan Boyle soared to stardom, and Tiger Woods tumbled to shame.

Meanwhile 80 percent of churches in North America have plateaued or are in decline because most of them don't know how to handle change or how to engage their culture. Many prefer to dig in and grasp the past rather than move ahead. Will we "leave this place and go" with God's presence before us (Exodus 33)?

Moreover, a shift in tasks and traditional roles impacts our sense of cultural identity. The proliferation of both Christian and non-Christian gay relationships, common-law living, divorce, "cougars," blended families, single-parent families, and avatar and Internet relationships cause us to feel uprooted and anxious. Our children tell us, "This is the way it is, not like it was when you were our age." As we drift in a moral quagmire, suicide, addictions, physical and sexual abuse, bullying, Internet pornography, depression, loneliness, and homelessness are prevalent signs of a

disintegrated culture shaped incessantly by the voracious appe-
tites of consumerism, the cult of personality and media satura-
tion. Welcome to the jungle!

Yet there is interest in Jesus and "spirituality," though many in
our culture disrespect Christians and don't want church.[9] Are we
the kind of people who will, with the Bible in one hand and a
newspaper in the other, face the onslaught of relentless missional
challenges in our culture?

Annie Dillard powerfully pictured the kind of challenge we
face when she wrote about Sir John Franklin's ill-fated expedition
in search of the Northwest Passage. Franklin left England in 1845
on two ships with a crew of 138 officers and men. He and the crew
knew they were headed out into unknown waters on a journey of
discovery, but they did not know what lay ahead. Not a single
member of the crew survived. Most of their bodies were eventually found in shallow graves dispersed across the frozen Arctic
wasteland. What happened? Alan Roxburgh suggests we consider
their manifest.

The manifest is a telling description of what these adventur-
ers understood to be important and necessary for the journey. It captures the narrative in which they lived, a narrative
that would destroy them because it made little sense in the
environment of the Arctic. Franklin equipped his ships with
a 1,200 volume library, a hand organ that played fifty tunes,
china place settings and expensive silver flatware.

These early Victorian era Englishmen took their world
with them. So important were these elements of their normal life in England that they only carried a twelve-day supply of coal for their auxiliary engines, knowing the journey
would last two to three years. Lodged deep inside them were
the habits and customs of their world, which determined
what they took with them when they abandoned ship to seek

help. Bodies were found lying out on the frozen ice or in shallow graves with their silver beside them. Despite their brave commitment to explore a new way through the North West Passage, Franklin and his crew went with the assumptions of a 19th Century English world and it killed them in the new space they entered.[10]

This is a pertinent image of the turbulent journey we face. The programs and techniques we can bring with us to innovate mission-shaped life are like the china plates and library books that provisioned Franklin's ship—symbols of what shaped his imagination. We easily underestimate the challenge, and when we attempt to predict the future based on the past, we bring useless baggage with us. When we rely on skills we learned in a twentieth-century analog world, we overestimate our ability to deal with the twenty-first-century digital world. We need a dynamic spirituality. We need to leave the familiar items behind and camp out as a mobile body of living people who journey together toward new horizons. Hans Küng writes,

> The Church is always and everywhere a living people, gathered together from the peoples of this world and journeying through the midst of time. The Church is essentially *en route*, on a journey, a pilgrimage. A Church which pitches its tents without looking out constantly for new horizons, which does not continually strike camp, is being untrue to its calling.[11]

Coming Home to Our Father's House

In a Greco-Roman world not unlike our own—a world of pluralism, oppression, massive social issues and disruptive change—enter twelve-year-old Jesus. Luke 2:41-52 records the only boyhood account of him: He and his parents made the journey to Jerusalem for the annual Feast of the Passover, which celebrated Israel's freedom from slavery in Egypt (Exodus 12). After the feast,

Joseph and Mary began the trip home while Jesus stayed behind in Jerusalem. They had gone about a day's journey before they realized he was not with them. After a frantic search for Jesus without success, they eventually returned to Jerusalem.

Finally, Joseph and Mary discovered Jesus sitting among the teachers in the temple as he listened and asked questions; all were amazed at his understanding and answers. When Mary saw him, she asked, "Son, why have you treated us like this? Your father and I have been anxiously searching for you" (Luke 2:48). His reply, the first recorded words of Jesus in this Gospel, challenged his mother's query with two questions: "'Why were you searching for me? . . . Didn't you know I had to be in my Father's house?' But they did not understand what he was saying to them" (vv. 49-50).

The Jerusalem temple—the Father's house—was the center of Jewish religious life. The world would experience radical transformation in one brief generation. Meanwhile Jesus' awareness of his unique relationship with his Father defined his identity and mission. William Hendriksen writes,

> It is clear from this answer that Jesus even at the age of 12 was deeply conscious of the unique relation between himself and his Father in heaven. Later on, he would refer to this marvelous theme repeatedly. It is he alone who thoroughly knows the Father, and the Father alone who thoroughly knows him (Luke 10:21, 22; cf. Matt 11:25-27). He was conscious of having been sent by the Father, whose will he always obeyed (John 6:37-40, 44, 57; 8:18, 28, 29, 38, 49, 54, 55). He is *one* with the Father (John 10:30, and read the intensely stirring chapter 17 of John's Gospel); and he finally commits his spirit to the Father (Luke 23:46).[12]

From an early age, Jesus carried a deep sense of mission, founded on his clear sense of identity. "His entire life was controlled by the 'divine must,' which was in complete harmony with his own desire (Ps 40:7; Jn 10:17, 18). The Gospels are full of this idea of *necessity*."[13] This missional necessity compelled Jesus to be about the Father's will and work. He *had* to be about his Father's affairs, in his Father's house (Luke 2:49). He did only what he saw his Father doing and taught only what he heard from him. Intimacy bonded Jesus to his Father. He was at home with the Father, secure in his family relationship. What about us?

Len's Homecoming

When Len and Betty left their church home in the fall of 2000 and ventured on a journey of discovery, they found that the church's role and rituals looked very different from outside the institution. They realized how insular and isolated church culture was. They had been so busy with other believers and events that they had no significant contact with non-Christians. They now found time to open their doors. On Sundays they ran a meal program for the poor. With few structures to rely on, they opened the Word for themselves and learned a new dependence on the Spirit. They slowed down enough to listen for the way back home.

Jesus said, "Make your home in me, as I make mine in you" (John 15:4 JB). God is our Father and we are children in his family, members of God's household (Ephesians 2:14; 1 Timothy 3:15). He invites us to come home. From Hallmark cards to Thomas Kinkade paintings, home is depicted as an enchanted place of warmth and beauty. In the movie *The Wizard of Oz*, Dorothy concluded, "There's no place like home." Leonard Sweet puts it this way: "We're headed home. We're headed toward wherever Jesus is, and wherever Jesus is that's home. . . . Our journey is a homecoming."[14] In American culture, a baseball diamond has a *home* plate. There are reasons home means so much to Americans. America was founded by a group of people who went there to create a new home. Americans have a strong sense of home and national pride, and their homeland has never been occupied militarily by another country.[15]

Do you long to come home? The word *home* carries powerful images and feelings, a sense of warmth, shelter, rootedness, safety and security. *Home is where the heart is.* Yet in this world, millions are homeless. Some are homeless because of inner pain. Others are driven from their hometowns and countries by violence. In refugee camps and overnight shelters we see homelessness. Still others, locked in urban and suburban concrete and steel, suffer in isolation. Yet Jesus invites us to come home.

We understand that the image of coming home and the image of father are not positive ones for many people. For some, *home* and *father* bring up terrible feelings and memories of abandonment, abuse, anger or alcoholism. We long for love, for security, for acceptance. We must bring our own story of brokenness into the biblical story that speaks of the Father's house as a place of wholeness, warmth and welcome.

The Father is accessible and lavish with love. He adopts us as his children into his new family system (Romans 8:15; Ephesians 1:5; 2 Corinthians 6:18). God's household is the church of the living God, the pillar and foundation of the truth (1 Timothy 3:15; Ephesians 2:19). The Canadian worship band Downhere chose their name to reflect the reality of a Father who comes down here to us. With Christmas, the Father came down through his only Son whom he gave up for us.

Perhaps the root issue is that many of us feel like exiles living in a world that can't satisfy our deepest longings. Tim Keller suggests that, like the prodigal son,

> we are all exiles, always longing for home. We are always travelling, never arriving. The houses and families we actually inhabit are only inns along the way, but they aren't home. Home continues to evade us. The message of the Bible is that the human race is a band of exiles trying to come home.[16]

The prophet Jeremiah preached of exile and homecoming. Many

believers share Jeremiah's sense of exile. They do not find their church experience a place of safety and welcome. We know scores of Jesus followers who keep the faith but long for spirituality and community and to live missionally, not frantically, in their culture. Perhaps, as Reggie McNeal suggests, "The North American church culture is not spiritual enough to reach our culture."[17]

A Missional Spirituality

From the perspective of first-century Jewish culture, there are several taboos violated in the story of Jesus and the Samaritan woman at the well in John 4. Jesus spoke with a woman in public: forbidden. Jesus accepted water from her. His actions preached a message. Jesus altered *everything*.[18]

He then announced, "Believe me, woman, a time is coming when you will worship the Father neither on this mountain nor in Jerusalem. . . . The true worshipers will worship the Father in spirit and truth, for they are the kind of worshipers the Father seeks" (vv. 21-23). He announced one of the most revolutionary theological changes ever to a Samaritan woman in public at noonday. That day, she came home to the Father. Many Samaritans also believed, and they came home too. The Samaritan woman drank from that spiritual well and became a spiritual spring herself.

The disciples returned and were surprised to find Jesus talking with this Samaritan woman in public. Astounded with Jesus, she left her water jar and ventured back to tell her story to the town folk in Sychar. She became a local missionary for Jesus who told her story to those in her own community. The disciples then urged Jesus to eat something. He replied, "I have food to eat that you know nothing about. . . . My food is to do the will of him who sent me and to finish his work" (vv. 32-34).

Jesus then made a missional connection for the disciples: "I tell you, open your eyes and look at the fields! They are ripe for harvest" (v. 35). The word *ripe* literally means "white." It could have referred to the streaming crowd of people dressed in white. Multitudes in Sychar became believers because of the woman's testimony (vv. 39-41).

What sustained Jesus while on mission? While on mission through Samaria, Jesus *fed* on the Father's will and work, and this produced a harvest. He invited his followers to enter his work. He connected spirituality and mission.

†

On a fall Tuesday morning in Edmonton, Alberta, in 2007, Roger sat in a meeting with a group of fellow pastors from the district where he served. The reading and discussion revolved around what it meant to be missional leaders in their district. The group discussed the John 4 passage above and how they needed to apply the words of Jesus to open their eyes and look at the ripe harvest fields in Edmonton. Only 13 percent of Canadians attend church on Sundays, and even though 80 percent of Canadians say they believe in God, they don't believe in the church.[19] In fact, the Christian and Missionary Alliance has officially declared Canada a mission field.

As the group talked, Dennis, one of the pastors, made a remark that shifted everyone's perspective: "Notice that spirituality is directly connected to mission: Jesus' food was to do the will of the Father who sent him and to finish his Father's work. God's will and work fed Jesus. We must feed on doing the Father's will and finishing his work." That statement caused a paradigm shift among them.

Roger mused before the group, "What does it mean for me to spiritually enjoy and nourish myself doing the Father's will and work to the same degree I enjoy and nourish myself on Boston Pizza?" This is missional spirituality in its essence. The extent to which we are transformed is the extent to which we can bring transformation. A missional spirituality moves from the inside out. Private piety must flow toward mission. N. T. Wright teaches,

> There is ultimately no justification for a private piety that doesn't work out in actual mission, just as there is ultimately no justification for people who use their activism in the social, cultural or political sphere as a screen to prevent them from facing the same challenges within their own lives—the challenge, that is, of God's kingdom, of Jesus' lordship, and of the Spirit's empowering. If the gospel isn't transforming you, how do you know it will transform anything else?[20]

Without a missional spirituality, we run the risk of becoming mere activists who simply engage in community service, justice-making or overseas missions projects. Reggie McNeal remarks, "Missional is a way of living, not an affiliation or activity. . . . To think and live missionally means seeing all of life as a way to be engaged with the mission of God in the world."[21] On the Missional Church Network website, Brad Brisco describes what it will take for the church to foster a missional posture. The first element is "start with spiritual formation":

> God calls the church to be a sent community of people who no longer live for themselves but instead live to participate with Him in His redemptive purposes. However, people will have neither the passion nor the strength to live as a counter cultural society for the sake of others if they are not transformed by the way of Jesus. If the church is to "go and be" then we must make certain that we are a Spirit formed community that has the spiritual capacity to impact the lives of others.[22]

We can't give what we don't have, and what we have to give is who we are. Christians must be real-life models of Christ's words and works. A missional spirituality is *fundamental to discipleship*, as Christ followers must become more like their Master, the founder and head of the church, the new humanity (Ephesians 2), and enlist in the movement of the Way. As apprentices and adherents of Jesus Christ, disciples engage in practices that help cultivate spiritual formation to assist them in the goal (*telos* in Greek) of becoming like him (Luke 6:40) to embody and propagate his kingdom message. We become everyday people on everyday mission right here and right now.[23] To be a disciple is to follow Jesus on mission, for he said, "Come, follow me, . . . and I will make you fishers of men" (Mark 1:17).

Missional spirituality is not primarily about self-improvement, spiritual disciplines, personal devotional life or even spiritual formation for our own sake. Spiritual formation, as Jeffrey Greenman defines it, "is our continuing response to the reality of God's grace shaping us into the likeness of Jesus Christ, through the work of the Holy Spirit, in the community of faith, *for the sake of the world.*"[24] Christian spiritual formation happens when the human spirit is formed into Christlikeness. Paul referred to this: "My dear children, for whom I am again in the pains of childbirth until Christ is formed in you" (Galatians 4:19). The word *formed* comes from *morphe*, which means "to shape." When combined with Greek prepositions, it is rendered "conformed" in Romans 8:29 and "transformed" in Romans 12:2.[25]

However, according to Eugene Peterson, "Somewhere along the way, most of us pick up bad habits of extracting from the Bible what we pretentiously call 'spiritual principles' or 'moral guidelines' or 'theological truths,' and then corseting ourselves in them in order to force a godly shape on our lives"[26] so we can live "Christianly." *Missional* means to participate in God's mission as he *and* we work out his will in the world. *Spirituality* means to live in and by the Holy Spirit. To be genuinely spiritual is not institutional. We are spiritual to the extent that the Spirit's presence permeates our lives and our churches in ways that can only be explained as his work. So, the goal of Christian spirituality is to be enlivened by God's Spirit.[27]

A *missional spirituality is a spirituality that forms and feeds mission.* Spiritual disciplines will *form* us, and doing the Father's work in community will *feed* us. We need disciplines of both abstinence and engagement, and we need the shared practices of communal life.[28] However, temple spirituality is a significant issue for us.

Temple Spirituality

Missional spirituality is not confined to buildings—in "God's house." That's temple spirituality. Temples represent settled religion. They are immobile and lend themselves to predictable forms. As Winston Churchill remarked, "We shape our buildings; and afterwards our buildings shape us."[29] Temple spirituality is dualistic: Sunday is sacred while Monday through Saturday are secular. Temple spirituality views God as a church-based deity whom we worship once a week, but Jesus was a seven-days-a-week mobile Messiah. Temple spirituality builds around priests and rituals; missional spirituality commissions priests to daily service in the world.

Though Jesus visited the temple, he revealed that his own body was the temple (John 2:19-22). And Stephen's words recorded in Acts 7:48-50 remind us that God "does not live in houses made by men." While we sometimes prefer this religious framework because it puts God on call for us, our God is wild and free. He invites us to live in the same freedom, in the awareness that the whole world is his footstool. The old temple was composed of bricks and mortar; the new temple is flesh and blood animated by the living Spirit (Ephesians 2:21).

The clash between the old physical symbol and the new reality came to a head at Jesus' crucifixion. The curtain in the temple was torn in two from top to bottom (Matthew 27:51). That became quite a theological visual aid. Gone was the need for temples, priests, altars and sacrifices. In A.D. 70, the Romans destroyed the entire Jerusalem temple. The church as God's people is now the spiritual temple (1 Corinthians 3:16; 2 Corinthians 6:16). Hugh Halter writes,

> Whereas the altar, tents, tabernacle, and temple held God's marginalized, on-the-run, wobbling Israelites together, the ecclesia of Christ was formed, not as a physical location or a building, but as a union of decentralized communities held together by the central life force of the Holy Spirit and the teaching of an apostolic band of leaders who gave direction to the communities.[30]

When Christianity moves from the center to the margins, it moves from temple to text, says Walter Brueggemann.[31] Those who recognize the inadequacy of temple spirituality recognize the need for an embodied scriptural life, the Spirit and a radical spirituality. Yet, like a giant Bible fixed on a Communion table at the front of the auditorium, the Scripture itself can become a fixed body or form of temple spirituality. When we attempt to "live by the Book," the Bible can become a fixed document like the Law, rather than the active, living Word of God that directs people to the living Christ and his mission.

Pastors and people can also occupy themselves with Bible sermons and studies that only serve the interests of church programs and church people. Priests and professionals, isolated too long in fortresses and temples can become insulated from the nonreligious world outside. We must rediscover that God makes us "competent as ministers of a new covenant" (2 Corinthians 3:6). God made his home in the tabernacle, then in the temple, then in Christ and now in the church. God always situates himself and his people in the world, the fullness of which is his. The task of God's people, then, is to be at home with God (in spirituality) as they also serve his agenda in the world (in mission).

Roger's Journey from Pagan to Pastor

On Roger's home office wall hangs a large print of Rembrandt's painting *The Return of the Prodigal Son*. His reading of Henri Nouwen's classic *The Return of the Prodigal Son: A Story of Homecoming* inspired him to request the painting as a graduation gift from his wife after he earned his doctorate. He chose it to remind him of his growing-up years as a prodigal pagan who lived in a fractured house of twice-divorced parents and squandered his life in Southern California squalor. He also chose it to remind him of his homecoming to the Father's house at age eighteen, when a welcoming, open-armed God "rescued [him] from the dominion of darkness and brought [him] into the kingdom of the Son he loves" (Colossians 1:13). A few years later, Roger heard the call and drove north with blind faith to Canada to study at a Bible college, and then back to the United States to seminary, to eventually become a Bible college teacher and then a pastor back in Canada.

But along with many pastors, he studied in schools driven by a Christendom model that largely teach us how to serve as *professionals* in the temple in a world that's quite different today.[32] We value our education, but we mainly learned to be competent as temple scholars (what the New Testament called scribes and teachers of the law) instead of as spiritual sages. We appreciate Dallas Willard's warning,

> Pastors need to have a vision of success rooted in spiritual terms, determined by the vitality of a pastor's own spiritual life and their capacity to pass that on to others. When pastors don't have rich spiritual lives with Christ, they become victimized by other models of success—models conveyed to them by their training, by their experience in the church, or just by our culture. They begin to think their job is managing a set of ministry activities and success is about getting more people to engage those activities.[33]

Many pastors and church leaders learn professional ministry adapted from business leadership models with assumptions of success measured by increased attendance, buildings and offerings, which can drive many of them to become workaholics focused on the church business.[34] We long to be competent as sons and daughters, not fortressed in temple spirituality, freed to venture out on reconnaissance with Christ on mission in the wide-open expanse of God's cathedral in creation and culture. We are learning what it means to be beloved sons and daughters of God, at home in our Father's house, a place of feasting and fellowship—where Jesus is "about [his] Father's business" (Luke 2:49 KJV). Like others, we need new maps, compasses and logbooks to navigate the turbulent oceans of cultural change and liminality.

We acknowledge the many resources that deal effectively with spiritual disciplines and spiritual formation offered by sages and scholars alike as we build on the rich heritage of Christian spirituality. However, we find it's common to practice spiritual disciplines for the sake of oneself as a consumer, with the view that biblical sanctification and the disciplines are meant to shape our morality and holiness. But as Robert Mulholland Jr. wrote, "Spiritual formation is a process of being conformed to the image of Christ *for the sake of others*."[35]

We believe that both the process and goal of a missional spirituality is to love God and others. In fact, Willard observed, "Failure to love others chokes off the flow of the eternal kind of life that our whole human system cries out for. The old apostle minces no words: 'He who does not love abides in death' (1 Jn 3:14). . . . The absence of love is deadly. It is withdrawal."[36] Christian spirituality is both relational and ethical, inward shaping for outward expression. The theater of this spirituality is missional as it both forms and feeds mission.

Personal transformation for the sake of others suggests a new paradigm. Earl Creps asks, "How can I be changed so that others will find me worth following in mission? The way to develop a missional ministry, then, is to be transformed into a missional person, 'so that everyone may see your progress.' In the end, my best practice must be me."[37] We suggest that *a missional spirituality is an attentive and active engagement of embodied love for God and neighbor expressed from the inside out*. In a missional spirituality, we love God and others as we invite them to come home to the Father's house of love.

As church leaders, we've spent our lives exploring the vast landscape of what constitutes effective church leadership and mission, discipleship and spiritual formation. But more than that, we've endeavored to practice and embody these in our personal and vocational lives, with failures and successes along the way. We've served in a number of capacities as laymen, pastors, teachers, and denominational and parachurch leaders, as we also continue to serve as husbands and fathers. Our personal journeys of liminality in the midst of rapid church and cultural changes cause us to reflect deeply on how to follow Jesus into *his* mission and ministry.

We know that our readers share similar journeys of exploration into the nature of effective church leadership, mission and spiritual formation, mingled with pain and feelings of disappointment and inadequacy. Like many of our readers, what challenges us almost daily is how we are to understand and work out the nature and mission of the church in our complex worlds.

To leave the organized church or to disdain current expressions of it is not an option for us. We love the church, even though we offer various critiques in our book. Instead, we suggest a theological and practical framework that will help our readers navigate the rough waters ahead and experience personal and corporate spiritual renewal in the midst of their own experiences of liminality.

At the core is not the need for more leadership development or methods for church growth and missional church. We need excellent leaders and missional churches. We need a dynamic spirituality, theologically grounded and connected to mission, and discipleship with practices that cultivate love for God and others. We invite you to venture along with us as we drill into the mine of what it means to love God and others from the inside out. Perhaps you will identify with us as you glean some insights that will help in your journey.

The Journey of a Missional Spirituality

In chapter two, we provide an overview of challenges to a missional spirituality that are largely rooted in disenchantment derived from an Enlightenment ethos. In chapter three, we suggest four theological foundations that will ground and provide a practical framework for a missional spirituality: (1) the Trinity, (2) the incarnation, (3) the priesthood of all believers and (4) the Jesus Creed/*Shema* or the Great Commandment. In chapter four we show missional spirituality in action as seen in the early church and in what we call classic Pietism, expressed through the Moravians, the Methodists, and the Christian and Missionary Alliance. In chapters five through nine, we offer practices for cultivating a missional spirituality that are tied to each of the elements of the Great Commandment to love the Lord our God from all our heart, soul, mind and strength, and our neighbor as ourselves. With these practices, we develop a missional spirituality through which we embody and express God's love from the inside out.

In chapter ten, we conclude with how a missional spirituality is played out as we embody the gospel as missionaries to our own communities and workplaces, and how we can exegete and engage our culture. Finally, in our appendices we offer suggestions for equipping for a missional spirituality in the church and academy and an example of missional spirituality in action with a local church. We begin with challenges to a missional spirituality.

Suggested Primers

1. Read through John 4:1-42. Observe and reflect on Jesus' actions as a paradigm for the development of your spiritual life connected to mission.

2. Regularly pay attention to the challenges and opportunities in your community. Endeavor to open your eyes to see where your community, just like Sychar, is "ripe for the harvest." Neil Cole suggests a daily prayer at 10:02 a.m., based on Luke 10:2: Ask "the Lord of the harvest . . . to send out workers into his harvest field."

3. Reflect on how your own private piety (spiritual life) might transform you to be a missionary (one sent on mission) to bring transformation in your community.

Discussion Starters

1. What is your response to the cultural challenges that Roger and Len identify and the personal challenges they faced? What does the imagery in Jesus' statement "I had to be in my Father's house" convey to you? How do you understand the term "temple spirituality"?

2. What are the transformational and missional implications of Jesus statement to you, "My food is to do the will of him who sent me and to finish his work"?

3. How would you describe the core characteristics of what the authors mean by a "missional spirituality"? What does the metaphor "coming home" communicate to you? How does it relate to missional spirituality?

2

Challenges for a Missional Spirituality

*After preaching to an earnest congregation at Coleford,
I met the Society. They contained themselves pretty well during
the exhortation, but when I began to pray the flame broke
out: many cried aloud; many sunk to the ground; many
trembled exceedingly; but all seemed to be quite athirst for
God, and penetrated by the presence of his power.*

JOHN WESLEY, JOURNAL

If you had a group of young adults and wanted to sponsor a movie marathon one weekend, replete with pizza, popcorn and pop, what set of four movies do you think they would prefer to watch? *The English Patient, Vanilla Sky, The Hours* and *Atonement,* or *The Lord of the Rings, Avatar, Inception* and *Voyage of the Dawn Treader?* Our guess is the second four. Why? These four films captivate the imagination and create intrigue with visual effects, the "spiritual" worlds, and the tension between good and evil. In a word, they offer *enchantment.*

Disenchantment

In *The Secular Age,* Charles Taylor asks one question: What occurred between 1500 and 2000—the modern age of Western society—when in 1500 it was impossible *not* to believe in God while in 2000 it became possible? His answer: *disenchantment*, which led to secularism.

A word repeated in Taylor's book is "disenchantment," derived from Max Weber, who saw Enlightenment reason turning into modern rationalization as intelligence is used not to get to the bottom of things but to organize life from the top down, through structures of hierarchy, specialization, regulation and control. Taylor agrees that this "disenchantment of the world" leaves us with a universe that is dull, routine, flat, driven by rules rather than thoughts, a process that culminates in bureaucracy run by "specialists without spirit, hedonists without heart."[1]

Look at the architecture and icons of medieval cathedrals and medieval art in museums in Europe and you'll see *enchantment*. The premodern world "still lived with Ptolemy's map of the world in their minds. Their universe was a three-layer structure—with an enchanted earth sandwiched between heaven and hell, the natural theater for the visits of angels and demons."[2] Taylor argues that the cumulative impact of Renaissance humanism (humans are the center), the Enlightenment (the mind is the center), the scientific revolution and, yes, the Reformation,[3] made it possible to explain the mystery and majesty of the world without God. Disenchantment discards the sacred, where wonder, worship and faith thrive.

Christianity itself suffered from the disenchantment of society because of seventeenth- and eighteenth-century British, French and American deism. This philosophy shoved God out of immediate interaction with his stars, sun and earth to exist in a vast impersonal universe run by the laws of physics. Religion became a private matter divorced from the public arena. "You can be a politician, but keep your beliefs to yourself." Taylor writes,

> This was inconceivable in previous centuries . . . where reli-
> gious values, practices, parishes, guilds, and influences per-
> vaded society. God, the Bible, churches, cathedrals, holidays,
> natural world, was a world "enchanted" with the spiritual
> world of God, spirits, demons, and moral forces.[4]

Christians today regularly refer to their culture as the *secular*
world—a dark and non-Christian place. It's where one holds a secular job, attends a secular university, listens to secular music and
watches secular movies and TV. Even though all cultures express
religion and spirituality in one form or another, the so-called secular world is often wrongly perceived as a separate realm *disenchanted*
from the sacred realm where the God way up there and Christian
faith reside. Some Christians place culture in one realm and place
the institutional church, Christian faith and their personal spiritual
life in another realm. This dualism is *secularization*.[5]

Peter Berger and others argue that the seeds of secularization
originated in the Enlightenment and Protestantism, whose theology
separated reality into tiers: natural/supernatural, reason/revelation
and science/faith.[6] Conrad Oswalt summarized Berger as saying,

> The biblical concept of a transcendent God leads to "disen-
> chantment of the world" and the separation of the world
> from the sacred realm. Later, as this transcendent philoso-
> phy developed into the Christian tradition, the tendency to
> create an oppositional relationship between religion and so-
> ciety was heightened by the institutionalization of the
> church. Berger argues when the church separated itself from
> the rest of reality by locating all "religious activities and
> symbols in one institutional sphere," it defined the rest of
> the world as separate, profane, and secular. Western religion
> sponsors the divided worldview that allows reality to be di-
> vided into secular and sacred realms in the first place.[7]

A missional spirituality cannot thrive in atmospheres of disenchantment, dualism and secularism that fail to view our heavenly Father at work in our culture, in city hall, in our workplaces. As did all the ancients, Jesus lived without this dualism. He did not separate the world into sacred and secular. He turned water into vintage wine at a wedding reception, had a noon-hour theological conversation with a Samaritan woman in public, touched and healed lepers, spent more time on the road than in the Jerusalem temple, announced that his own body was the temple of God, told lots of down-to-earth stories, came eating and drinking wine to the point that people said, "Here is a glutton and a drunkard, a friend of tax collectors and 'sinners'" (Luke 7:34). Finally, Jesus scandalized religious leaders, who then executed him.

As pastors, we've both struggled with dualism and disenchantment. We, like most ordinary Christians, believe in prayer and the supernatural. Yet we are just as apt to apply business and sociological principles to see growth in our churches and are just as apt to seek medical attention before we seek God in prayer for healing. We believe the devil and demons exist, and yet we are just as apt to organize our churches or counsel our people into wholeness before we would engage in spiritual warfare or deliverance. We look at our own lives and preaching and we wonder where the power of God that Paul mentions is present.

And yet Christmas, the ministry of Jesus and the crucifixion were all enshrouded in deadly, enchanted, cosmic battles between God and Satan. While we can't entirely disenchant the crucifixion, we can unfortunately disenchant Christmas. In December 2009, a local church ran a nativity drama and art event. It consisted of the middle section of the nativity story: from the angels making the announcement to the birth of Jesus. It was light-hearted and included song and dance. The quality was impressive; skilled dancers and vocalists performed beautifully. But it lacked core biblical truth about what really occurred in the New Testament account.

This nativity play was cleansed of all conflict. It was superficial and lacked tension and risk. There was no battle between darkness and light concerning the newborn Jesus, whom Herod tried to murder. This and other historical details of the Christmas story were disenchanted in the play. It also lacked connection to real life: friends with cancer, unemployment, depression and addictions. Many years ago, Malcolm Muggeridge commented on the typical nativity celebration among Christians: "Truly, we human beings have a wonderful faculty for snatching fantasy from the jaws of truth."[8]

Missional spirituality will avoid a common tendency to consign culture to the devil and huddle into the safety of Christian ghettos and subculture, replete with its own copied versions of music and movies, services and superstars, concerts and cruises.[9] The cosmos and culture throb with God's will and work. All of life is sacred when we relate and submit all aspects of life to him. King David affirmed that God is everywhere and that we can't escape his presence. He asked, "Where can I go from your Spirit? Where can I flee from your presence?" (Psalm 139:7). It's in God that we "live and move and have our being" (Acts 17:28).

Popular films can help us with theological reflection. One such film is the comedy-romance *Chocolat*. The story is set in a small French village dominated by a religious, traditional, overbearing mayor, the Comte de Reynaud. The village is colorless and austere, drab and dusty; neither plants nor trees grow there. The people mirror the town: colorless, lifeless and dominated by fear, with fractured relationships and repressed lives.

Into this dismal place venture Vianne and her daughter, who open a chocolate store. They arrive dressed in bright-red capes, blown "by a sly wind from the north." Vianne is a beautiful woman in a town where passion of any kind is unwelcome. Coincidentally, she arrives at the beginning of Lent, when the townsfolk must deny themselves certain pleasures. The mayor himself refuses all food. As the *chocolaterie* window showcases every chocolate delight imaginable, the contest between enchantment and grace and its opposite, disenchantment and law, is set.

It would be easy to write the movie off as a battle between Christianity and paganism. But that would miss its deeper significance. Vianne is the missionary, less concerned about selling her chocolates than about building relationships that offer healing and freedom. She's warm, compassionate and inclusive as she shakes up the rigid morality of the community. She's involved in the community and revels in creativity and good food. Vianne helps the townsfolk learn to celebrate life as a gift from God. Meanwhile, Comte de Reynaud uses religion as a stern veneer of righteousness while he exercises control over the town and banishes threats to its moral stability, maintaining its disenchanted faith. Like the movie *Babette's Feast*, *Chocolat* offers compelling spiritual insights.

Excarnation

The consequence of a disenchanted faith is what Taylor calls an *ex*carnational faith—one that lives more in the head than in the heart, in the brain than in the body—opposite to *in*carnation. He writes, "Official Christianity has gone through what we can call an 'excarnation,' a transfer out of embodied, 'enfleshed' forms of spiritual life, to those which are more 'in the head.' It follows in parallel with 'Enlightenment,' and modern unbelieving culture in general."[10]

To safeguard objective truth, an excarnational faith is wary of aesthetics, intuition, spiritual discernment and gut feelings. In addition, art, poetry and music are second fiddle to reading, 'riting and 'rithmetic. The inside of an average evangelical church, designed for teaching, looks bland, abstracted and disenchanted. Bible studies, sermons, academic theology, doctrine and classes tended to become the primary *food* for evangelical faith and life.

Even though these are valuable, Reggie McNeal states, "We have very little evidence that academic or conferential learning changes behavior."[11] Have we emptied our hearts to fill our heads?

We both love books, study, academics and theology, with earned doctoral degrees in leadership and spiritual formation. We can write dissertations, books and articles, and we appear quite spiritual as we research and wrestle with deep truths. But this can become a liability. We can live in a world of ideas and words as we teach, preach and communicate information that primarily reaches people's heads. We suffer from our own brand of excarnation as we long to become more holistic and incarnational.

A major challenge for a missional spirituality is to develop a holistic approach that does not succumb to an excarnational, knowledge-based approach to spiritual formation. Doug Pagitt writes, "I believe that the knowledge-based spiritual formation of the 20th century has so reduced the call of Jesus to right belief that many become confused about why mere profession of belief does not bring life change."[12] We pump enormous amounts of biblical information into the minds of people through studies and sermons. How many, after being told the truth, can apply it? We all know about proper nutrition yet continue to eat in unhealthy ways, even when our lives are at risk. Doug describes the practices of his church, where "they forget about working on a part of a person's life, and instead work with people as if there is no distinction between the spiritual, emotional, physical, social, professional, and private aspects of life."[13]

Abstraction

An excarnational faith has roots in abstraction. Abstraction is the process in which you distance ideas from objects or subjects. For example, love, justice, faith and community become ideas we can analyze and study apart from actual people who embody them as subjects. We can discuss what it means to be a missional *church*, but it's an abstraction if we don't discuss what it means to be a missional *people*. We can preach and study spiritual formation and discipleship at an intellectual level, but if this doesn't translate into and emerge out of actual practices, we preach abstractions. Jesus taught abstract ideas but brought them down into concrete realities in his parables, showing us that there's value in going up and down the ladder of abstraction. In fact, Jesus the Word (abstract) became Jesus incarnate (concrete), who taught and lived out of who he was, not out of intellectual ideas distanced from him as a subject. We must ground a missional spirituality in practices and people, not merely in ideas and information.

Abstraction has its roots in the Enlightenment worldview—the engine of Modernity—an optimistic value placed in the potential of reason[14] and industrial progress to improve the conditions of humankind with a stress on the individual rather than on the community. The Age of Enlightenment was a period in Western philosophy and cultural life forged during the eighteenth century, when the primary source of authority was reason. A forerunner to the Enlightenment was the invention of the printing press in the fifteenth century. It opened the possibility for common people to be able to read. The shift went from hearing a live person speak to reading words on a page divorced from the body language, tone and personality of an author. Then, for the next four centuries, this new print culture helped promote a Modern worldview in which medieval enchantment became disenchantment and abstraction. Shane Hipps writes,

> By the 17th century, the [print] medium had become the dominant means of communication. These conditions embedded the bias of the printed medium deeply into the Western worldview and gave rise to the modern mindset that represented a dramatic departure from medieval European thought. This newly entrenched worldview was character-

ized by a strong emphasis on individualism, objectivity, abstraction, and reason, in contrast to the medieval worldview characterized by an emphasis on tribal, mystical, and sacramental experiences.[15]

Where previously knowledge had been transmitted verbally, face to face, print culture fostered a detached individualism. This promoted abstract thinking, linear reasoning and analysis. The messenger is separated from the message; the world is abstracted according to words on a page; and the whole is ordered into parts—in effect, the medium is the worldview.[16]

In abstraction, theology focuses on propositions. It becomes "systematic" and offers the tidy cause-effect application of principles instead of radical obedience to Christ. Living faith in a Person can become an intellectual system of beliefs, in which management replaces mystery, strategic planning replaces prayer, and the individual priesthood of the believer replaces the priesthood of the believing community.

We realize that in this book we present some abstract material, including some in this chapter. In some ways we can be self-defeating as we seek to present ideas abstracted from concrete realities in our lives. We are on a journey of renewal ourselves as we seek to integrate faith and life in which to love God and neighbor is not a concept we study but a life we must live in the daily rounds of our life. Nevertheless, our tendency at times is to diagnose life and leadership like a medical doctor diagnoses a patient. Even an emphasis on church health, where leaders diagnose church systems to grow the church, can be a form of scientific abstraction. These may be modern concerns but they are not the primary concerns of the New Testament. The New Testament measures church maturity not church health,[17] and only God can grow the church (1 Corinthians 3:6-7).

An abstracted faith and culture is free to turn Christian symbols, values and practices into religious commodities or conduct shorn of their biblical meaning and substance. This can result in strange contradictions. Someone can wear a cross as jewelry or tout biblical verses in movies and music but not believe in the Christ who died on that cross or what these verses convey. Another can place a leather Bible on a coffee table as a religious ornament but never read it. One can point upward after a touchdown or thank God at the Oscars but not worship God. One can earn a PhD and teach New Testament but not obey its teachings. Another can shop around for good music, preaching and children's programs and not follow Christ in mission.

Consumerism

Like you, we have our homes, our cars, our flat-screen high-definition TVs and our MasterCards to buy whatever whenever we want. Because we both work from our computers and cell phones, we have a yearning to own the latest version of our computers, software and iPhones. It's as difficult for us as it is for you to stand against the tsunami of a consumer culture whose mission is to convince us that more is better. Just like millions, we feel the pull to purchase more at the mall because of such good sales the day after Christmas. How do we cultivate missional spirituality in such a world? Skye Jethani warns, "Consumerism is the dominant worldview of North America. As such, it is competing with the kingdom of heaven for the hearts and imaginations of God's people."[18] Abstraction is an issue.

One aspect of abstraction is separating the world into subject and object, depersonalizing the world. It works by creating distance. One outcome of that distance is helpful: we often see clearer from a distance because we see with less personal bias. But a negative outcome of distance is the possibility of reduced ownership of the outcome. We tend to forget that only people make decisions and only people have responsibility. If we forget these things, we can become detached from our world rather than engaged in it as stewards. This outcome plays very well into a consumer culture.

In *Being Consumed*, William Cavanaugh rightly points out that there's nothing wrong with material goods per se, but the problem is consumerism, the perpetual cycle of dissatisfaction and desire with the quest to turn everything into a commodity.[19] Like Simon, who offered money to buy the gift of the Holy Spirit and the working of miracles from Peter to profit his magic business (Acts 8), we can become prosperity preachers who turn ministry into religious merchandising for profit.

In the secular world, an agent can market celebrities with products that bear their names and images. One woman said, "Those of us who are fans, we use these celebrity lives in ways that transform our own. I sometimes think that these are our gods and goddesses, these are our icons, and their stories become kind of parables for how to lead our lives."[20] A Chinese woman in Shanghai was so keen to win back her ex-boyfriend that she planned to have plastic surgery to transform herself into his favorite Hollywood actress, Jessica Alba.[21] The TV show *60 Minutes* ran a segment about the largest gambling addiction in the United States—to the new digital slot machines. They noted that there are over 850,000 slot machines in the United States (double the amount of ATM machines), with casinos in thirty-eight states, where people spend more money on slot machines than on movies, baseball and theme parks combined.[22] Consumption is addictive, win or lose.

There's a danger for Christian ministry to become another cultural form of consumerism, where

> a consumer-focused approach to ministry successfully attracted crowds, but it has failed for the most part to transform lives or construct the significant personal relationships that provide encouragement, spiritual growth, accountability and avenues for Christian ministry. . . . More and more

people spend their time just shopping around, looking for diversion while avoiding commitment.[23]

Alan Hirsch argues that if we use a seeker approach to evangelism and entertainment to attract people to Christ, the fact that we gather more religious consumers shouldn't surprise us. We can't entertain people into discipleship. Even before we come to Christ, pop culture has already formed us, discipling us through the medium of advertising, which appeals to the religious longings for identity, meaning and purpose. But church can become a mall that offers Christian goods and services that generate steady income (tithes) from satisfied customers. We must develop practices that counteract culture and conform us to Christ.[24] We cannot make missional disciples who are consumers, because they are committed only to their needs and wants.

Entitlement

Here's what can happen. If not trained in New Testament discipleship, consumer-oriented pagans who become Christians can morph into consumer-oriented church members who feel entitled to what the church offers. They can innocently become consumer advocates who submit product critiques to the "customer service" department, usually staffed by pastors or the board. Discipleship can become service to the church rather than service to the person of Jesus Christ and the local community in mission.

We've listened to countless pastors bemoan this challenge. One pastor changed the order of service so that the offering and comment cards were collected at the conclusion of the service. He said most Mondays were dreadful as the secretary and lead pastor read the comment cards with their criticisms about the music, sermon and service. He now has the offering and comment cards collected in the middle of the service, hoping to change the practice of waiting to use the comment cards like an anonymous customer-satisfaction survey. He discards anonymous cards and meets with people face to face who have legitimate complaints. This new lead pastor's vision is to stimulate rigorous discipleship and spirituality, New Testament style.

Bill Easum warns, "In an entitled system, membership, not servant-hood, is the primary goal."[25] Elected church members can gain unspiritual authority. Pastors can be hired to provide preaching, programs, care and counseling for church club members who feel entitled to have their spiritual needs met. Like shareholders, elected boards coupled with democratic votes from the members can control the "company" and its stock. But the New Testament speaks of non-elected servants and slaves rather than voting and entitled members and boards. Easum says, "Imagine a church where non-members are entitled to everything a church has to offer and the members are servants who have given up all entitlements."[26]

Extraction

For years, we've felt the overwhelming gravitational pull that church ministry has on us as pastors. We earned our degrees in theology, set up shop in local churches and soon realized that the legitimate needs in every local church are like a black hole. The never-ending demands of people's broken lives, board and committee meetings, study for preaching and teaching, counseling and crisis management, organizing weekend services, marrying and burying people, is more than a full-time job. There's little time left to engage the community and connect with unsaved people on their turf in a way that's relational and incarnational. Leading church life becomes "the ministry." However, as we serve in the temple, we are removed from the world and our mission to it.

What happens when our main goal is to assimilate people into the church and help them become good church members? Extraction. When we remove people from their natural habitat and insert them into church life, we create an artificial environment that's separate from real life. We do this with animals, taming them and creating environments that are similar to their real life. But we remove the wildness and dangers from their new habitat and end up with bored, lazy animals. We also domesticate people, leading them to become good members in the temple. This occurs when we extract them from their networks and workplaces to primarily serve in church ministries. They learn to become ministers here but not missionaries there. Rather than train members to be ministers, what if we train members to be missionaries? In most churches in the West, people can attend services and be active members and never take their faith outside the church building. No wonder we see little connection between membership and sacrifice, discipleship and dying, spirituality and mission!

Good leaders can end up on boards and committees that have no missional or spiritual focus, get buried in brain-numbing micromanagement and become rear-echelon bureaucrats disconnected from the front lines. Good people can end up as volunteers for Sunday school and the nursery, and leaders of small groups and worship, overburdened with endless church meetings. We must unleash the church to run in the holy wild, free and fruitful.

Mutant Pietism and Programism

Pietism (from the word *piety*) was a spiritual reform movement in the seventeenth and eighteenth centuries that began as a reaction to lifeless German Lutheran religion and sterile orthodoxy. Influenced by Lutheran pastor Philip Jacob Spener and his book *Pia Desideria*, or *Pious Desires*, first published in 1675, Pietism intended to balance the head with the heart. It focused on inner personal conversion, religious experience and sanctification, requiring outward evidences of the fruit of regeneration. It placed the authority of Scripture above church creeds and dogmas as the source for church and personal life. At its core, Pietism contained a *love* theology that promoted a strong missional emphasis on charity and good deeds along with the belief in the priesthood of all believers. Classic Pietism, as we'll see in chapter four, was a river of missional spirituality in action that irrigated, among others, the Moravians, the Methodists, the Christian and Missionary Alliance, and evangelical spirituality.

Enlightenment rationalism that flourished in the eighteenth century paralleled Pietism. The Pietist focus on personal Bible study and prayer, subjective experience, personal morality, and democratic authority vested in the individual paralleled the Enlightenment ethos that assumed individual human potential. During the nineteenth to twentieth centuries, Pietism mutated into various streams of evangelical spirituality that emphasized personal holiness, personal devotions and a personal relationship with Christ. The corporate dimensions of Christian life and mission and the practice of the priesthood of all believers generally receded. What resulted was an inner and individualized spirituality of "the monastery apart from the marketplace." Today, pietism generally means inward spiritual devotion and disciplines.

Renewal movements usually begin as a reaction to frustration with systems of sterile religious life. God's people tire of religion and lifeless Christianity. They want to experience joy as the Methodists did during the Second Great Awakening in America (ca. 1776-1810). A conversation between the Methodist circuit rider Francis Asbury and his apprentice, Charles, makes the point.

> "Heard you went to a Methodist meetin'," [Charles said
>   to Francis].
> "Sure did."
> "Any shoutin'?"
> "Some."
> "Why do Methodists shout?"
> "Because they're happy!"

"Can't see how anyone could be happy in church. Whenever I go I feel like a corpse."[27]

Though Pietism claims a rich heritage, its classic form needs renewal today. The challenge in today's evangelical church is *not* to foster spirituality along the lines of "the monastery apart from the marketplace." A mutant pietism restricted to personal devotions, prayer and holiness will generally not produce a missional spirituality. Rather than engage in a spirituality for the road—a missional spirituality—Christians retreat into what Reggie McNeal calls "refuge thinking" or "deeper life spirituality," where they settle into mere Bible study.[28] While we need to retreat and reflect, we also need to engage and act.

We were taught to have personal devotions with Bible reading and prayer, and tried numerous methods to build structure and rhythms into our spiritual lives. We own dozens of books on prayer, spiritual formation and community. We've experimented with *lectio divina*, contemplation and intercession. Maybe you feel as feeble and frustrated in your spiritual lives as we do, dragging yourself out of bed Monday morning after a demanding weekend to face a snowstorm and the frenzied world outside. Maybe you skipped your devotions and couldn't find a thing for which to thank God. The main temptation here is to embrace a mutant pietism, an interior and retreat spirituality, disengaged from the world.

Another challenge is *programism*. The assumption is, if we offer an array of good programs, studies and small groups, and get people to participate, they will grow spiritually. Attendance is a measure of success. Willow Creek Church did a research project to find out which programs and activities of their church helped people mature spiritually and which did not. In 2007, they published the results in *Reveal: Where Are You?* The Reveal study sought to answer the question "Does church activity drive spiritual growth?" How does Willow Creek define and measure spiritual growth?

Their survey, influenced by a business consultant, asked behavioral questions about serving, Bible study, small-group involvement, spiritual practices including prayer and solitude, attendance at services and anything that tied into their spiritual lives.[29] Executive pastor Greg Hawkins said, "Participation is a big deal. We believed the more people participating in these sets of activities, with higher levels of frequency, will produce disciples of Christ." Their philosophy of ministry for thirty years was this: the church creates programs and activities; people participate in them; the outcome is spiritual maturity. "The research revealed that increasing levels of participation in these sets of activities does not predict whether someone's becoming more of a disciple of Christ. It does not predict whether they love God more or they love people more."[30]

When he spoke at the Leadership Summit that summer, Willow Creek pastor Bill Hybels mused that they should have taught believers how to become self-feeders who can read the Bible and do the spiritual practices for themselves.[31] "In other words, spiritual growth doesn't happen by becoming dependent on elaborate church programs but through the age old spiritual practices of prayer, bible reading, and relationships. And, ironically, these basic disciplines do not require mulit-million dollar facilities and hundreds of staff to manage."[32] Willow Creek influenced thousands of churches with their program-driven, attractional, seeker-sensitive, business models of leadership. In 2009 Barna Group verified the problem with programism:

> Nine out of ten senior pastors of Protestant churches asserted that spiritual immaturity is one of the most serious problems facing the Church. Few pastors have a written statement to define spiritual maturity, how it's measured, the strategy for facilitating maturity, or what scriptures will help foster maturity. *Those pastors who made an attempt to measure maturity were more likely to gauge depth on the basis of par-*

ticipation in programs than to evaluate people's spiritual understanding or any type of transformational fruit in their lives.[33]

Our language shows our theology: we reach "unchurched" people and "bring them to church." Is the goal for them to become
"churched"? How about, we find wandering people and bring
them to Jesus? Reggie McNeal quipped, "[Jesus] did not say, 'I
have come to give you *church*, and give it to you more abun-
dantly.'"[34] Are Willow Creek and other program-driven churches
simply artifacts of temple spirituality?

There is, of course, a legitimate place for good church programs.
The challenge is to repurpose the programs and ministries to include those who need to "come home," who need the feast and the
fellowship that those already home enjoy.

The challenges for a missional spirituality are complex.

The West is transitioning into post-Christendom. In Christendom, the church occupied a central and influential place in
society as it shaped culture with Christian theology. In post-
Christendom, the church no longer occupies this central place of
authority and influence. Rather, it is on the margins of society as
one option in a pluralist, postmodern landscape. Yet we maintain confidence in Christ, his cause and his church.

Suggested Practices

1. How does fear limit your ability to live as one sent into the
   world for Jesus? Ask God to lead you beyond your comfort zone.
   Follow up with a plan to try something new.

2. With a friend or group, fast for three days as a counter-formation against the tyranny of consumption. Use the time you save
   in preparing food to pray for justice in the world. Take the cash
   you save and give it to an organization that promotes justice.

Discussion Starters

1. Summarize the main ideas in the challenges presented, including disenchantment, excarnation, abstraction, consumerism, entitlement, extraction, mutant pietism and programism. What do they have in common? Do you agree with these challenges or not? Where do you go from here? Reflect on John Wesley's quote at the beginning of the chapter.

2. Watch the movie *Chocolat* or *Voyage of the Dawn Treader* with some people. Interpret the story in the light of Scripture, and through the lenses of personal growth and outward service. How might these movies inform your missional spirituality?

3. What practices have you developed to resist consumerism? What has helped or not helped?

3

Theological Foundations

*The purpose of theology is mission. The commands to love
God, be transformed, discipline our thoughts, and be ready to
account for our hope are all connected to the calling and the
participation of the church in the mission of God. This
missional vocation should shape and orient all the beliefs
and practices of the Christian community.*

JOHN R. FRANKE, THE CHARACTER OF THEOLOGY

In his primer on theology, Swiss Reformed theologian Karl Barth
told the story of a series of lectures he gave in the summer of 1946
in the post-war ruins of the Kurfürsten castle in Bonn, Germany.
A rebuilding project was underway. Every morning at seven they
met to sing a psalm or a hymn to cheer each other up. By eight
o'clock, "the rebuilding of the quadrangle began to advertise itself
in the rattle of an engine as the engineers went to work to restore
the ruins."[1]

This is where we accomplish vigorous theological work: in the
ruins of an old world but with an active hope for a new world. In
the last chapter we explored the challenges to missional spirituality. In this and the following chapters, we move to the possi-

bilities and practices of a missional spirituality that has solid theological foundations.

Christian theology guides and nurtures the vocational identity, function and practices of the church as God's ambassador and witness as whole people. Therefore, "the chief purpose of theology is whole-person formation for mission. Because it addresses the whole person, theology is inherently spiritual. Because it concerns God's mission to the world, theology is inherently missional."[2] In this chapter we offer four sides of a theological foundation on which coming home to a missional spirituality can rest: the Trinity, the incarnation, the priesthood of all believers and the Jesus Creed.

The Trinity

Though the word *Trinity* is absent in Scripture, the church formulated the doctrine as a central theological foundation of the Christian faith. Paul's benediction offers a glimpse: "May the grace of the Lord Jesus Christ, and the love of God, and the fellowship of the Holy Spirit be with you all" (2 Corinthians 13:14). What is unique about the Trinity? Our God is a divine *community* whose essence is holiness, love and fellowship. The Trinity describes a relational family of three divine Persons in one eternal essence: Father, Son and Spirit. Christian spirituality is relational and trinitarian. What difference does the Trinity make for a missional spirituality?

In the early fifth century, Patrick was appointed as the first British missionary bishop to take the gospel to the Celtic peoples of Ireland. He launched a contextual, missional church-planting movement, and in two or three generations Ireland had become substantially Christian. The Trinity became foundational in Celtic spirituality, fitting well with the importance they placed on the number three.[3] As Ian Bradley explains in *The Celtic Way*, "The Celts saw the Trinity as a family. . . . For them it showed the love that lay at the very heart of the Godhead and the sanctity of family and community ties. Each social unit was seen as an icon of the Trinity."[4] The Celtic Christians had a flow to their lives that included three elements:

- a contemplative devotional life that strengthened their belief in God

- a desire to live and belong in community with like-minded souls on their journey

- a sense of mission that drove them to show compassion and bless the world[5]

Even before creation, God was a community of three divine Persons who existed and loved each other in a trinitarian family. John tells us, "God is love." Incredibly, God invites us to participate in his family of love, which is fundamentally relational. God is personal. He flourishes in friendship. This attribute of God warmly touches a need in postmodern people who crave connection. Witness the astonishing rise of social networks through Facebook, Twitter, texting and blogs. All people desire to belong and be known. As theologian Lesslie Newbigin put it, "Interpersonal relatedness belongs to the very being of God. Therefore there can be no salvation for human beings except in relatedness."[6] Being made in God's image, we are created for community, for relationship, for family. Christian spirituality is relational and formed in love.

Missional spirituality is trinitarian. In the Great Commission, Christ followers are sent on mission to make disciples as they baptize people into the Trinity and teach them to obey the commands of Jesus (Matthew 28:18-20). John 14–17 reveals the deep unity and relationship that Christ followers, Father, Son and Spirit experience together. Jesus' high-priestly prayer reinforces the connection between spirituality and mission: "Sanctify them by the truth; your word is truth. As you sent me into the world, I have sent them into the world" (John 17:17-18). The Father sent the Son into the world, and the Son sends his followers into the same world. We could say that *missio Dei* is essentially "Trinity-in-mission." We could also say that the church is a community in mission, which produces communities of *shalom*.

In his first resurrection appearance, Jesus connected mission and shalom, God's restoration of the wholeness of all things. This sending is trinitarian. Jesus declares, " 'Peace be with you! As the Father has sent me, I am sending you.' And with that he breathed on them and said, 'Receive the Holy Spirit' " (John 20:21-22). All three members of the Trinity act as Jesus declares shalom, the coming of God's peace. He sends his disciples as he breathes on them the Spirit. Robert Webber says, "Spirituality is our mystical union with God through Jesus Christ by the Spirit that results in our participation in the life of the Triune God in the life of the world."[7]

Mission is the ministry of the Son for the Father through the Holy Spirit *for the sake of the world.* In self-absorbed cultures—especially in the West, where many have a sense of entitlement—pain and loss seem more irrational than ever. People wonder, *Why me, God? Where is God when it hurts? If God is loving and powerful, why doesn't he prevent undeserved tragedy?* There is a current resurgence of trinitarian thought, not only in missional literature but also in popular literature that reenchants a cold and mysterious world with a relational God. The bestselling novel *The Shack* is an example.[8] It offers an unconventional portrait of the Trinity as it deftly tackles the problem of pain, loss and evil. It grounds a trinitarian spirituality in suffering that leads to love and grace that leads to healing.

In times of reformation, new questions emerge about the nature of what it means to be human. Yet while *community* is a buzzword, it remains an elusive experience. We all hunger to belong, but community is not built in meetings and events. Rather, community is *nurtured* in mutual service and interdependence, in significant interaction and vulnerability, in shared stories and common purpose. Some Christians leave a church because they do not discover community with other Christians there, but they seldom leave because they couldn't tolerate unbelievers. Or maybe they do not find the type of community they want or are not willing or not able to foster it. The church ought to be a place of community where people can come home.

When we understand God as trinitarian, we ask new questions about the meaning of people created in his image and likeness. What does it mean for a missional spirituality that people bear God's image and likeness? Paul teaches that Christ followers are "being renewed in knowledge in the image of [their] Creator" (Colossians 3:10), and they invite others to come home to a new family. Why? Because God is love. Stephen Seamands writes, "Out of the dynamic of self-communicating love *within* the circle of the Trinity flow God's love for the world *outside* the circle."[9] God is on mission. That mission is embodied in Jesus and then in his church.

The Incarnation

Apart from the incarnation, there would be no mission of God in the world, no redemption and no meaning to the prayer "May your kingdom come on earth." Incarnation means literally "in the meat," in the flesh, God *embodied*. What difference does it make that God the Son took the limitations of flesh, became a Jewish man to live, work and walk in Israel? What does it mean that he died and then arose in a transformed physical body? What difference does the incarnation make for a missional spirituality? Dallas Willard revolutionized a theology of the spiritual disciplines when he showed how the incarnation is a tangible model of what the life of salvation should look like. Jesus shared a human body as all human beings do. The human body is the focal point of human existence. And all spiritual disciplines and Christian mission are carried out in the human body.

Jesus entered our world and became a model for us as the perfect human person who lived according to the Spirit.[10] God became *embodied* in Jesus. He was not a generic human being, but very specific. Jesus was God *contextualized* in human, male, Jewish, Galilean,[11] first-century, Greco-Roman form, born to a virgin teen and circumcised on the eighth day. God did not reveal himself through ideas but through concrete realities and actions. In Jesus' life there was no division between sacred and secular, spiritual and physical, clean and unclean. He enjoyed parties, wine and food. The goodness of the physical body is proven because God became incarnate through Jesus Christ the Word (John 1:1-18; Philippians 2).

The ultimate theological foundation for a missional spirituality is the incarnation, where Christians continue a similar process where they contextualize God's presence:

> The Incarnation is a process of becoming particular, and in and through the particular the divinity could become visible and in some way (not fully, but in some way) become graspable and intelligible. It follows quite naturally that if that message is to continue to touch people through our agency, we have to continue the Incarnation process. Through us, God must become Asian or African, black or brown, poor or sophisticated, a member of twentieth-century secular suburban Lima, Peru or of the Tondo slum dweller in Manila, or able to speak to the ill-gotten affluence of a Brazilian rancher. Christianity . . . must continue God's Incarnation in Jesus by becoming contextual.[12]

Missional spirituality is embodied in daily life. The church as a living temple is the body of Christ in the world. But this temple is not made of concrete and steel. When we become real-life examples of Jesus for people, we can invite our family and friends, our fellow employees at work, our neighbors, to come home. We incarnate the Spirit of Jesus in the world. Robert Webber writes, "In Jesus we see what a human being who participates in God looks like. The spiritual life, like the incarnation, is participation in this world, this life, this place, in our day-to-day relationships in family, work, church, and leisure."[13] The church is not just a mystical universal body in the world but also the physical expression of Christ in the world.

God loves the physical because he created it and pronounced it good. Spiritual formation is connected to the physical. Our culture understands the importance of the physical life as expressed in marketing and advertising. In a section titled "The Cultural Power of Discipline Formation" in his book *Who's Afraid of Postmodernism?* James K. A. Smith describes how these mechanisms shape us:

> Disciplinary mechanisms in our society *do* make humans into certain kinds of people who are aimed at particular goals. Many Americans are defined by the primary goal of consumption. Television programs were invented to gain an audience for commercials and marketing is driven by products with social, sexual, and even religious value and fundamental human desires for meaning and transcendence to satisfy human longings. Marketing forms us into the kind of persons who want to buy beer to have meaningful relationships, or buy a car to be respected, or buy the latest thing simply to satisfy the desire that has been formed in us. These disciplinary mechanisms transmit values and truth claims covertly. Through a range of practices, they teach the body, as it were.[14]

Smith points to the necessity of counter-formation by counter-disciplines that form us into the kinds of people God expects as the *telos* (goal) of sanctification and human vocation as image bearers of God in the world. Apart from physical practices, we will not form the habits that equip us to counteract MTV and television commercials, for example.

In the incarnation, God drew close. Why would God do this? Why would a safe trinitarian God send the Son to move into our neighborhood only to live and die on a Roman cross? There is only one possible answer: the burden of God's love compelled him to act. God loves us because we are his family members created in his image and likeness. We bear God's image and likeness with immense dignity and worth. Unlike any other created thing, humans are both physical and spiritual. As King David wrote,

What is man, that you are mindful of him,
the son of man that you care for him?
You made him a little lower than the heavenly beings
and crowned him with glory and honor.
    You made him ruler over the works of your hands.
        (Psalm 8:4-6)

Love for people who are made in God's image and a little lower than God compels a missional spirituality that is embodied, incarnational. Alan Hirsch wrote,

By living incarnationally we not only model the pattern of humanity set up in the Incarnation but also create space for mission to take place in organic ways. In this way, mission becomes something that "fits" seamlessly into the ordinary rhythms of life, friendships, community, [and hospitality] and is thus thoroughly *contextualized*.[15]

As Jesus mediated the mission of God incarnationally as high priest, all believers, in conversion, are ordained to his priesthood. They are commissioned to incarnationally mediate God's mission to invite lost people to come home.

The Priesthood of All Believers

On Halloween, October 31, 1517, a massive theological tsunami slammed the shores of the Holy Roman Catholic Church. One of its German monks, professor Martin Luther—gripped by a fresh understanding of salvation by faith and grieved by the corruption of the papacy—launched a new movement within Christendom, later called the Protestant Reformation. On that day, he particularly protested the sale of indulgences as he nailed his "Ninety-Five Theses" to the Wittenberg castle church door in Germany.

Eventually, a revolutionary doctrine emerged from the Reformation: the priesthood of all believers. It challenged the hierarchical and exclusive papal system. While Luther did not use this exact phrase, he recognized that in the teaching of the New Testament all baptized believers are priests and spiritual in God's sight. His doctrine cleared the way for non-clergy (laity) to practice their own vocational callings and use the gifts of the Spirit as their priestly service to God.

What comes to mind when you hear the word *priest* or *priesthood*? A man or group of men wearing black shirts with white tabbed collars who marry and bury? A man with a gray beard wearing a long, multicolored garment and oblong shaped headdress, who swings an incense censer and chants monotone prayers? A special order of holy men who received a call to the ministry to serve God? What about a twenty-two-year-old political science university student in London who recently gave her heart to Jesus Christ? A fifty-six-year-old executive who works in the oil and gas industry in Alberta? A thirty-four-year-old single parent of three who works at Wal-Mart in Butte, Montana? A sixty-year-old retired and widowed schoolteacher in Perth, Australia? A fourteen-year-old, blind Christian girl in your hometown? Did you think of yourself or your neighbor as a priest, or did you default to the image of a minister or pastor? A quote from the character Eliza Doolittle in *My Fair Lady* speaks for us:

> You see, Mrs. Higgins, apart from the things one can pick up, the difference between a lady and a flower girl is not how she

behaves, but how she is treated. I shall always be a common flower girl to Professor Higgins, because he always treats me like a common flower girl, and always will. But I know that I shall always be a lady to Colonel Pickering, because he always treats me like a lady, and always will.[16]

Could it be that the reason so many believers don't act like priests of Jesus is because they are treated like *the laity*? Can you see yourself as a member of a royal priesthood at work, in your neighborhood, in your community and in your culture? Paul understood that one of his priestly duties was to proclaim the gospel to the communities to which God led him: "I have written you quite boldly on some points, as if to remind you of them again, because of the grace God gave me to be a minister of Christ Jesus to the Gentiles with the *priestly duty* of proclaiming the gospel of God, so that the Gentiles might become an offering acceptable to God, sanctified by the Holy Spirit" (Romans 15:15-16, italics ours).

Dean, a house church–planting pastor at Pathway Christian Communities in Grande Prairie, Alberta, offers one snapshot of how they practiced the priesthood of all believers in a corporate sense:

> Like the Apostle Paul, we as a church community feel God has given us this same privilege and opportunity as well. With each member of the church exercising the spiritual gifts God has given them, we have together reached out into our community to proclaim the gospel (our priestly duty) in collective actions as well as words. In one instance a need in our community came to our awareness. We knew of approximately 120 street folks who would be without access to food over a several day period. We began praying together to see what God would have us do in light of the fact that there were legal, logistical, financial, and time issues to overcome. We desired to minister to these folks in a practical and timely way.

To offer food to a group of 120 people (we are a house group movement, we own no building) we needed to find a venue that would be big enough to host the 120 people and distribute food to them in a legal manner that met national food preparation and serving guidelines. God provided a restaurant that would normally be closed that day because it was a holiday. He used a Muslim restaurant owner who because he was observing the month of Ramadan (it is a religious mandate of a devote Muslim that during the month of Ramadan he do something for the poor) offered his venue to serve these folks. This Muslim owner respected us as a Christian group of believers as in the past we have prayed for him and his business. So God provided food to serve the homeless!

We needed to come up with the money to fund this outreach as well. Those of the church who could give financially did so. Other folks in the church came out to serve food to the people while others went around offering tea and coffee to the people. Our street friends were blown away as they felt like important guests at a fancy restaurant. Still others in the church sat down with folks to listen and pray with them. Out of this collective priestly sacrifice for God another opportunity in the community unfolded. Folks from an inner city elders shelter were at this event and opened the doors for us as a church to minister to them on a weekly basis to play games, sing, listen, and share the gospel.[17]

When we teach on missional leadership and spirituality, we place a mirror at the bottom of a covered box beforehand. We ask the question "What do you think a missional Christian [or royal priest] looks like?" We then pass the box around for all to look inside and see themselves. The reactions are fun to watch. Most people laugh. One person exclaimed, "Scary!" The priesthood of all believers, when practiced, removes a hierarchical dualism of ordained clergy and non-ordained laypeople, pros and amateurs, and dismantles notions of spiritual aristocracy within the church. It suggests a missional adventure for entire congregations who have direct access to God *and* who mediate God to their communities. A theology of vocation and of place includes those local places where missional spirituality is practiced by the priesthood of all believers at work, in the neighborhood, in the community and in the wider culture. It's where every member is a *missionary* rather than just a *minister.* Alan Roxburgh writes,

> Across the varieties of today's models of ministry, there remains this underlying notion of church leadership functioning as specialized professionals. . . . *This view effectively eclipses the gifts for leadership in the non-ordained contingent of God's sent people,* those known in Christendom as the laity. Ministry remains identified with the static roles of clergy as priest, pedagogue [teacher], or professional, all dispensers of spiritual resources. *Even where the priesthood of all believers stands as a theological conviction of an ecclesiastical community, it is rarely practiced in the church.*[18]

Unfortunately, churches that apply the doctrine of the priesthood of all believers merely to church polity through congregational government fail to capture its core theological intent, which is spiritual and missional, not institutional. It has little to do with democracy at church business meetings where a majority vote supposedly determines God's will for a congregation and yet may produce very unspiritual results.[19] Granted, all believers have immediate access to God and can hear directly from him; pastors should consult people when making decisions; and corporate discernment is a good safeguard when seeking God's guidance. However, the priesthood of all believers provides a stronger foundation for missional spirituality than for church polity.

Foundational Texts for the Priesthood of All Believers: 1 Peter 2:4-5, 9-12

Read this passage carefully. Theologians (and Luther) tend to focus on verse 9 ("But you are a chosen people . . ."). But the full context reveals the corporate nature and function of the church as a people, not as individuals. In fact, no individual in the New Testament is ever called a priest. *Priest* is always used in a corporate sense, and the responsibilities of the priesthood are never confined to a special class in the church. It is priesthood of *all* believers not of *each* believer.[20] It is a *royal* priesthood with a spiritual task of ruling. Peter showed that the church is now both the temple and the priesthood begun with Israel:

> As you come to him, the living Stone—rejected by men but chosen by God and precious to him—you also, like living stones, are being built into a spiritual house to be a holy priesthood, offering spiritual sacrifices acceptable to God through Jesus Christ. . . .
>
> But you are a chosen people, a royal priesthood, a holy nation, a people belonging to God, that you may declare the praises of him who called you out of darkness into his wonderful light. Once you were not a people, but now you are the people of God; once you had not received mercy, but now you have received mercy. Dear friends, I urge you, as aliens and strangers in the world, to abstain from sinful desires, which war against your soul. Live such good lives among the pagans that, though they accuse you of doing wrong, they may see your good deeds and glorify God on the day he visits us.

In verse four, "As you come to him" is frequently translated in the Greek Old Testament (Septuagint) as "drawing near to God" to hear him speak or to enter his presence to offer sacrifices. It's translated in Hebrews as "drawing near to God" in worship.[21] Believers have direct access to God through Jesus Christ their High

Priest (Hebrews 4:14-16; 7:25; 10:1; 12:22).

According to verse five, believers, "like living stones, are being built into a spiritual house," formerly God's house—the Jerusalem temple—and are "to be a holy priesthood" now ordained as priests in God's kingdom. N. T. Wright said, "Jesus and his followers as the 'living stones' . . . bring the presence of God into the wider world, carrying forward the mission of declaring God's powerful and rescuing acts."[22] Believer-priests exist incarnationally and offer spiritual sacrifices of themselves and their gifts. It is interesting to note that the title *Pontifex* comes from the Latin meaning "bridge-builder," and thus a priest—a pontiff—ideally is a missional bridge from God to people.

In verse nine, "But you are a chosen people, a royal priesthood, a holy nation, a people belonging to God" is a clear allusion to Israel (Exodus 19:5-6; 23:22; Isaiah 43:20-21) and now attributed to the church as a covenant community, "that you may declare the praises of him who called you out of darkness into his wonderful light." Proclamation and praise result as the church participates in the redemption of the fallen creation. We both mediate and live for Christ in the world as recipients of God's mercy (1 Peter 2:10) and as those who extend his rule (Revelaton 5:10). Some scholars suggest that 1 Peter 2:9-10 might be a hymn that was sung at baptismal services in the early church. If so, baptism shaped the theological identity and missional function of new believers.

As a *chosen* people, *holy* priesthood, holy *nation*, we *belong* to God. These are theological images of covenant relationship, consecration, intimacy and identity. National identities disappear and one new nationality forms. Zechariah prophesied that many nations would become God's people (Zechariah 2:11). When this was fulfilled, the Jerusalem church leaders realized that God had gathered "a people for himself" from among the Gentiles (Acts 15:14). Mission participates with God as he establishes his kingdom from all the nations on earth.

Verses eleven and twelve read, "Dear friends, I urge you, as aliens and strangers in the world, to abstain from sinful desires, which war against your soul. Live such good lives among the pagans that, though they accuse you of doing wrong, they may see your good deeds and glorify God on the day he visits us." The spirituality of royal priests and a holy nation is mobile and missional. We as "resident aliens" and foreigners in this world are to avoid sin and embody the charm of good living in ways that point to God (Matthew 5:16). N. T. Wright argued that royal priests are God's *rulers*, who live together in such a way that the crucified and risen Jesus is seen as the world's true sovereign and who by Christian virtue reveal God's glory to the world.[23]

This passage identifies the vocation of this royal priesthood and holy nation: to be vice-rulers of God who practice worship that leads to mission supported by observable holiness of character and good deeds in the world. This is the new humanity, restored to the image of God.

According to a paper produced for the 2004 Lausanne Forum, missional congregations reflect the priesthood of all believers.[24] Ordinary people, not just ordained people, constitute the priesthood of all believers, empowered by the Spirit in mission. In Christ, a new and living temple emerged, made not with concrete and steel, but with real people. N. T. Wright wrote,

> The Temple was never supposed to be a retreat away from the world, a safe holy place where one might stay secure in God's presence, shut off from the wickedness outside. The Temple was an advance sign of what God intended to do with and for the whole creation. When God filled the house with his presence that was a sign and foretaste of his ultimate intention, which was to flood *the whole world* with his glory, presence and love. Just as in Exodus 19, God tells the Israelites that all the world belongs to him before telling

them that they are to be a special people with a ministry to that world so the tabernacle and the Temple were an anticipation of a much larger reality yet to come.[25]

The body of Christ is the temple in whom God's Spirit lives, and believers are the priests who serve in the world. As mobile priests and living temples, they orient their lives and vocations around their Father's household affairs. For the first few centuries, the church practiced all the gifts of the Spirit for both ministry (inward life) and mission (outward life). Even a century before Constantine, church life had become a settled experience, and mission was something "over there." The roles of apostles, prophets and evangelists were marginalized, and roles of pastor and teacher became central, as they are to this day in most churches.[26] What began as a Master of Divinity degree for the *pastoral* role became a *professional* degree for a management role. But with God's new temple, distributed gifts throughout the priesthood of all believers should displace an elite professional, pastor-teacher role.

Leaders practice the theology of the priesthood of all believers when they equip, release and trust the laity to serve vocationally in ministry wherever they are.[27] Leaders help them imagine and, as permission-granting leaders, also say yes to their ideas.[28] What could happen if we ordained people for daily mission?[29] A pastor leads a rural church near Edmonton, Alberta, that continues to grow, and he can't keep track of everything. His people practice simple hospitality and invite their neighbors into their homes, small groups and other gatherings. The atmosphere is charged with God's presence. Priests build bridges between God and people, and show the way home. The theology they practice is found in the Jesus Creed.

The Jesus Creed: Shema Spirituality

We come now to the core theological foundation of a missional spirituality—what Scot McKnight calls "the Jesus Creed," which is contained in Mark 12:28-34.[30] This creed reveals the overarching substance for life's meaning, mission and spirituality. It's a theological structure that begins with God to supply the biblical worldview.

According to Mark, as Jesus walked the temple courts in Jerusalem, a group of religious leaders confronted him with cynical questions about his authority, paying taxes to Caesar and the resurrection (11:27–12:27). As recorded in Mark 12:28-31, a conversation ensued:

> One of the teachers of the law came and heard them debating. Noticing that Jesus had given them a good answer, he asked him, "Of all the commandments, which is the most important?"
>
> "The most important one," answered Jesus, "is this: 'Hear, O Israel, the Lord our God, the Lord is one. Love the Lord your God with all your heart and with all your soul and with all your mind and with all your strength.' The second is this: 'Love your neighbor as yourself.' There is no commandment greater than these."

This question came from a law scholar (or scribe) who posed a significant question to Jesus. In the religious climate of the day, differentiations were made between commandments of greater and of lesser weight. The core issue was to establish which commandment, which overarching absolute, superseded all commandments. Jesus placed the greatest weight on one commandment followed by another: love God and then love others.

Jesus stoutly quoted from two Old Testament passages: Deuteronomy 6:4-5 and Leviticus 19:18. He cited the *Shema*, a creed named after the first Hebrew word (*shema*, "hear") in Deuteronomy 6:4. Pious Jews since the second century B.C. had recited the creed every evening and morning.

In the context of an ancient Near Eastern world with a belief in many gods, Moses called Israel to *hear* (heed, pay attention to the fact) that Yahweh was their covenant God and their one and only God—"the Shema speaks not only of *uniqueness* but also of the *unity* of God."[31] Israel's God is personal ("the Lord *our* God") and also a unity ("the Lord is *one*"). Israel was to love him with all their heart, soul and strength, and these commandments were to be on their hearts (Deuteronomy 6:5-6).[32] This is what Alan Hirsch calls "Shema spirituality"—the epicenter of what it means to be a disciple.[33] The point in both Deuteronomy and Mark is that we are to love God completely and totally, with no room left for any other gods.

The word *heart* in Scripture is the seat of the will, the emotions and the mind—the command center of a person. The word *soul* in Scripture means the person or living being. The Hebrew word *meod*, translated as "strength" in Deuteronomy 6:5, has an Akkadian root that means "muchness" or "property" and carries a two-fold implication: ability (i.e., power and strength) and means (i.e., wealth).[34] Jesus added that we must love God from our minds— the faculty of intelligence, thought, perception and judgment. Love for God begins at the inner level of the heart and mind and strength and then moves outward through to others. John Piper summarized the meaning well:

> These four faculties overlap in meaning. But they are not identical. "Heart" highlights the center of our volitional and emotional life without excluding thought (Luke 1:51). "Soul" highlights our life as a whole, though sometimes distinguished from the body (Matt. 10:28). "Mind" highlights our thinking capacity. And "strength" highlights the capacity to make vigorous efforts both bodily and mentally (Mark 5:4; Luke 21:36). The function of these faculties and capacities in relation to loving God is to demonstrate that love.[35]

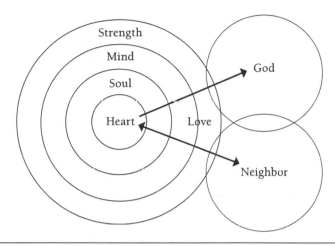

Figure 3.1.

Though there are distinctions between heart, soul, mind and strength, we should view them as constituting the totality of one's being and resources. So from our total being we must love God and love our neighbor as ourselves, *from the inside out.*[36]

Now one more point from Mark. The Greek translation is that we are to love God *from out of* (*ek*) the heart, soul, mind and strength. The Greek preposition *ek* governs each commandment and denotes the source from which an action proceeds rather than the instrument used. So, we are called to love God *from out of* all our heart, soul, mind and strength rather than *with* or *by means of* our heart, soul, mind and strength.[37] Mark used the preposition *ek* similarly when he declared, "For from within, out of men's hearts, come evil thoughts, sexual immorality, theft, murder, adultery" (Mark 7:21).

We love God *from* our whole being. For those in the Father's house, William Lane notes, "The love which determines the whole disposition of one's life and places one's whole personality in the service of God reflects a commitment to God which springs from divine sonship."[38] The fourfold repetition of *all* conveys totality.

We love God out of unity and totality, just as God is a tri-unity. Missional spirituality is *embodied* love for God and people—a commitment and a loyalty to God, worked out in love for people.

Jesus then brought Leviticus 19:18, set within the context of the Law of Holiness, together with Deuteronomy 6:4-5. He expanded the connection between love for God and love for neighbor (which, until Jesus, referred only to fellow Jews and relatives). The law scholar asked which commandment superseded all, but Jesus supplied *two* because they are inseparable. God requires both. Love for God establishes the correlative of love for others. Two commands fulfill one will (1 John 4:20-21).

This is the theological foundation for the Golden Rule, set not in humanitarianism or ethics but in devotion to God. Our love for God partners with our love for others. "If we love our neighbors as we love ourselves, we shall want for them the treatment we should want for ourselves, were we in their place."[39] The two sections of the Ten Commandments reveal the structure of love for God and neighbor (Exodus 20:1-11, 12-17). Love is the fulfillment of the law (Romans 13:8-10; Galatians 5:14). Spiritual disciples love God and people and one another (John 13:34). The essence of spirituality is not spiritual gifts, power or discipline but love. Spirituality is relational. Jon Stewart said, "Remember to love your neighbor as you love yourself. And if you hate yourself, then please—just leave your neighbor alone."[40]

We suggest that *a missional spirituality is an attentive and active engagement of embodied love for God and neighbor expressed from the inside out.* And now, the telling conclusion to this conversation in Mark 12:32-34:

> "Well said, teacher," the man replied. "You are right in saying that God is one and there is no other but him. To love him with all your heart, with all your understanding and with all your strength, and to love your neighbor as yourself

is more important than all burnt offerings and sacrifices."

When Jesus saw that he had answered wisely, he said to him, "You are not far from the kingdom of God."

Jesus brought insight to the law scholar who then saw the synthesis between loving God and others as weightier than ritual offerings and sacrifices that "potentially undermined the primacy of the temple establishment itself." [41] Though this was already a theme in the Old Testament (1 Samuel 15:22; Hosea 6:6), this scribe now viewed love in a superior position. James Edwards commented, "Even the most sacred duties may not take precedence over *agape* love, and they have no meaning unless they are an expression of it." [42] Jesus' reply showed how this theological conversation was missional at its core: "When Jesus saw that he had answered wisely, he said to him, 'You are not far from the kingdom of God'" (Mark 12:34).

Tony Campolo suggests that the kingdom of God is a party.[43] He writes, "Everybody was invited to the party, from widows who hadn't had a fun night out for a year, to poor kids who couldn't have come up with the ticket money to whatever was the ancient equivalent of Disneyland. Prostitutes and tax collectors were invited."[44] He cites Matthew 22:1-5 *(The Message):*

"God's kingdom," [Jesus] said, "is like a king who threw a wedding banquet for his son. He sent out servants to call in all the invited guests. And they wouldn't come!

"He sent out another round of servants, instructing them to tell the guests, 'Look, everything is on the table, the prime rib is ready for carving. Come to the feast!'"

The festivities of the Father occur in his house of love. We all need to come home. It's less about a vertical love for God and then a horizontal love for people. Rather, it's an all-inclusive love from the inside out, for God and for people.

Suggested Primers

1. In what ways is the Trinity a key theological foundation for a missional spirituality? What are some key biblical texts? Read *The Shack* and critique it.

2. How do you understand what incarnation means? In what ways is incarnation a theological foundation for a missional spirituality? What are some key biblical texts?

3. How do you understand what the priesthood of all believers means, and in what ways is it a theological foundation for a missional spirituality? What is a key biblical text?

Discussion Starters

1. Read and reflect on John 17:15-18; 20:20-22; and Matthew 28:18-20. How do these passages inform your theological understanding of the trinitarian and incarnational implications for a missional spirituality? How would you practice this theology in your life and work as a pastor, leader, church planter, student or parishioner?

2. Read and reflect on 1 Peter 2:4-5, 9-12. Consult a couple of good commentaries on this passage. What images and implications come to mind? How would you actually practice this theology in your life and work as a pastor, leader, church planter, student or parishioner?

3. Read and reflect on Mark 12:28-34. What does it mean to love God and neighbor from the inside out? What are the implications of this text and how does it affect your understanding of a theological structure and substance for an all-encompassing missional spirituality?

4

Missional Spirituality in Action

What if we looked at our world as Julian of Norwich learned to, "with pity and not with blame"? What if we heard God's call to evangelize out of love instead of fear, hope instead of judgment? What if we saw sin for the complex mixture it is, grounded in wounds and unmet needs? In short, what would it mean to read our world with a hermeneutic of love?

ELAINE A. HEATH, THE MYSTIC WAY OF EVANGELISM

Pastor Jeff and his board from North West Community Church in Calgary held a planning weekend. As leaders of a ten-year-old church that had started to stagnate somewhat, their goal was to evaluate their maturity as a church and then refocus their missional lens. Their philosophy of ministry had been to run around the bases of the purpose-driven diamond diagram developed by Pastor Rick Warren of Saddleback Church, which Saddleback uses to explain its education and assimilation process to its members. Each base represents a completed class and a deeper level of commitment.

The leaders at North West confessed that their on-base percentage and runs scored were mediocre in the areas of conversion growth and intentional disciple making. Though the church met in a school and they wished for a permanent facility, they began to see their location's possibilities rather than liabilities as a kingdom outpost in a neighborhood of ten thousand residents. The pastor and board knew that most people are not looking for a church and most churches are not looking for people. And they discovered during the planning meeting that their church had no clear mission.

After a few months, they developed this mission statement: "To be Christ in our community and bring our community to Christ." Jeff and North West Community Church now endeavor to put missional spirituality into action.

We discussed the challenges of a missional spirituality in chapter two and the theological foundations of a missional spirituality in the last chapter. We now launch into an overview of a missional spirituality in action. We begin with the early church in Acts.

The Early Church

Though many cite Acts 2:41-47 to depict the ideal elements for a healthy church, let us offer it once again to support our point. In many ways, it's a summary of a missional spirituality with core practices.

> Those who accepted his message were baptized, and about three thousand were added to their number that day. They devoted themselves to the apostles' teaching and to the fellowship, to the breaking of bread and to prayer. Everyone was filled with awe, and many wonders and miraculous signs were done by the apostles. All the believers were together and had everything in common. Selling their possessions and goods, they gave to anyone as he had need. Every day they continued to meet together in the temple courts. They

broke bread in their homes and ate together with glad and sincere hearts, praising God and enjoying the favor of all the people. And the Lord added to their number daily those who were being saved.

Notice baptism and Communion, Scripture, prayer, Spirit and relationships, enchantment (supernatural ministry), generosity and gratitude, hospitality and service, community and worship. As these practices streamed from inside the church out to the community, they collectively spawned favor. The Lord blessed the church's missional spirituality in action with notable results: "the Lord added to their number daily those who were being saved" (v. 47). This is a typical pattern in the book of Acts.

In Acts 16:6-15 we again see missional spirituality in action. After the Holy Spirit kept Paul and his companions from preaching in the province of Asia and from entering Bithynia, Paul had a vision of a man in Macedonia who begged him to come over and help them. At once they traveled to the Roman colony of Philippi in Macedonia, where they met Lydia, a Gentile businesswoman, and other women gathered by the river for prayer. After she listened to Paul, the Lord opened her heart to respond to his message, and she and her household were baptized. Lydia then opened her home to them. That's how the Spirit planted the church in Philippi.

By the way, Paul never planted a church. He planted the gospel. Churches then emerged as the fruit of that seed sowing.[1] It started with his obedience to a vision through the Spirit's guidance.

Acts is full of supernatural missional action through the Spirit.[2] Such action is not for charismatics and Pentecostals only, but for the whole church, "being built together to become a dwelling in which God lives by his Spirit" (Ephesians 2:22).[3] During approximately thirty years, lively missional spirituality was in action from Jerusalem to Rome. Empowered by the Holy Spirit, it started with a prayer meeting in Jerusalem that ventured to Judea, to Samaria and to the ends of the earth (Acts 1:8). The early church lived the Jesus Creed in such a way that the Greco-Roman-Jewish culture recognized its *embodied* truth. The practical love and piety of those early believers caught the attention of unbelievers. But the miraculous ministry of the church also caught their attention. The first church historian, Eusebius (A.D. 263-339), recounted how, around the turn of the first century in the province of Asia,

> there were many who amplified the Message, planting the saving seed of the heavenly kingdom far and wide in the world . . . evangelizing . . . with God's favor and help, since wonderful miracles were wrought by them in those times also through the Holy Spirit. As a result, assembled crowds, every man of them on the first hearing, eagerly espoused piety toward the maker of all things.[4]

By A.D. 300 Christianity had become a revolution that stampeded from a small Jewish sect in Jerusalem to a global movement that traversed and transformed the Roman Empire.[5] It was less a social than a spiritual phenomenon. It was not coordinated through a central organization but through a spontaneous missional spirituality with a theology of enchantment, embodied by ordinary people bonded together by social networks and apostolic leadership.[6]

Classic Pietism

Here we must pass sixteen centuries of church history from which we could profit in our study of missional spirituality.[7] Due to its pervasive influence, we move to what we call classic Pietism, which began in Germany and prepared the way for evangelical renewal, revival, missions and spirituality. As we mentioned in chapter two, the publication of *Pia Desideria* by Philip Jacob Spener was instrumental. It was a welcomed reaction to the cold and formal theological establishment of the German Lutheran church. In its first edition in 1675, Spener proposed a *heart religion* to replace the dominant *head religion* of his day.

The book addressed defects in the civil authorities, clergy and common people, and offered six proposals to correct the conditions in the church. These included a more extensive use of the Bible, exercise of the spiritual priesthood of believers, practice versus mere knowledge of Christianity, and conduct in controversies. He also sought to reform clergy education, with less focus on academic theology and greater focus on the example, piety and practical preaching of the clergy.[8] Though Spener's teaching would not appear radical today, it was in his day. His book gave rise to the term *Pietists*, a name critics originally used to mock the movement. (The Methodists got their name in the same way.)

Though classic Pietism faced criticism for individualism, subjectivism and its lack of a theological center grounded in justification, it was a spirituality based in the Jesus Creed that bridged love of God and neighbor from the inside out. It also owed much to Puritan strands. The priesthood of believers coupled with missional practices launched Pietism as a renewal, revival and disciplemaking movement. We will trace its progress from its founder on through the Moravians, Methodists, and Christian and Missionary Alliance—missional streams generated by the river of Pietist spirituality.

Through his book *True Christianity*, Lutheran theologian Johann Arndt (1555-1621) is considered the founder of German Pietism. He sought to apply Luther's theology and to *practice* the Christian life. His writings were the initial impetus for Jacob Spener, whose devout godmother had him read *True Christianity*. Influenced by Thomas à Kempis and other mystics, Arndt made Catholic mysticism available to Lutherans.[9] He argued for a mystical union with Christ, daily renewal and repentance, and a rigorous, Spirit-activated faith expressed in strong social concerns based on love.

Arndt argued, "True Christianity consists, not in words or in external show, but in living faith, from which arise righteous fruits, and all manner of Christian virtues, as from Christ Himself." He asked, "What is Christian faith without a Christian life?"[10] His book is still a rich read for today's pastors, leaders and students of spirituality.

The more credited leader for Pietism was Lutheran pastor and theologian Spener (1635-1705), with his *Pia Desideria*. Spener practiced his ideas for five years before he published his book. He proposed mid-week Bible studies called "colleges of piety," and lay ministry with an emphasis on morality and on works of love and charity. He sought to nurture the interior life of heart religion and the practice of the priesthood of all believers.

Spener in turn influenced pastor and professor August Hermann Francke (1663-1727), who landed a teaching post at the University of Halle in Germany—the chief academic center of Pietism. His older sister, Anna, encouraged him also to study Arndt's *True Christianity*. Francke developed the social side of classic Pietism. He reinforced the doctrine of repentance that leads to conversion, which results in joy and assurance, also a feature in John Wesley's theology.

Francke had a heart for the destitute and helped found a school for the poor, an orphanage, a hospital, a widow's home, a teacher's training institute and a Bible school. He also trained some of the first Protestant missionaries to leave Europe. One of his students was Count Nicolaus Ludwig von Zinzendorf (1700-1760), a Lutheran Pietist and reformer of the Moravian movement.

Pietism, with its varied expressions, endured numerous criticisms that identify it with mysticism, individualism, subjectivism, legalism and separatism. Its doctrine of justification and sanctification is rooted in a *love theology* for God and neighbor expressed in spiritual service as a priest. With its underlying motif of new birth, Pietist theology viewed people as either regenerate or unregenerate. It was governed by the Bible more than by creeds and church dogma, by profession of faith rather than by cultural Christendom and by the illumination of the Spirit enlivened by personal piety expressed in good works. With its recurring references to "the indwelling Christ," Pietism was also missional.

> The Pietist milieu resulted in desires to transform the living conditions of the poor and oppressed, reform prison systems, abolish slavery, remove class distinctions, establish a more democratic polity, initiate educational reforms, philanthropic institutions, and missionary activity, obtain religious liberty, and propose programs for social justice.[11]

Classic Pietism also influenced the Methodist movement and through it many Wesleyan branches, such as the American Methodists, Salvation Army, Church of the Nazarene, Missionary Church USA and Evangelical Missionary Church Canada. Pietism also influenced Mennonites, Quakers, European Reformed Churches, the Evangelical Covenant Church and the Evangelical Free Church. It made its enduring mark on Jonathan Edwards, Francis Asbury, George Mueller, Friedrich Schleiermacher, Phoebe Palmer, D. L. Moody, Hannah Whitall Smith, Andrew Murray, R. A. Torrey, A. B. Simpson, the Keswick renewal movements in the United Kingdom, and the Holiness and Pentecostal movements in the United States and Europe.[12] It was a missional spirituality in action with a dramatic impact on the Moravians, the Methodists, and the Christian and Missionary Alliance.

The Moravians

What is the origin of all of this? Let's venture back to back to the Pietist leader Count Nicolaus von Zinzendorf. He studied at the Universities of Halle and Wittenberg and was Jacob Spener's godson. In 1722 he permitted a small sect called the *Unitas Fratrum* (Unity of the Brethren) from Moravia near the Czech border to live on his nearby estate in Berthelsdorf, Germany. This underground, exiled church traced its origins to Czech reformer John Hus, who broke with the Roman Catholic Church and was burned at the stake in 1415.

This church established a new colony called *Herrnhut* ("the Lord's watch," based on Isaiah 62:1, 6-7) about two miles from Berthelsdorf, which united under Zinzendorf to renew the *Unitas Fratrum*. Between 1722 and 1726, three hundred Reformed, Separatist, Anabaptist and Catholic refugees streamed to *Herrnhut*. Key leaders were Germans Peter Bohler, who became a Moravian missionary and bishop in America and England, and August Spangenberg, who became a bishop and founder of the Moravian church in America and Zinzendorf's successor.

The community was conflicted until Zinzendorf drew up a rule of life called the "Brotherly Agreement." He divided the community into bands of two or three people of the same gender to meet and pray for one another. The community elected twelve elders and night watchmen. On August 13, 1727, during a Communion service, *Herrnhut* experienced a "Moravian Pentecost." The Spirit moved their hearts with love toward the Lord and one another. The Spirit's power flowed, including through divine healing. Factions dissolved. A twenty-four-hour continuous prayer watch was established with forty-eight men and women who prayed in pairs for one hour, seven days a week. It continued for more than a century.

Herrnhut was a strict experiment in organized Pietism that led to a movement of modern missions and the establishment of more than thirty settlements globally, based on the *Herrnhut* model. It spawned hundreds of small renewal groups that operated within the existing churches of Europe, known as "diaspora societies." These groups encouraged personal prayer and worship, Bible study, confession of sins, and accountability.

Moravian missionaries were the first large-scale Protestant missionary movement comprised mostly of laypeople. In 1732 the

first Moravian missionaries, who were peasant farmers and trades-
men, ventured to the West Indies. By 1760, 226 Moravian missionaries had ventured to the Caribbean, North and South America,
the Arctic, Africa, Egypt, and the Far East. They were the first to
send non-clergy laypeople, the first to intentionally reach black
slaves and the first missionaries in many countries of the world.[13]
Pietist Moravian missional spirituality also greatly impacted the
Methodists.

The Methodists

Ordained Anglican priest John Wesley (1703-1791) pressed his
theology and piety into the service of spirituality, mission and disciple making, with early influences from Jeremy Taylor's *The Rules
and Exercises of Holy Living and Holy Dying*, Thomas à Kempis's
Imitation of Christ, William Law's *A Serious Call to a Holy and Devout Life* and Henry Scougal's *The Life of God in the Soul of Man*.[14]
Later Wesley would republish an abridged edition of Arndt's *True
Christianity*.

While teaching at Oxford, Wesley aimed for inward holiness,
and in 1729, he established and led the "Holy Club" with his
brother Charles, George Whitefield and one other. They practiced
methodical Bible study, prayer, weekly Communion, twice-weekly
fasting, reading of the classics and works of charity. They were
mockingly called "Methodists." On his way to Georgia to serve as
a missionary to American Indians, Wesley and some Moravians
were aboard a ship caught in a storm. Impressed by their courage,
he searched his soul concerning salvation. Upon his return in
1738 while in London, he conversed much with Moravian Peter
Bohler from early February to early May about the state of his soul
and the nature of faith and salvation.

On May 24, 1738, Wesley went unwillingly to a Moravian society meeting at Aldersgate Street in London. When Luther's preface
to the epistle to the Romans was read, Wesley felt his "heart

strangely warmed" and trusted Christ alone for salvation with an assurance that Christ had removed his sins. Soon after, Wesley visited Pietist centers in Germany such as Halle and *Herrnhut*, where he met Zinzendorf.

By 1739 Wesley had set out to promote practical religion and to spread scriptural holiness. After being rejected in Anglican churches, he preached to the poor in open-air meetings and taught that justification by faith imputed righteousness and that sanctification by faith imparted righteousness and "intended that sanctification should be a disposition of the mind or a condition of the heart from which spring all good works."[15] According to Albert Outler, for Wesley, "the Christian life is a 'devotio,' the consecration of the whole man to God and neighbor in the full round of life and death."[16] Wesley championed anti-slavery measures, prison reform and other social issues, such as aid to the disadvantaged. Most of the conversions and discipleship came through a network of classes, bands and societies.

> The requirement for joining a Methodist class was "a desire to flee from the wrath to come." Most conversions took place in the classes rather than through the field preaching. The classes were also the disciplinary unit of the movement. Inquiry was made into the state of each member's soul, and unrepentant offenders were removed from the fellowship. Howard Snyder describes the classes as "house churches" meeting in the various neighborhoods where people lived. The class leaders (both men and women) were pastors and disciplers. All Methodists were class members. Those who were clearly converted moved on to join the "bands." While the major focus on the class was on conversion and discipline, the focus of the band was on confession and pastoral care. The "societies" were composed of all class and band members within a local area.[17]

Methodism was largely a lay movement of non-ordained preachers and pastors.[18] It grew among members of England's working class who did not fit the refined Church of England culture. Methodist spirituality emphasized hospitality, music, Bible study, prayer, confession and discipline in inward and outward holiness for mission.

Wesley believed that Christians are called into, not out of, battle with principalities and powers with "real faith working by love." By the time of his death in 1791, there were 72,000 Methodists in the United Kingdom and 57,000 in America.[19] Wesley, who was only five feet three inches tall and weighed 128 pounds, achieved large results.[20] He "did more to transfigure the moral character of the general populace, than any other movement British history can record."[21]

In 1784 Wesley named Francis Asbury and Thomas Coke as co-superintendents of the work in America, which began the Methodist Episcopal Church of the USA, later to become a large component of the United Methodist Church. For the next thirty-two years, Asbury led the Methodists in America. Like Wesley, he preached in all sorts of places: courthouses, public houses, tobacco houses, fields and public squares. He rode an average of six thousand miles each year, preached virtually every day and conducted meetings and conferences. Under his direction, the Methodist church grew from 1,200 to 214,000 members and 700 ordained preachers.

"Methodism became the largest Christian movement in North America by the mid-nineteenth century because of the power of its class and band meetings to form Christian disciples . . . whose social justice advocacy reformed American culture," according to Elaine Heath.[22] Methodists insisted that salvation required Christian mission to the world. Holiness is more than personal piety; love of God is linked with love of neighbor and justice in the world. In both the Moravian and Methodist contexts, biblical community was central.

The Christian and Missionary Alliance

In the United States during the mid-nineteenth century, the Wesleyan-Holiness revival emerged as a reaction to the prevailing shallowness of conversions devoid of consecration. This movement

> followed Wesley's teaching of entire sanctification when the Methodist churches had lost interest in it. Many evangelicals felt a longing for "something more" than the justification by grace they had experienced at conversion. They found the power to live the new life expected by these groups, a life of holiness, avoiding the pleasures of the world and devoting themselves to evangelism and social reform. They found power in an experience of total surrender to God and, according to the Methodist branch of the movement, a life of sinless perfection thereafter.[23]

One stream that flowed from this Wesleyan-Holiness river was the Christian and Missionary Alliance, shaped by A. B. Simpson. Incorporated in 1897 in Old Orchard, Maine, the Christian and Missionary Alliance was a merger of two organizations: the Christian Alliance and the Evangelical Missionary Alliance (later renamed the International Missionary Alliance). It is known for its practice of spirituality and missions structured by its theology of the Fourfold Gospel: Jesus as Savior, Sanctifier, Healer and Coming King.

A. B. Simpson (1843-1919) was a Canadian-born Scottish Presbyterian influenced by the Wesleyan-Holiness movement. Out of his pastoral frustrations in Hamilton, Ontario; Louisville, Kentucky; and New York City, emerged Simpson's emphasis on the deeper life and divine healing, which led to missional service motivated by premillennialism. Puritan books such as Richard Baxter's *Saints Everlasting Rest* and Philip Doddridge's *Rise and Progress of Religion in the Soul* disciplined Simpson's soul as a young boy.[24]

The Christian and Missionary Alliance and the Pentecostal movement of the twentieth century both have their roots in the Wesleyan-Holiness revival. Also, "the issues that gave rise both to Holiness independency and to Pentecostalism can be attributed to the aims of the original promoters of the nineteenth century revival, who traced the church's malady to lack of sanctification," according to Stanley Burgess and Gary McGee.[25] Furthermore, Simpson's influence regarding sanctification and missions surges deep into Pentecostal theology. According to Assemblies of God historian Carl Brumback,

> The Pentecostal movement owes the CMA a sevenfold debt: (1) doctrines borrowed from the Alliance; (2) the hymns of Simpson; (3) the books of Simpson, Pardington, Tozer, and others; (4) the terminology "Gospel Tabernacle," which, when supplemented with "Full" became a popular name for churches among Pentecostals; (5) the polity of the early Alliance Society; (6) a worldwide missionary vision; and (7) numerous leaders converted and trained in Alliance circles.[26]

In addition,

> Aimee Semple McPherson's "Foursquare Gospel," which she claimed was given directly to her by divine revelation, was noticeably similar to A. B. Simpson's "Fourfold Gospel." The emblem of the Foursquare movement, which included a cross, a laver (representing healing), a dove, and a crown, bore a marked resemblance to the already existent Alliance symbol, which included a cross, laver (representing sanctification), a pitcher of oil, and a crown.[27]

Out of Simpson's Missionary Training Institute came Pentecostal leaders such as John W. Welsh, Noel Perkins, William I. Evans and Frank M. Boyd.[28] Central to the theology of sanctification for Simpson was the deeper life initiated by what Wesley referred to as "the second blessing" and to which Pentecostals traditionally refer as baptism in, or by, the Holy Spirit, followed by the sign of speaking in tongues—a position that Simpson did not hold.

Certain New Testament texts were foundational in Simpson's theology.[29] Theological and practical applications emerged from Simpson's study: an integration of conversion and sanctification, theological reflection on abiding in Christ, prayer and stillness, all leading to an energetic missional spirituality. His 1925 book *Wholly Sanctified* promoted the structure for sanctification based on 1 Thessalonians 5:22-24: "Avoid every kind of evil. May God himself, the God of peace, sanctify you through and through. May your whole spirit, soul and body be kept blameless at the coming of our Lord Jesus Christ. The one who calls you is faithful and he will do it." The key was a willing mind and a surrendered heart, obedience to Christ, abiding in the spirit of prayer (union with Christ) and fellowship with the Holy Spirit—all centered in abiding in Christ.[30] The Christian and Missionary Alliance DNA connects spirituality and missions:

> The C&MA began as a deeper life and missionary movement initiated by Dr. Albert B. Simpson in 1887 to mobilize the under-utilized lay forces and resources of the churches to "take the whole Bible to the whole world." He believed that a life completely yielded to Christ was one in which service to Christ would be of paramount importance. A person controlled by the Holy Spirit has no choice but to be involved in bringing the Good News to others, either as an overseas missionary or as a missionary at home.[31]

Through his deeper life and missions conferences, Simpson recruited leaders and raised money for missions. In 1882, he started the Missionary Training Institute—the first Bible college in North America and forerunner to Nyack College and Alliance Theological Seminary—and the Berachah Home (House of Blessing), one expression of the Alliance's healing ministry and a respite for sufferers. By 1895, more than three hundred Alliance missionaries were serving overseas.

On September 10, 1899, at the conclusion of the Nyack Convention, Simpson gave a message titled "Aggressive Christianity." In it, he appealed for a deeper and a larger faith and for unselfish and aggressive work. He said, "All missionary enterprise must have its source in a deeper spiritual life," and "no soul can receive this deep, divine and overflowing life and henceforth live unto himself. . . . It makes the world our parish and irresistibly flows out like water to the deepest place of need."[32] According to him, to dwell in Christ was the core of Christianity. "Christ in you" was the central and dominant truth of his missional spirituality.[33] Simpson saw no distinction between missions at home and abroad—the white harvest field was everywhere.[34] Viewing Jesus as our missional model, Simpson wrote,

> Even still on His ascension throne He is continually employed in ministries of active love. No consecrated Christian can be an idler or a drone. "As my Father hath sent me even so send I you." We are here as missionaries, every one of us with a commission and a trust just as definite as those whom we send overseas.[35]

Gordon Smith remarks, "It is more accurate to affirm that the C&MA is radically Christ-centered,"[36] and that "sanctification is a consecration of our lives and service for God and His kingdom. In this sense, sanctification is profoundly linked with service and activity in the world. We are, in some sense at least, sanctified *for* service."[37] The Alliance today has thousands of churches and hundreds of missionaries, with relief efforts and microenterprise projects around the world. However, as with many evangelical denominations with roots in classic Pietism, the missional spirituality of the original Alliance vision needs continuous renewal.

Lessons for Today

We can see from this brief historical overview that both the early church and classic Pietism contained the essential theology and practices for a fruitful missional spirituality in action. A recovered classic Pietism, latent though mutant in modern evangelicalism, contains all the elements for a present-day renewal of missional spirituality across all evangelical denominations. Several time-tested themes occur:

1. We must be grounded in a *love theology* for God and neighbor, nurturing that life with spiritual practices that feed the heart and shape our actions outward to the poor, the marginalized, the oppressed and the hurting, and not just inward to ourselves.

2. We must empower men and women, boys and girls, to practice and to be the priesthood of all believers to the people around them.

3. We must place Scripture, prayer and the Spirit at the center of our piety *and action*, where discipleship is shaped from consistent responses to the Holy Spirit's initiatives.

4. We must cultivate biblical community for spiritual formation through small groups whose purpose is discipleship and mission, and we must connect spirituality to mission.

5. We must connect and converse with the wider ongoing story reflected in the diversity of Christian traditions that advance the mission of God in the world.

6. We must recover a comprehensive process of evangelical conversion whereby the theology of justification and sanctification are lived through the *praxis* of union with Christ, for the *telos* of continuing transformation and mission.[38]

Suggested Practices

1. One hour each week, let your imagination soar as you contemplate, in prayer and reflection, how to practice scriptural holiness and sanctification in your daily life at home, in front of the computer and while at work. Reflect how to cultivate a willing mind and a surrendered heart as places of virtue in your life. Keep a daily journal to record your reflections.

2. Regularly identify the needs of the poor, oppressed and marginalized in your community, and find specific ways to assist. In a small group, practice silence and waiting on God. Ask him to show how you as a group can practice missional spirituality in action with your time, talents and treasure. Perhaps you could volunteer once a month at a food bank or women's shelter, or sponsor an orphanage in India and visit as a group of volunteers.

3. Like Wesley's "Holy Club," try the practice of methodical Bible study, prayer, weekly Communion, twice weekly fasting, reading spiritual classics and doing works of charity.

Discussion Starters

1. Read the book of Acts and note how it depicts a missional spirituality in action. Develop a teaching outline, teach it or preach it, and make follow-up questions for people to discuss.

2. Start a small group, a kind of "college of piety" or "band," and read Arndt's *True Christianity* together. For a lite version, read Spener's *Pia Desideria*. Discuss how these leaders can shape your understanding and actions for a missional spirituality.

3. Reread this chapter and select the quotes, themes and relationships you see that enrich your understanding of a missional spirituality in action. Review the "Lessons for Today" section, and discuss it with others.

5

Your Heart and Soul 1

Our desire for God is the desire that should guide all other
desires. Otherwise, our bodies, minds, hearts, and souls
become one another's enemies and our inner lives become
chaotic, leading us to despair and self-destruction. Spiritual
disciplines are not ways to eradicate all our desires but ways to
order them so that they can serve one another and together
serve God.

HENRI NOUWEN, BREAD FOR THE JOURNEY

There's an old joke about a young man who stood in Times Square
in New York City with a violin case under his arm. As a visitor to
the Big Apple, he didn't know his way around the vast city and was
lost. "How do I get to Carnegie Hall?" he asked a policeman. Without blinking an eye, the policeman replied, "Practice, my dear
man, practice."

The Practice of Theology

As God's people engage in tangible practices (habits, disciplines)
of inward and outward life, they are formed according to the culture of the Father's house. We need to integrate individual and

communal practices in which both individual and communal transformation will occur. The word *practice* now appears regularly in the missional and spiritual formation literature. Since we intend to use it frequently ourselves, we must begin with a description. Craig Dykstra writes,

> Practices of the Christian faith . . . are not . . . activities we do to make something spiritual happen in our lives. Nor are they duties we undertake to be obedient to God. Rather, they are patterns of communal action that create openings in our lives where the grace, mercy, and presence of God may be made known to us.[1]

We don't merely *believe* our way into spirituality. We must *practice* our way. Knowledge without action stunts spiritual growth. We can listen to sermons and attend good Bible studies, but until we put Christian truth into practice, little transformation will occur. A faithful inner world sustains a fruitful outer world (see Matthew 7:17-18; 15:11-20; 23:25-28). As doctors practice medicine and attorneys practice law, God's people must practice theology from a clean heart. As all successful athletes and musicians can attest, practice is essential for mastery. The practices of a missional spirituality form character and conduct toward love for God and neighbor. Like learning another language, after the sustained training of practice, becoming fluent is second nature. Tim Morey describes practices this way:

> A spiritual discipline is any practice that enables a person to do through training what he or she is not able to do simply by trying. They are the practices, relationships and experiences that bring our minds and bodies into cooperation with God's work in our lives, making us more capable of receiving more of his life and power.[2]

A practice is a task or action that applies a theory or skill. To pray or to read Scripture regularly is a practice. *Praxis* involves practices, but when you are engaged in the practices, you discover meaning as *truth in action*. We learn obedience as we practice obedience. We learn humility as we practice humility. We learn truth as we practice Scripture. We learn to love God and neighbor through various practices whose meanings are discovered and revealed in actions. The church embodies its theology through *praxis*.

The final purpose or goal of something is its *telos*. The *telos* for a Christian is to become mature in Christ (Colossians 1:28). *Praxis* is an action or practice that includes the *telos* of its truth. A biblical foundation for praxis is John 3:21: "But whoever lives by the truth comes into the light, so that it may be seen plainly that what he has done has been done through God."[3]

The Practices of Heart and Soul

Imagine the scene. Assembled before King David is a vast crowd of Israelite officials and warriors summoned to witness his charge to Solomon, the next king and temple builder. It is a defining moment in Old Testament history. Hushed people listen. David advises, "And you, my son Solomon, acknowledge the God of your father, and serve him with wholehearted devotion and with a willing mind, for the LORD searches every *heart* and understands every motive behind the thoughts" (1 Chronicles 28:9, italics ours). The Hebrew term for "wholehearted devotion" is literally a "heart of shalom"—a whole and complete heart. A missional spirituality seeks to love God and people from the whole person, not from isolated parts. Evelyn Underhill writes,

> For a spiritual life is simply a life in which all that we do comes from the center, where we are anchored in God: a life soaked through and through by a sense of His reality and claim, and self-given to the great movement of His will. Most of our conflicts and difficulties come from trying to deal

with the spiritual and practical aspects of our life separately instead of realizing them as parts of one whole.[4]

In many ways, a missional spirituality is about enlarging the size of our hearts. It's

> moving from the preferential love (*phileo*) of friends and family, to the unconditional love (*agape*) that is wide and boundless. What prevents us from engaging people in greater depth and frequency is the size of our heart. It is our limited heart size that limits our capacity to selflessly serve others. Our hearts do not grow stronger before we exercise but only after we exercise.[5]

Spiritual practices will exercise and enlarge our hearts. "How we spend our days is, of course, how we spend our lives," Annie Dillard mused.[6]

In the following section, we offer daily practices that can help align our desire for God to guide and order all other desires as parts of one whole. To love God from all our heart and soul coordinates and compels missional practices.

Because they are so inseparable and yet biblically distinguishable, we place heart (or spirit) and soul together, with Mark 12:30 as our point of departure, for it is the heart and soul of the matter. Together heart and soul set and store the desires for a missional spirituality that loves God and neighbor.

> Your heart is the center of your inward life—the deepest place of your emotions, desires, reason, and will—the location of feeling and faith. It's your interior site of purpose and passion. The heart is the command center of life. Proverbs 4:23 declares, "Above all else, guard your heart, for it is the wellspring of life." The center of your journey with God is the way of the heart.[7]

In Mark 12:30, the Greek word for "soul" is *psyche* (life, heart, self). The soul is that dimension of the person that interrelates all other dimensions; it encompasses the whole person, one's life (see Mark 8:35-36).[8] In spiritual formation—or heart and soul formation—we must train, shape and incline both our heart and soul in their desires and practices to love God. Jonathan Edwards taught, "True religion consists, in a great measure, in vigorous and lively actings of the inclination of the will of the soul, or the fervent exercises of the heart."[9] Our union with Christ coordinates all our affections and practices.

The Practice of Union with Christ

John 15:1-17 contains the vine and branches metaphor in which Jesus described the essential element for fruitful discipleship: remaining in him. As we shall see, this means living in a home where love flourishes into fruitfulness, friendship, answered prayer and joy.[10] Henri Nouwen captured the sense: "Speaking of himself as the vine and of his disciples as the branches, Jesus says: 'Make your home in me, as I make mine in you.' (Jn 15:4). This is an invitation to intimacy."[11]

Imagine that Jesus arrives one day at your front door and asks if he can live there with you. Imagine how your life would be different if Jesus moved in as a rent-paying tenant. Then imagine Jesus as a landlord who moves in with you: he owns your home because he purchased it (1 Corinthians 6:20; 7:23; 1 Peter 1:18-19). His new address is your life. Jesus said, "If anyone loves me, he will obey my teaching. My Father will love him, and we will come to him and make our home with him" (John 14:23). We come home to a place of love.

The key word in John 15:1-17, *remain*, occurs there eleven times. To *remain* means to dwell in, continue in, live in, lodge, stay, to make oneself at home in. According to Acts 27, on his way to Rome, Paul was trapped in a storm in the Adriatic Sea along with Roman soldiers and sailors. The sailors feared the storm would dash their ship against the rocks, so they let the lifeboats down to escape. But Paul warned, "Unless these men stay with the ship, you cannot be saved" (v. 31). The word *stay* is the same word as *remain* in John 15. A missional practice is to stay in union with Christ, to dwell in him, to live in him. Yet, it is not we who live, but Christ who lives in us by faith (Galatians 2:20).

To dwell in or make our home in Jesus is important for a missional spirituality because he made it a requirement for fruitfulness: apart from him, we can do nothing (John 15:5). Stephen Seamands suggests that we are able to depend only nominally on the Holy Spirit. It's more natural to depend on ourselves—our training, personality, skills, past experience and knowledge. He quotes Wesley Duewel: "If you rely on training, you accomplish what training can do. If you rely on skills and hard work, you obtain the results that skills and hard, faithful work can do. When you rely on committees, you get what committees can do. But when you rely on God, you get what God can do."[12] We must live a life worthy of the Lord and please him in every way, "bearing fruit in every good work" (Colossians 1:10). Jesus said, "This is to my Father's glory, that you bear much fruit, showing yourselves to be my disciples" (John 15:8).

Discipleship is a common and yet misunderstood word in our Christian vocabulary. What is a disciple? What is discipleship or disciple making? If you do a concordance search on the word *disciple* in the Gospels, you'll discover what Jesus taught. There's enough content there to both inform your biblical understanding and form a foundation for a discipleship process for your church, group or personal life. The evidence of true discipleship, according to Jesus, is when we bear much fruit. The key is that we learn how to *live* in Christ not just *learn about* Christ. Imagine the potential if we developed as the core curriculum in our newcomer orientation classes and small groups biblical teaching and practices that equipped people to dwell in Christ.

Imagine the fruit of such a focus!

How do we practice *dwelling* in Christ? Notice two key elements: love and obedience. "As the Father has loved me, so have I loved you. Now remain in my love. If you obey my commands, you will remain in my love, just as I have obeyed my Father's commands and remain in his love" (John 15:9-10). Love and obedience are core practices in God's family system. To remain or dwell in Christ's love does not mean we try to act more lovingly with a coworker or a child. Rather, we become the kind of people who from our heart and soul choose to be loving people. Our motivation is that Christ loves us as the Father loves him. This is not mere morality but the very basis of life itself. Imagine a world without love. We learn to love as we *practice* love.

Jesus also said, "You are my friends if you do what I command. I no longer call you servants, because a servant does not know his master's business. Instead, I have called you friends, for everything that I learned from my Father I have made known to you" (John 15:14-15). This text was a foundational text for the Quakers, the Society of Friends. There are no family secrets in our Father's house. We are friends and family with Jesus, and we get to know what he knows from the Father. We get to know our father's business and share in his rich inner life.

We remain in Jesus' love by *obeying* his commands—also a missional practice. The key command in John is that we love others. Jesus does not say that we will produce fruit when we attend church services, volunteer, tithe and attend Bible studies. Rather, we learn how to dwell in Christ, and we bear much fruit as a natural result. John writes that when we love, "God lives in us" (1 John 4:12, 15, 16).

In addition, when we make our home in Christ and he makes his home in us, prayer becomes effective. We enjoy fireside chats with him! Jesus promised, "If you remain in me and my words remain in you, ask whatever you wish, and it will be given you"

(John 15:7) and "You did not choose me, but I chose you and appointed you to go and bear fruit—fruit that will last. Then the Father will give you whatever you ask in my name" (John 15:16). As you remain in Christ's words, you learn his ways, bear fruit and see your prayers answered. You contemplate more deeply and pray more effectively. Len once journaled,

> I have been moving too fast lately. It makes listening difficult. I lose track not just of God, but also of my self. The center unravels. I no longer know who I am. And then in that place, my attention is divided. There are many distracting voices, and each seems to offer hope of an identity—but not mine. And because I haven't heard the One voice that speaks peace to my inner self, I can't offer an authentic word to anyone else either. I become merely a mirror, or an echo chamber. I am filled with noise. So, paradoxically, today, I choose solitude, so that my participation in the community will be vital and authentic, coming from a still place in my own soul where I have been named. This morning I seek to find myself in You so that I can offer true hospitality to others.

There's spiritual solidarity among intimacy, obedience and fruitfulness as we dwell in Christ's love that then flows into mission. Henri Nouwen noted, "As surely as solidarity arises out of true intimacy, mission emerges from fecundity [fruitfulness]."[13] The life of the vine feeds and bears fruit through the branches. We understand this image because we've both lived in the luxuriant Okanagan Valley in Kelowna, British Columbia, home to numerous picturesque vineyards that produce world-class wines. There's always mission in mind for a vineyard: to make the best wines for national and international markets.

In 1958, David Wilkerson founded Teen Challenge to reach troubled youth in New York City. Operating in eighty-two countries, this missional community seeks to provide faith-based residential drug and alcohol rehabilitation. It boasts a 70-percent success rate over five years for its participants—"success" being not returning to drugs or alcohol. How does Teen Challenge achieve this? By instilling rigorous spiritual practices in the residents as part of its mission. The residents learn to dwell in Christ in community through obedience, worship, prayer, Bible reading, classes, work and service. Life in Christ is at the center of the program. They practice a missional spirituality.

Roger spoke in chapel at a Teen Challenge camp situated southwest of Calgary. After an energetic worship time where the dozen men watched and sang along with a Hillsong United live DVD, he preached on John 15:1-17. They already knew the passage and knew that apart from Christ they could do nothing. They knew that they had to love God from heart and soul and to dwell in Christ to overcome their addictions. They were learning how to foster a missional spirituality in which they fed on the Father's will and bore fruit in their lives and could also help nourish others. Afterward Doug introduced himself and told his story:

> My parents divorced when I was 12 and my brother and I lived with my mom. I started in a new school in grade 6, began smoking pot, and hung out with the wrong crowd. The day I turned 16, I got my driver's license and decided I didn't need school anymore. I bought my first car and 11 hours later, I fell asleep driving home from work. The accident left me in a coma. I wasn't expected to live through the night. I woke up several weeks later unable to walk or talk. For years, I blamed God for my accident.
>
> When I was 25, my girlfriend and I had a son. It didn't work out, so I started to raise him alone when he was 10 months old. A few years later, I was introduced to crack cocaine. When my son went away on weekends, I would start using as soon as he left. Eventually, I decided to go back to

school to get my high school education. This is where I met my wife, and she invited me to her church. This was a life-changing experience for me. We were married and I stayed clean for a while, but eventually returned to smoking marijuana heavily.

My psychologist told my wife about Teen Challenge. I decided to stop being so selfish and entered the program. My thinking has changed dramatically! I'm reading my Bible and praying regularly. *It seems that God has taken permanent residence in my life.* I am learning valuable lessons every day and I am excited about my future![14]

Doug's face glows and his eyes gleam. He has come home to the Father. He's determined to help other drug and alcohol abusers when he graduates from the program. He's on mission as he radiates joy. Nouwen observed, "After speaking about intimacy and fecundity [fruitfulness], Jesus said to his disciples, 'I have told you this, so that my joy may be in you and your joy may be complete' (John 15:11). 'Complete joy' is the reward of intimate and fruitful life in the house of God."[15] A missional spirituality thrives when we are at home, where love, spiritual friendship, fruitfulness, answered prayer and joy nourish love for God from all our heart and soul. The practice of obedience sustains the practice of union with Christ.

The Practice of Obedience

Obedience is fundamental to a fruitful life. We recall the story of Mary and Joseph frantically searching for and then finding Jesus at the temple. His reply was, "Why were you searching for me? . . . Didn't you know I had to be in my Father's house?" (Luke 2:49). This astonishing statement follows: "Then he went down to Nazareth with them and was obedient to them" (v. 51). Jesus as an earthly son obeyed his human parents. As the divine Son, he learned obedience to his heavenly Father (Hebrews 5:8).

Making our home in Jesus requires that we learn and practice obedience as well. Obedience comes from faith, is an antidote to evil desires and is the basic substance for walking (living) in love (Romans 1:5; 1 Peter 1:14; 2 John 6). It's *obedience* to Jesus' commands, not just learning his commands, that's at the heart of discipleship and thus missional spirituality (Matthew 28:20).

Obedience is an attitude of submission to God that results in acts of service. James wrote, " 'God opposes the proud but gives grace to the humble.' Submit yourselves, then, to God" (James 4:6-7). We must arrange or rank ourselves under God. This implies that all other aims in life are removed and replaced with the single aim of living our life under God's authority. Humility drives submission as we empty ourselves and make space for Christ to live in us. *The spiritual life is the surrendered life.*

How does coming home to the Father connect with surrender? It's not an attitude of resignation to a Father who says, "As long as you are living under my roof . . ." It's more an attitude of relinquishment to a Father as we say, "Not my will, but yours be done" (Luke 22:42) and "May it be to me as you have said" (Luke 1:38). When we surrender we relinquish our control to a heavenly Father who is love. He's safe. We can trust him because he's mindful of our deepest needs. We offer willing worship in view of God's mercy as we sacrifice ourselves (Romans 12:1).

Loving God from all our heart and soul is unsustainable without practices. These help shape our ordinary responses so that we can be vulnerable and available to the Father. The practice of *obedience* should serve as a primary vow or as the basis for a rule of life to order all our desires toward loving God. It's what Richard Foster calls the discipline of submission, which means we give up our rights and control through self-denial, subordination, and service to others and God.[16] When we come home, obedience is basic to our trust in Christ. Dallas Willard writes:

The idea that you can trust Christ and not intend to obey him is an illusion generated by the prevalence of an unbelieving "Christian culture." In fact, you can no more trust Jesus and not intend to obey him than you could trust your doctor and your auto mechanic and not intend to follow their advice. If you don't intend to follow their advice, you simply don't trust them. Period.[17]

The word *obedience* can carry old-fashioned connotations like duty, compliance or rule keeping, and can even call dog training to mind. It is derived from the Latin word *oboedire*, meaning "to hear, to listen toward." A key Greek root for the word "obey," is *hupakouo*, which means "to hear under." We hear under Jesus.

John Calvin wrote, "All right knowledge of God is born of obedience."[18] And Dietrich Bonhoeffer said, "Only he who believes is obedient, and only he who is obedient believes. . . . Faith only becomes faith in the act of obedience."[19]

Another Greek word translated as "obey" is *tereo*. It means "to guard, watch over, observe, keep in view, or keep." This word appears frequently in John's writings, where it essentially means to keep or observe the word, commands or teachings of Jesus (John 14:23; 17:6; 1 John 2:5; 3:22-24). As we noted earlier, Jesus taught, "If you obey [keep] my commands, you will remain in my love, just as I have obeyed [kept] my Father's commands and remain in his love" (John 15:10).

A man once offered to pay Roger ten dollars an hour to meet each week and teach him how to study the Bible. Roger agreed to meet with him but said, "Give the money to the food bank. You need to obey Jesus and what the Bible teaches, and learn to help others." His reply, "That's easy for you to say. You get paid to obey Jesus!" The practice of obedience is a hard sell for some Christians.

Some non-Christians, in their search for meaning, will obey something or someone, whether it's the Bible or a celebrity. A. J. Jacobs, an agnostic Jewish editor of *Esquire*, decided to obey the Bible literally for one year. He documented his quest in *The Year of Living Biblically*.[20] In 2008, Robyn Okrant lived her life completely according to the advice of Oprah for one year. Her website offers her blogs and her book about her ongoing experience of "living Oprah."[21] What compels non-Christians to obey the Bible or Oprah for one year while some Christians aren't compelled to obey Jesus for one month? Willard argues that many Christians do not intend to obey Jesus' teachings because they don't really trust him.[22]

The Practice of Humility

"Humility is simply the disposition which prepares the soul for living on trust," Andrew Murray wrote.[23] The taproot for the practice of obedience is the practice of humility, "the sovereign virtue, the mother and root of all virtue," John Calvin said.[24] This is a difficult subject to write about because it's difficult to practice. And yet humility is a core attribute of God himself. Humility also gets God's attention (Isaiah 66:2). The Father sent his Son Jesus on mission. Jesus left the fellowship of the Trinity to become a man to serve, die and redeem the world as the resurrected Christ. To accomplish this mission, he had to humble himself; the goal was to become a *servant*, literally a *slave* (Philippians 2:7-8).

In our churches, we often ask people to become volunteers. But Jesus doesn't invite us to become his volunteers. He calls us to follow him and become his servant-slaves. A volunteer can quit at will and is not subject to a master as a servant-slave is.

The word *humility* is from the Latin root *humus*, which means "ground." The Greek word group for "humility," from the root *tapeinos*, means "low." Someone said, "Pride is dust defying itself." To practice humility is to decrease ourselves, to go low to ground level; "humility is to the soul what fertilizer is to a garden."[25] It's a place of sub-mission (under mission). Slaves obey and serve in submission.

Of humility, Jonathan Edwards wrote,

The eminently humble Christian is as it were clothed with lowliness, mildness, meekness, gentleness of spirit and behaviour, and with a soft, sweet, condescending winning air and deportment; these things are just like garments to him, he is clothed all over with them (1 Pet. 5:5; Col. 3:12). . . . Pure Christian humility has no such thing as roughness, or contempt, or fierceness, or bitterness in its nature; it makes a person like a little child, harmless and innocent, that none need to be afraid of; or like a lamb, destitute of all bitterness, wrath, anger, and clamor; agreeable to Eph. 4:31.[26]

We speak of the culture of a family, business or church—the feel or ethos. What's the culture of our Father's house? Self-abandonment and gain through loss shapes that culture, in which the way up is down: "Humble yourselves before the Lord, and he will lift you up" (James 4:10), and "All of you, clothe yourselves with humility toward one another, because, 'God opposes the proud but gives grace to the humble.' Humble yourselves, therefore, under God's mighty hand, that he may lift you up in due time" (1 Peter 5:5-6).

We must wear the garments of humility—unfettered lowliness like that of Mother Teresa and Pope John Paul. Bill Hybels suggests, "If you want to be truly great, then the direction you go is down. You descend into greatness. Greatness is not a measure of self-will, but rather self-abandonment. The more you lose, the more you gain."[27] Even in the secular business world, humility or self-effacement is considered a feature of leaders who take a company from good to great, leaders who are a blend of personal humility and professional will.[28] Singer-songwriter Peter Mayer expressed humility like this:

What if the highest destination of any human life
Was not a place that you could reach if you had to climb

Wasn't up above like heaven, so no need to fly at all
What if to reach the highest place, you had to fall?[29]

Andrew Murray asserted, "Christ is the humility of God embodied in human nature; Jesus was the Incarnate Humility."[30]
The practice of humility finds its theological substance in the
incarnation detailed in Philippians 2, the basis of missional-
incarnational service.

> Do nothing out of selfish ambition or vain conceit, but in
> humility consider others better than yourselves. Each of you
> should look not only to your own interests, but also to the
> interests of others.
> Your attitude should be the same as that of Christ Jesus:

> Who, being in very nature God,
>   did not consider equality with God something to be
>   grasped,
> but made himself nothing,
>   taking the very nature of a servant,
>   being made in human likeness.
> And being found in appearance as a man,
>   he humbled himself
>   and became obedient to death—
>   even death on a cross! (Philippians 2:3-8)

We could call this "nothing spirituality" or "self-emptied spirituality." The Greek word for "made himself nothing" in Philippians 2:7 (*kenosis*) simply means "to empty."[31] What did Jesus empty?
He emptied himself of his status as equal with God. The question
is, how do we practice humility?[32]

We meet many faithful Jesus followers on the street: people
hesitant to look a young professional in the eye, yet who trust
Christ and can report his daily care for them. Meanwhile, in
middle-class churches we meet many who are ready to declare

God's goodness while they protect their rights and comforts, and neglect the poor.

A homeless woman needed a safe place to stay, and the shelter was full. At first Len resisted having her stay at his home: "Why do I have to share my home with this person I don't know? I'm a writer and I need my space." She spent five nights with him and Betty, and her faith and unpretentiousness challenged his faith.

"Consider others better than yourselves." To understand the meaning of these words we must *practice* them. Gordon Smith wrote, "The outcome of true humility is that we are capable of love toward others; the virtue of humility enables us to turn from self-centeredness and pride and embrace the way of love."[33] Humility is often inconvenient and aggravates our sense of entitlement.

"We don't become humble as much as we learn to practice humility," Gary Thomas says.[34] To practice humility does not mean we are to think less *of* ourselves but less *about* ourselves. We choose to become less than others. Humility is for the sake of others. God is less interested in people who perform outward religious sacrifices than he is with righteous people who "act justly . . . love mercy and . . . walk humbly with [their] God" (Micah 6:8).

Philippians 2:5 is the key: we need an *attitude*—"Your *attitude* should be the same as that of Christ Jesus." Literally, "let this mind be among you as also in Christ Jesus." Humility is how we "work out [our] salvation with fear and trembling" (Philippians 2:12-13). To "work out" means to cause to function or to show the results of. The practice of humility is a function and result of our salvation.

William Law says that every day is a day of humility. And how does it come about? As we condescend to serve others.

Condescend to all the weaknesses and infirmities of your fellow creatures, cover their frailties, love their excellencies, encourage their virtues, relieve their wants, rejoice in their prosperities, compassionate their distress, receive their

friendship, overlook their unkindness, forgive their malice,
be a servant of servants, and condescend to do the lowest
offices to the lowest of mankind.[35]

Good Christian leadership is an imitation of Christ. If we seek to
imitate Christ, we must imitate both his person and his practices.
He came among us as Lord and Master, but he then set an intentional example of suffering service. If we look to his position or
being, we view him as heroic. If we look to his word and his example, we see him as host. He was over us as Lord and Master and
Creator. He was lowly and vulnerable as a servant. He calls us not
to lord it over one another. To lead as a Jesus follower is to lead
from among and from below, not from above.

Given Jesus' example and the biblical emphasis on attitudes
of humility and submission, the weight of evidence against any
top-down, CEO model of leadership within the community of
faith is overwhelming. The problem with mixed models in
churches today—welding the business and the faith-community
models together—is that they are not in line with the New Testament model and they subvert the culture of kingdom leadership. Christian leaders must resist the pressure to lead from
above.

Xinwei, a Mandarin-speaking Chinese leader with a PhD in bi-
ology, left mainland China in 1998 to work at the University of
Alberta in Edmonton as a research professor. After their move, his
wife, a member of the Communist Party, became a Christian
through the influence of a friend who invited her to a Mandarin-
speaking church. In time, Xinwei also became a Christian, and
they were both baptized on the same Sunday morning. Eventually
he left his position to study at Taylor Seminary to earn a Master of
Divinity degree and train for pastoral work. He is now a dedicated
Christ follower.

After graduation, Xinwei's church commissioned him to plant

a church in Calgary. Today that church numbers around one hundred Chinese people, mostly new converts. After six years, his mother church in Edmonton invited him to return as their new senior pastor. When you sit and talk with him, or see him serve, you feel the glow of his humility. His soft-spoken demeanor, character and grace flow from an attitude of servanthood, which is considerate of others and submissive. He is a missional leader who practices a missional spirituality as he loves God and people.

Suggested Practices

1. Monthly read John 15:1-17 in *The Message* and then Galatians 2:20 in two or three translations. Imagine what it means to practice union with Christ, to be at home in Christ with the Father, where Christ is also at home with you, living in you. Daily practice the presence of Christ in your heart and mind by faith, and "pay absolute unmixed attention" to his words.

2. Watch *The Soloist* with some friends. Talk about what you saw and felt. What did you learn about helping relationships, giftedness and friendship? Ask the Lord if you could become a friend to someone who is outside your normal comfort zone. Consider volunteering with a church or agency that works with the poor, marginalized or destitute.

3. Identify areas in your life where you might value position, power and prestige, and where you notice times when you look after your own interests first before the interests of your family members, friends, work associates and others. Practice condescending to others, and focus on small ways to daily serve and support the interests of those around you. Surrender. Meditate on St. Benedict's twelve steps to humility (see <http://www.osb .org/rb/text/toc.html>, starting in chapter seven).

Discussion Starters

1. Henri Nouwen wrote, "Speaking of himself as the vine and of his disciples as the branches, Jesus says: 'Make your home in me, as I make mine in you' (John 15:4). This is an invitation to intimacy." What images does this convey to you? What does it mean to make your home in Jesus as he makes his home in you? What does it mean to be a friend of Jesus?

2. The words *obey* and *obedience* can often carry negative connotations. Based on the discussion in this chapter, how would you describe the nature of biblical obedience and how is it a key to fruitful discipleship? Respond to this quote: "The spiritual life is the surrendered life." What would this look like in your personal life as it flows into your public life?

3. What do you think of the statement "God is a servant"? Why is humility essential in the spiritual life, and what does it mean to have the same attitude that Jesus had in Philippians 2? In what ways did Jesus model humility as connected to a missional spirituality? Compare and contrast what it means to follow Jesus as a "volunteer" or as a servant-slave. What are some practical ways to practice humility at home, at work, at school?

6

Your Heart and Soul 2

O Thou to whom I owe the gift of this day's life, give to me also,
I beseech Thee, the spirit to use it as I ought. Forbid that I
should stain the brightness of the morning with any evil
thought or darken the noontide with any shameful deed. Let
Thy Holy Spirit breathe into my heart today all pure and
heavenly desires. Let Thy truth inform my mind. Let Thy
justice and righteousness make a throne within me and rule my
errant will. Let Christ be formed in me, and let me learn of
Him all lowliness of heart, all gentleness of bearing, all
modesty of speech, all helpfulness of action, and promptness in
the doing of my Father's will.

JOHN BAILLIE, A DIARY OF PRIVATE PRAYER

The essential practices for a missional spirituality provide a dynamic interface among Scripture, prayer, the Spirit and relationships. An evangelical tendency is to separate spiritual disciplines into the inward and the outward. It's helpful to isolate and cultivate specific practices such as prayer, solitude, fasting, study, worship, fellowship and service, but a missional spirituality must integrate inward dimensions of the heart and mind with outward dimensions of the physical and social. Paul prayed, "May God himself, the God of peace, sanctify you *through and through*. May your whole *spirit*, *soul* and *body* be kept blameless at the coming of our Lord Jesus Christ" (1 Thessalonians 5:23, italics ours). Another evangelical tendency is to view spiritual formation mainly in terms of Bible study and prayer. These aren't wrong, and we affirm both Scripture and prayer in this section. But we agree with Earl Creps that these two disciplines entail several dilemmas:

> *Practicality*: these two disciplines tend to operate in isolation from real life, serving as the "national anthem" before the ball game that starts whenever we go to work.

> *Character*: to speak for myself, I've met too many bad people who pray and read their Bibles rigorously and are unchanged by their efforts.

> *Mission*: churches are filled with people who are committed to prayer and Scripture but either have no concern for mission or actively resist the changes that it requires.

Most of the dilemmas spring from the way prayer and Scripture study are isolated from the rest of the Christian life. If they are to have any transforming effect, the effect must be found in the ordinary junctures of human life. In other words, our practice of the disciplines tends to be undisciplined.[1]

The Practice of *Missio* Reading and Prayer

We encourage a disciplined approach where the practice of *obedience* to Scripture is integrated with the practices of prayer, attentiveness to the Spirit, in the context of relationships, which will feed and facilitate mission located in the ordinary junctures of life. We call this the practice of *missio* reading and prayer. (The Latin word *missio* means "mission.") It's inadequate to settle into an inward, pietistic spirituality that can lead to a journey merely of self-improvement or, as Dallas Willard says, "sin management."

Rather, spirituality must be a natural part of salvation expressed in discipleship and mission.[2] A missional spirituality involves loving God and others from the inside out. Mission is the context for the Bible. Christopher Wright argues,

> The whole Bible is itself a "missional" phenomenon. The writings that now comprise our Bible are themselves the product of and witness to the ultimate mission of God. . . . A missional hermeneutic or missional reading of biblical texts is to see how a text often has its origin in some issue, need, controversy or threat that the people of God needed to address in the context of their mission . . . of being a people with a mission in a world of competing cultural and religious claims.[3]

A *missio* reading of Scripture will inspire our obedience to its truths in all of life—the home, the workplace, the neighborhood, the wider culture. Jesus placed the sanctifying Word of truth in the context of mission. His followers are set apart from evil and the world for mission: "My prayer is not that you take them out of the world but that you protect them from the evil one. They are not of the world, even as I am not of it. Sanctify them by the truth; your word is truth. As you sent me into the world, I have sent them into the world" (John 17:15-18). The Holy Spirit, who inspired all Scripture, guides Christians into all truth, illuminates the truth of Scripture and seals its meaning in their hearts, and bears witness to Jesus Christ, the living Word. The Scriptures and the Spirit work inseparably in our lives. Robert Webber offers initial counsel in how to practice spiritual reading:

> As you read the Scriptures that lead you into a walk with the Spirit, open your heart and mind to the voice of God met in the words and images of Scripture. Take time to reflect, to ruminate, to chew on what you hear: Have a good walk and allow yourself to be formed more deeply by your companion, the Holy Spirit.[4]

King David prayed, "Teach me to do your will, for you are my God; may your good Spirit lead me on level ground" (Psalm 143:10). The Word is not a record only of what God *spoke*, but of what God *speaks*. It's not only a narrative of what God *did*, but of what God *does*. Stanley Grenz remarks,

> Scripture is one aspect of the Spirit's mission of creating and sustaining spiritual life. He both authors and speaks through the Bible, which is ultimately the Spirit's book. By means of Scripture he bears witness to Jesus Christ, guides the lives of believers, and exercises authority in the church.[5]

As we endeavor to listen to the Spirit through Scripture, prayer places us on a wavelength to hear his voice in stereo. Or to put it another way, when we are home, prayer occupies the great room, serving as host to the Scripture and the Spirit. Jesus declared, "Is it not written: 'My house will be called a house of prayer for all nations'?" (Mark 11:17). As he cited the Old Testament, Jesus did not say God's house is a house of preaching, teaching or study per se; rather, prayer is the channel for worship, learning and missional spirituality "for all nations." The Jews saw the temple primarily as a place of sacrifice, but Jesus saw it as a place of prayer (see 1 Kings 8:27-30). It was to be "for all nations," not just for the Jews or for the religious. True prayer is itself a sacrifice to God (Psalm 141:1-2). As the temple of the Holy Spirit, the church is now the living house of prayer, where the Spirit dwells and intercedes in accordance with God's will for believers in times of weakness and wordlessness (Romans 8:26-27).

Prayer requires the discipline of an Epaphras, who was "always wrestling in prayer" for the Colossians (4:12). Someone said, "Prayer is the gymnasium of the soul." It's by or in the Spirit (Ephesians 6:18). It often carries an intercessory missional focus for the spiritual benefit of individuals and churches and for the advance of the gospel. Prayers ascend to heaven as incense with answers that descend from heaven as lightning (Revelation 8:3-5), what Mark Buchanan calls "perfume and bombs."[6] Feel the passion in Paul's exhortation "Never be lacking in zeal, but keep your spiritual fervor, serving the Lord. Be joyful in hope, patient in affliction, faithful in prayer" (Romans 12:11-12).

Richard Foster declares, "All who have walked with God have viewed prayer as the main business of their lives."[7] Alan Hirsch and Darryn Altclass suggest, "Within the practice of prayer we would include solitude, silence, contemplation, and petition, as well as confession"[8]—and, we add, intercession.

A resurgence of the medieval practice of *lectio divina* (divine reading), or praying the Scriptures especially according to Benedict's Rule, is a welcome corrective we can practice both individually and corporately. *Lectio divina* uses four practices: *lectio* (read the text); *meditatio* (meditate on the text); *oratio* (pray the text); *contemplatio* (contemplate the text). However, it does not primarily foster a missional spirituality, because it concentrates more on inner disciplines that seem to stay there without an outlet into the world, without a contemplation of and movement toward people. We also know few people who actually practice *lectio divina*.

As we approach obedience to Scripture with a *missio* reading, knowing that Christian spirituality is relational and missional, our hearts and souls are nourished. The Spirit shapes reading in which the mind descends into the heart—from mere information to formation—where God can address and shape us *for the sake of others*. We must embody the text, share the text, pray the text and apply the text in the context of relationships. Eugene Peterson says this "is a way of reading that becomes a way of living"[9] as we foster union with Christ. The Spirit enlivens and directs *missio* reading and prayer relationally as we love God and others from the inside out.

When we practice *missio* reading and prayer, we pay attention to how the Spirit convicts, corrects or enlivens growth and oppor-

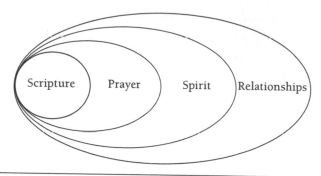

Figure 6.1.

tunities in our relationships with people in our families, workplaces, neighborhoods and communities. The practice of *missio* reading and prayer focuses on *obedience* to Scripture, integrated with the practice of prayer and attentiveness to the Spirit, in the context of relationships for mission. This empowers us to love God and others.

Embodying God's Love from the Inside Out

Evelyn Underhill wrote, "The action of those whose lives are given to the Spirit has in it something of the leisure of Eternity."[10] Unfortunately, widespread disenchantment, *ex*carnation, programism and abstraction in modern rationalistic church cultures often sterilize and de-supernaturalize the practice of Bible reading and prayer. A common result is that they are reduced to intellectual studies, shopping lists and organizational systems.

There's a place for intellectual study, but only insofar as it equips us to handle or expound the word of truth correctly—literally "to cut a straight path" (2 Timothy 2:15). As if on a road that goes straight to its destination, we are to search for the truth of Scripture without getting sidetracked into wordy debates or impious talk and to look not only for meaning but for obedience (Ezra 7:10). Spiritual knowledge joined with vital piety—the religious affections transformed by Scripture, prayer and the Spirit in the context of relationships—forms a holistic missional spirituality. We offer a method for the practice of *missio* reading and prayer from John Wesley:

> This is the way to understand the things of God: Meditate thereon day and night; so shall you attain the best knowledge, even to "know the only true God, and Jesus Christ whom he hath sent." And this knowledge will lead you "to love Him, because he hath first loved us;" yea, "to love the Lord your God with all your heart, and with all your soul, and with all your mind, and with all your strength." . . . If you desire to read the Scriptures in such a manner as may most effectually answer this end, would it not be advisable,
>
> 1. To set apart a little time, if you can, every morning and evening for that purpose?
>
> 2. At each time, if you have leisure, to read a chapter out of the Old and one out of the New Testament; if you cannot do this, to take a single chapter, or a part of one?
>
> 3. To read this with a single eye, to know the whole will of God, and a fixed resolution to do it? In order to know His will, you should,
>
> 4. Have a constant eye to the analogy of faith, the connexion and harmony there is between those grand, fundamental doctrines, original sin, justification by faith, the new birth, inward and outward holiness;
>
> 5. Serious and earnest prayer should be constantly used before we consult the oracles of God; seeing "Scripture can only be understood through the same Spirit whereby it was given." Our reading should likewise be closed with prayer, that what we read may be written on our hearts;
>
> 6. It might also be of use, if, while we read, we were fre-

quently to pause, and examine ourselves by what we read, both with regard to our hearts and lives. . . . And whatever light you then receive should be used to the uttermost, and that immediately. Let there be no delay. Whatever you resolve begin to execute the first moment you can. So shall you find this word to be indeed the power of God unto present and eternal salvation.[11]

Roger was part of a men's group that met weekly from 7 to 8 a.m. For one year all the men did was read daily Bible selections in the Old and New Testaments from a one-year Bible and record their reflections in their journals. They read the same passages at home daily, and then on the Wednesday morning of their meeting day, they read the passage for that day and quietly journaled for about twenty minutes. Then each man shared his reflections with the others. In community, they virtually practiced John Wesley's reading program, and there were astonishing results: times of tears and laughter, holy prayer for one another, awestruck silence from the observations, and prayers read from journals.

Over time, there was a felt need to open the group to others. One day, one of the men (we'll call him John) felt compelled to offer a ride to a man (Will) he saw walking on the side of the road on his way into town. They met a few days later for coffee. Will said he needed a place to stay, so John offered him the small guesthouse on his property. He also invited him to the men's group, where Will began to share his life and story, felt loved and accepted, and eventually gave his heart to Christ. Six months later Will asked Roger to baptize him. So one Wednesday morning, that men's group met down at a local lake at 7 a.m. to witness Will's baptism. Afterward the spiritually charged men's group went for breakfast to celebrate their journeys into Jesus as a "band of brothers." They practiced *missio* reading and prayer, with the Spirit, in relationships, as always.

The Practice of Worship

The shortest route to deeper and richer worship is
a clearer theology.

P. D. MANSON

What is the organizing practice—the center of gravity—of a people who wish to dwell in Christ, obedience, humility, *missio* reading and prayer? What does a chosen people, a royal priesthood, a holy nation, a people belonging to God *do*? Peter taught that the church is to "[offer] spiritual sacrifices acceptable to God through Jesus Christ" and "declare the praises of him who called [them] out of darkness into his wonderful light" (1 Peter 2:5, 9). We practice *worship*. In all of Scripture, there's only one thing the Father actively seeks: worshipers who worship him in Spirit and truth (John 4:23). And we must *learn* to worship: "Blessed are those who have learned to acclaim you, who walk in the light of your presence, O LORD" (Psalm 89:15).

Worship is a verb. It involves both attitudes and actions. Biblical worship contains images of worshipers bending the knee, bowing down and lying prostrate before the Lord. The outward positions express the inward postures; they bowed down in submission. Worshipers do not "appear before the Lord empty-handed" (Deuteronomy 16:16). They offer spiritual sacrifices of praise, financial gifts, doing good and sharing with others as they declare his worth (Philippians 4:18; Hebrews 13:15-16). They "worship the Lord [their] God, and serve him only" (Matthew 4:10). Believers offer themselves as living sacrifices before God as worship (Romans 12:1). Vance Havner remarked, "Every Christian is a priest, not offering a sacrifice for sins—since that has been done once and for all—but offering their person, praise and possessions."[12]

Worship for believers today in both Reformation and revival

settings can suffer from defective theology that can lead to defective practice. Reformation worship can cause believers to intellectualize their faith, keeping them in the posture of a student in a lecture-hall, while revival worship can cause believers to emotionalize their faith, keeping them self-absorbed as if in a concert hall.[13] In the milieu of Enlightenment rationalism, the Reformation placed highly reasoned exegetical preaching as the centerpiece of worship and removed the artistic, imaginative, mystical and experiential aspects. While the Word is central in Reformation worship, the Spirit is central in revival worship. It can focus on the emotional and experiential, emphasizing triumph but overlooking trial. Perhaps we should reinstate the Psalms in worship, which ground us theologically in both triumph and trial. Stanley Grenz stated, "What Christians believe shapes the content and approach of their worship, and their worship reflects what they believe."[14]

Typical evangelical worship songs frequently use the words *I* and infrequently use the words *we* and *us*. Instead of a God focus and corporate focus, many songs have a human and individual focus.[15] According to pollster George Barna's research, 50 percent of all adults who attend church services don't experience God's presence. Furthermore, he states, the majority don't consider worship a top priority in their lives, while they believe that the goal of worship is for personal benefit and pleasure.[16]

Defective views of God ("bad" theology) lead to unorthodox worship. Missional worship tends not to be a prominent feature or practice in either conservative or charismatic worship contexts. While worship is a vertical act toward loving God, it emerges from inward piety. Biblically, it's also horizontal and outward toward others through service as a royal priesthood. Orthodox worship is private *and* public, personal *and* communal, for both ministry *and* mission.

Sally Morgenthaler documented and opened wide the subject of worship evangelism.[17] She argued that orthodox worship should connect edification with evangelism. Worship should build up believers while it also builds bridges to the world. In other words, orthodox worship is missional. Psalm 96:3, 10 instructs, "Declare his glory among the nations, his marvelous deeds among all peoples. . . . Say among the nations, 'The LORD reigns.'" David vowed, "I will praise you, O Lord, among the nations; I will sing of you among the peoples" (Psalm 57:9).

In Acts 2:47 we see the effects of the community life and worship of the early Christians: they "[praised] God and [enjoyed] the favor of all the people; and the Lord added to their number daily those who were being saved." In 1 Corinthians 14:25, Paul advised that proper use of prophecy and tongues in worship could be a vehicle for unbelievers present to "fall down and worship God, exclaiming, 'God is really among you!'"

In Romans 15:9-11, Paul used Old Testament texts to support missional worship: "Therefore I will praise you among the Gentiles, I will sing hymns to your name" (Psalm 18:49); "Rejoice, O Gentiles, with his people" (Deuteronomy 32:43); "Praise the LORD, all you Gentiles, and sing praises to him, all you peoples" (Psalm 117:1). Gerrit Gustafson said, "Worshippers, don't just enjoy God's wonderful presence for yourselves. Call others to join you there through faith in Christ. And those of you who want to see the world come to Christ, don't just call men and women to believe, call them to worship."[18] Worship and mission are connected where the inner circle and the outer circle are integrated. Jim Wallis remarked,

> Scripture judges the value of worship, the inner circle, by looking at the shape of the outer circle, or the daily obedience it produces. Our worship should spread from the inner circle to the wider circle of our everyday lives as Christians, and our daily speech and acts and attitudes are ordained to

be a wider and transformed worship.[19]

This reframes our worship from the purely spiritual to include the physical and social. We love God and others in tangible ways. We are hospitable, we share our homes, and we are good neighbors. In worship we bless the Lord who blesses us to venture out and bless others.

Missional worship is the organizing practice for all of life—the God-life. A major challenge is to recapture a theological imagination and a heart for God and his kingdom. Our media-saturated consumer culture imposes a relentless array of idols that compete for God's position in our hearts: the desires for unrealistic beauty, sexuality, materialism, food and drink, fitness, recreation and status. In *Desiring the Kingdom*, James Smith argues that the "liturgies," or worship practices, of the market and the mall, and their extensions through television and advertising, form people's hearts—the seat of desire and what people love.[20] Drink Guinness, drive a Lexus, look like a supermodel, indulge in unrestrained romance and sexuality, experience exotic vacations and charge them to MasterCard.

Behind these practices is a secular goal of life—a secular *telos*—a vision of the "good life." These "shape and constitute our identities by forming our most fundamental desires and our most basic attunement to the world. In short, liturgies make us certain kinds of people, and what defines us is what we *love*."[21] If our *telos* is to live the good life rather than the abundant life in Christ, our imagination and heart will be attuned to that goal. We then become like that which we love.

We cannot simply teach more information and expect heart change. A goal of worship is not more head information but heart transformation. Smith writes,

> Being a disciple of Jesus is not primarily a matter of getting the right ideas and doctrines and beliefs into your head in

order to guarantee proper behavior; rather, it's a matter of being the kind of person who *loves* rightly—who loves God and neighbor and is oriented to the world by the primacy of that love. We are made to be such people by our immersion in the material practices of Christian worship—through affective impact, over time. . . . The liturgy is a "hearts and minds" strategy, *a pedagogy that trains us as disciples precisely by putting our bodies through a regimen of repeated practices that get hold of our heart and "aim" our love toward the kingdom of God.*[22]

The good life is to love God from all our heart, soul, mind and strength, and our neighbor as our self. Private worship should be an extension of public worship. The Spirit fosters a lively missional *Spirit*-uality in which corporate worship is a gathering point from which God's people emerge, directed by Jesus, strengthened by the Spirit, to join the Father's mission throughout the week.

Temple spirituality views the church as those who gather to worship God as a weekly routine in fixed structures. A missional spirituality will view the church as those who gather to worship God, who then *sends* them into the daily routines of worship as service in the community as a royal priesthood. Because of a transformed heart, they seek to "loose the chains of injustice and untie the cords of the yoke, to set the oppressed free and break every yoke; . . . to share [their] food with the hungry and to provide the poor wanderer with shelter—when [they] see the naked, to clothe him, and not to turn away from [their] own flesh and blood" (Isaiah 58:6-7).

The Practice of Enchantment

People travel there from all over the planet to Southern California to experience the marvel of its sun-drenched beaches, stately palm trees, star-studded Hollywood and, of course, Disneyland. These pilgrims become immersed in a vacation wonderland. But when you live there a while, the "wow" becomes "whatever." You endure the grind of traffic jams, hot smoggy days and fast-food diets, high taxes and little green space, urban congestion and crime. A visitor's wonderland adventure is far different from a resident's everyday life.

Similarly, some Christians lose their wonder and endure the sometimes dull familiarity of church life—devoid of the "wow" because they've lived there a while. Perhaps they settled for a colorless theological imagination and awelessness that resulted from *disenchantment*. This is where mystery and miracle, dreams and visions, Spirit and sacrament are merely showcased in what some call a primitive ancient world that we must demythologize or dispensationalize for a modern word-based world.

Like the children who ventured into the magical world of Narnia through the wardrobe, we can venture into a wonder-filled world of worship through the practice of *enchantment*—where we are attentive to God's handiwork. Elizabeth Barrett Browning expressed the theological imagination behind this practice:

> Earth's crammed with heaven,
> And every common bush afire with God;
> But only he who sees, takes off his shoes—
> The rest sit round it and pluck blackberries.[23]

Through the practice of enchantment we view God's world as a sacramental place that reveals his tangible and yet hidden presence, his nearness and transcendence. The practice is an active and attentive, prayerful spirituality of the everyday. Simone Weil depicts prayer as "pay[ing] absolute unmixed attention."[24] Paying such attention enables us to see the sacred in creation and culture through the discipline of awareness in the sacrament of the present moment. A. W. Tozer remarked, "You can see God from anywhere if your mind is set to love and obey him." This practice makes daily life sacramental.

Abraham Joshua Heschel asked, "How does one find the way to an awareness of God through beholding the world here and now?" He suggested that we see the world as the Bible sees it, through *enchantment*, with attention to the sublime and mysterious, in wonder and awe. Nature's power, beauty and grandeur command our attention.[25] The perception of beauty is a path on which we experience the sublime that arouses in us a sense of wonder, "a way in which things react to the presence of God."[26] The presence of God and his handiwork are everywhere visible and even invisible, in the beauty and bounty of both creation and culture: "The heavens proclaim the glory of God. The skies display his craftsmanship" (Psalm 19:1 NLT). The cathedral of creation houses icons of God's artwork full of multisensory vastness and inexhaustible variety. We can read God's poetry in male and female, made in his image, living icons of his dominion and glory. We can contemplate the creation to discover the extraordinary in the ordinary and "see all things, persons and moments as signs and sacraments of God."[27]

We can see the sacred also in culture. Though culture is fallen, God's common grace refracts the colors of enchantment through the prism of culture: the opening extravaganza of the 2010 Vancouver Winter Olympics; David Foster and Friends, U2, and Celine Dion concerts; *Fiddler on the Roof;* birthday parties and weddings; *Extreme Makeover: Home Edition;* school Christmas plays; potluck dinners with friends. We need receptive hearts to perceive God's energies in culture, where "our search for God and His search for us meet at windows in our everyday experience."[28] We can even learn from Mick Jagger's song "God Gave Me Everything." As Jagger sings, you can see "it" (the presence of God) in the sky and sand, women and babies, lovers and the sun, races and storms, wine and fathers, in symphonies and in love shown.[29]

When we practice enchantment, we "pay absolute unmixed attention" to God's artwork revealed and we see God in the daily rounds of life. Elizabeth Dreyer addressed clergy, writing,

> For everyone, the spiritual life involves the connections we make between the divine and the human. But the lives of clergy and professional ministers are steeped in explicit, public, religious symbols and activity that have God as their direct and proper object. However, most members of the church spend their days in a world that is not explicitly religious. Therefore, it becomes imperative that this wider lay community be empowered to see God on its daily rounds— wherever that may be.[30]

To glorify God is the *telos*, the end purpose of life and creation. God's glory is the radiance of his magnificent holiness, perfection, honor and works. In Hebrew and Greek, God's glory (*kabod* and *doxa*) includes his beauty, which shows itself in the cosmos. Psalm 19 trumpets, "The heavens declare the glory of God; the skies proclaim the work of his hands. . . . The law of the LORD is perfect, reviving the soul. The statutes of the LORD are trustworthy, making wise the simple." Verses 6-14 move from the glory in creation to the glory in the law (vv. 1-5). King David linked the beauty of creation to obedience to the law that results in moral excellence— *virtue*. Virtue—the beauty of the moral life—reflects God's beauty. Jonathan Edwards wrote,

> Virtue is the beauty of those qualities and acts of the mind, that are of a *moral* nature . . . that true virtue must chiefly consist in love to God. . . . For as God is infinitely the greatest Being, so he is allowed to be infinitely the most beautiful and excellent: and all the beauty to be found throughout the whole creation, is but the reflection of the diffused beams of that Being who hath an infinite fullness of brightness and glory.[31]

He continues, "True virtue . . . is that *consent*, propensity and union of heart to [God's] being in general, which is immediately exercised in a general good will."[32] Beauty exists when things fit together, when they "consent" to God's being. Virtue aligns with the beauty of God's being and God's cosmos. Does not a hike into a rugged mountain range or a gaze into a vast summer evening sky inspire something of virtue and transcendence in us?

We can see the sacred in painted skies and shooting stars, in golden prairies and speckled deserts, in a dog's wagging tail, in an infant's gurgling smile, in a *Riverdance* performance. A virtuous life glorifies God. The practice of enchantment helps us apprehend God's beauty with a response of *being* a person of virtue, of godly beauty.

Basic morality is not virtue or spirituality. There are moral people who are not virtuous or spiritual. Virtue is moral excellence developed from consistent practice that transforms a person's character through union with Christ. A missional spirituality cultivates virtue for the sake of others through regular practice until it becomes natural.

We can cultivate virtue only when we know the human *telos*—the goal or ultimate aim of human life—and what it means to be fully human as God designed us. Virtue is those qualities of character forged through regular choices and thinking that help us achieve that *telos*. When we know the *telos* of human life, we know how all the parts either contribute to or don't contribute to its achievement.[33] God's original design was for humans to reflect his image and likeness as those who rule and reign over creation and are fruitful and multiply (Genesis 1:26-28). Humans were to be icons, image bearers, who would represent and reflect God's rule in creation. The theme of rule also comes out in the vocation of the church as a royal priesthood and holy nation (1 Peter 2:5, 9)—the church serving as priests and rulers who mediate God's presence and reign in the world.[34] In the age to come, that vocation will continue: "You have made them to be a kingdom and priests to serve our God, and they will reign on the earth" (Revelation 5:10).

The New Testament continues the theme of image bearing in terms of practices that cultivate virtue: "Put to death, therefore, whatever belongs to your earthly nature . . . since you have taken off your old self with its practices and have put on the new self, which is being renewed in knowledge in the image of its Creator" (Colossians 3:5, 9-10). True humans are renewed image-bearers of God. The *telos* for the Christian life is that believers would become complete, mature, *teleion*, in Christ (Colossians 1:28) and be perfect and complete, as their heavenly Father is perfect, *teleios* (Matthew 5:48).

The Greek word for virtue is *arete*, meaning "moral excellence."[35] Christian virtues are those characteristics that reflect God's beauty, which believers must choose to think about and make every effort to possess in increasing measure. Paul wrote, "Whatever is true, whatever is noble, whatever is right, whatever is pure, whatever is lovely, whatever is admirable—if anything is excellent [arete] or praiseworthy—think about such things" (Philippians 4:8). And Peter gave the pattern: "For this very reason, make every effort to add to your faith goodness [arete]; and to goodness, knowledge; and to knowledge, self-control; and to self-control, perseverance; and to perseverance, godliness; and to godliness, brotherly kindness; and to brotherly kindness, love. For if you possess these qualities in increasing measure, they will keep you from being ineffective and unproductive in your knowledge of our Lord Jesus Christ" (2 Peter 1:5-8).

To be like Jesus Christ is the *telos* of life: "Dear friends, now we are children of God, and what we will be has not yet been made known. But we know that when he appears, we shall be like him, for we shall see him as he is. Everyone who has this hope in him purifies himself, just as he is pure" (1 John 3:2-3). We can cultivate virtue according to the conventional wisdom "Sow a thought and reap an action; sow an act and reap a habit; sow a habit and reap a character; sow a character and reap a destiny." Aristotle said, "Excellence is an art won by training and habituation. We do not act rightly because we have virtue or excellence, but we rather have those because we have acted rightly. We are what we repeatedly do. Excellence, then, is not an act but a habit."[36]

Those who practice enchantment also pay attention to the Bible's depiction of the world as a place where supernatural activities choreograph kingdom life. Genesis to Revelation clearly portrays real, not mythical, spiritual warfare between the kingdom of light and the kingdom of darkness. Angels do appear to people, demons do possess people, miracles and healing do touch people, and dreams and visions do guide people. Interpret the Bible with enchanted hermeneutics.

"Jesus went throughout Galilee, *teaching* in their synagogues, *preaching* the good news of the kingdom, and *healing* every disease and sickness among the people" (Matthew 4:23, italics ours). According to Barna, three-quarters of all pastors see themselves as gifted either in preaching or in teaching. Jesus' ministry had three components: preaching, teaching and *healing*.[37] Samuel Chadwick said, "A ministry that is college-trained but not Spirit-filled works no miracles." And Eugene Peterson wrote, "The secularized mind is terrorized by mysteries. Thus it makes lists, labels people, assigns roles, and solves problems. But a solved life is a reduced life. These tightly buttoned-up people never take great faith risks or make convincing love talk."[38] A gift-based team ministry validates and seeks to foster all the gifts: teaching, healing, faith, helps, mercy, prophecy and miracles.

But in a world of enchantment, we must locate spiritual formation, and what we term missional spirituality, precisely in the world of the Spirit. With Paul, "we regard no one from a worldly point of view" (2 Corinthians 5:16). We must consider how to practice spiritual warfare, pray for the sick and cast out demons, facilitate prophecy and intercessory prayer, listen for God's voice, and develop supernatural gift-based ministry and guidance. Furthermore, in a world full of addictions and dysfunctions, we must consider how to disciple and help people through supernatural means, not just through natural ones.

A missional spirituality is eschatological, organized around kingdom life in this age, a foretaste of the age to come (Hebrews 6:4-5). Hebrews 2:4 states, "God also testified to it [the gospel message] by signs, wonders and various miracles, and gifts of the Holy Spirit distributed according to his will." The word *testified* implies that miracles and gifts of the Spirit are an ongoing reality today. We should do what Jesus did (John 14:12); we should practice the Gospels, Acts and 1 Corinthians. Supernatural ministry in the fullness of the Spirit is normal kingdom life in an enchanted world (see Acts 4:31; Galatians 3:1-5).

During his senior year of college, Trevor and his buddy Josh bought memberships at a gym in the basement of the local recreation center, also used by local hockey clubs for fitness programs. A junior hockey team was one of them. Here's a narrative from Trevor, now twenty-six:

> Josh and I got to know some of the players by name and started to attend their home games. One day on our way home from the gym, the Lord simultaneously burdened our hearts for a ministry with these hockey players. We started to brainstorm big about ideas that we wanted to see God do. We dreamed of three things: (1) get Bibles for every player, (2) pray with the guys before their home games, (3) sing together during the chapel times. So instead of jumping right in, which is natural for our personalities, we set out to pray every night together for two weeks to seek the Lord's face about the possibility of start-

ing a chaplaincy program with this team.

While we prayed, our senior class invited a pastor from Josh's home church to come and teach a leadership class for two weeks. During that time, we shared our hearts with the pastor and his son-in-law, who was also there taking the course. Immediately the son-in-law said we should contact a guy he knew who is the regional rep for HMI (Hockey Ministries International), the biggest hockey ministry in the world. We contacted him and shared our vision. He loved the idea. He told us that he was actually praying and looking for a pastor to start a chaplaincy program and that although we weren't pastors we were the guys for the job. He also had a son who played for the team.

He advised us to meet with the coach and let him know that we represented HMI. After the coach agreed to a meeting, we praised God over and over for opening these doors for us, even though there was a possibility the coach would refuse us. We left it in the Lord's hands. As we shared with the coach, he not only gave us permission but also said that if we needed anything to let him know. It turns out that he was a coach in the west coast, where all of their teams had chaplains through HMI.

The next step was to meet with the whole team and introduce ourselves and our new ministry opportunity. The regional rep came down for the meeting and shared about HMI, and then it was our turn. We assured them it was not mandatory and that all we wanted to do was share Christ's love with them and give them a different perspective to life than what the world offered. We left it at that.

As we approached the door of their dressing room, where the chapels occurred, we took a deep breath and opened it. Sixteen of the twenty-one players sat there. Some consistently came weekly. Some came once to feel it out, and others came sporadically. They all had the gospel seed planted in their hearts. At the end of the first chapel we pitched our idea about praying with them before the game on Friday. They all agreed.

As we entered the dressing room on Friday night all the coaches and players were there. We didn't know what to expect. I said, "Anyone who wants to pray can come and meet us in the hall." Over half the team came out, and there we were, a group of guys with one common bond—love for the game of hockey—huddled in a circle praying to the God of the universe for safety, protection, and fun. What a feeling!

That was our routine for five months. God provided amazing answers to prayer. After we prayed in the hall before only two games, a player who never came to the chapels spoke up for the whole team and invited us into the room to pray. So for the rest of the season Josh and I walked in before the games where every player removed their helmets, bowed their heads, and prayed with us. Just before the Christmas break, Josh's home church sponsored the team and shipped us enough embossed Bibles for every player and coach.

Lastly, the guys agreed to learn songs during chapel. They started off timid and shy, but by the end of the season we could hear them sing over the guitar. God is *so* good! What was also pretty cool was that we were the only chapel group in hockey in the world that our rep knew of where the players themselves regularly sang in chapel.

We know four of the players gave their lives to Christ. We helped some guys through hard issues and personal loss throughout that year. We travelled to different churches with the guys from the chapel program so they could have a church home to attend the next season when we wouldn't be there. Josh and I had an opportunity to share our ministry with over 300 men during a Men's Conference at school. The team also had a bus accident in a snowstorm that could've been worse. Every player plus three coaches appeared at the next chapel.

When God burdens our heart with something, it's for a reason. He wants to bring life change through us. This hockey ministry started with an idea in our hearts followed by fervent effective prayer. The most fulfilling Christian life is one that seeks God's plans, strives to accomplish them, and therefore leaves no room for asking "what if?" Think big. Believe big. Obey big. Pray big. Don't be surprised when God does big things as a result.

Suggested Practices

1. Read through John Wesley's program and practice *missio* reading and prayer for three months as a spiritual experiment and then evaluate and make adjustments. As you read and pray, be attentive to how the Spirit leads you into mission as a result.

2. Listen to the worship song "Lifesong" by Casting Crowns. Notice how it communicates the call to a lived theology of worship. Determine to practice life worship in your love for God.

3. Hike through a wilderness area or camp out overnight in a national park, and ponder the beauty and enchantment of the creation. Absorb its beauty into your heart and reflect on ways God's beauty inspires you to be a person of beauty, of virtue.

Discussion Starters

1. How do you view *missio* reading and prayer as one integrated practice? Is there a connection between them? Discuss how Bible reading and prayer, in the Spirit, in the context of relationships can foster a missional spirituality.

2. Evaluate the worship in your personal life and in your church life. What are the strong areas and the weak areas? Why? Do you agree that there is such a thing as missional worship? Discuss specific ways you can grow in the practice of personal and corporate worship.

3. Reread the section titled "Disenchantment" in chapter two and then reread the section titled "The Practice of Enchantment" in this chapter. What is the connection? How can you grow in a supernatural missional spirituality? What is the connection between beauty and virtue? Discuss specific things that are essential to enable you to grow in virtue.

7

Your Mind Matters

"For who has known the mind of the Lord that
  he may instruct him?"
But we have the mind of Christ.

1 CORINTHIANS 2:16

We've discussed what it means to love the Lord your God from
all your heart and soul with practices that help you nurture this
adventure. We will now discuss the mind. Let's return to the conversation between Jesus and the scribe about *Shema* spirituality:

> [Jesus said,] "'Love the Lord your God with all your heart
> and with all your soul and with all your mind and with all
> your strength.' The second is this: 'Love your neighbor as
> yourself.' There is no commandment greater than these."
> "Well said, teacher," the man replied. "You are right in
> saying that God is one and there is no other but him. To love
> him with all your heart, with all your *understanding* and with
> all your strength, and to love your neighbor as yourself is
> more important than all burnt offerings and sacrifices."
> (Mark 12:30-33, italics ours)

In verse 30, Jesus said to love God with all your mind, or *dianoias*.

In verse 33 the scribe substituted that word *mind* with the word *understanding*, or *suneseos*, which refers to insight. In verse 34 Jesus acknowledged that he answered "wisely" or "thoughtfully," or *nounechos*. Practicing love for God from your mind means your thoughts, understanding and insights originate in and are directed toward him. It does not primarily mean you accumulate biblical information or become astute in Christian reason, apologetics and academics. Rather it means you place God at the center of your mental orientation toward life, and you practice *faith thinking* driven by the desires of a godly heart toward understanding. Your mind matters.

What Is the Mind?

Our modern view of love is that it is largely emotional, sentimental and sensual, with *eros* at its core. Because God is love, all dimensions of his being reflect love. Just as we are made in his image, we must reflect love from all dimensions of our being, including the mind. *Mind* in Mark 12:30 refers to understanding, the activity of thinking and intelligence. The English translations of various Hebrew and Greek words denote the human capacity for contemplation, judgment and intention. *Mind* may also signify your mindset, attitude or characteristic point of view (for example, see Philippians 2:2-5). In both the Old and the New Testaments, "heart" is often used as the equivalent of "mind" and is sometimes translated as *mind* (for example, in Isaiah 65:17; Jeremiah 19:5).[1] *Heart* and *mind* are terms that overlap and signify the deepest parts of who we are and our inner disposition and orientation toward God and his laws (see Hebrews 8:10; 10:16).

Your thoughts shape your theology and then your spirituality, which ultimately shapes your character and conduct. Marcus Aurelius stated, "The things you think about determine the quality of your mind. Your soul takes on the color of your thoughts."[2] Leonard Sweet writes:

Cognitive theorists tell us that you and I generate at least sixty thousand thoughts a day. That amounts to one thought every 1.44 seconds. That thought may be true or false, noble or debased, just or unjust, pure or impure, lovable or spiteful, gracious or offensive, excellent or cheap, admirable or shameful. Since every thought reverberates bio-chemically throughout the body, our thoughts shape our souls in ways we have only begun to imagine.[3]

How you think shapes how you behave. James concluded that a double-minded person is unstable in all he or she does (James 1:8). Paul said that believers should not conform to the pattern of the world but be transformed by the renewing of their minds (Romans 12:2). The New Living Translation renders this verse as, "Let God transform you into a new person by changing the way you think." Paul also wrote, "Once you were alienated from God and were enemies in *your minds* because of your evil behavior" (Colossians 1:21).

The brain contains about two hundred billion neurons, which compose a series of electrical highways interconnected by synapses. John Ortberg writes,

Researchers have found that tennis players can improve their backhands simply by rehearsing them *mentally*. Neurons that will change you are firing in your mind. Over time, those pathways between neurons were shaped in ways that are absolutely unique to you. . . . Which synapses remain and which wither away depends on your mental habits. Those that carry no traffic go out of business like bus routes with no customers. Those that get heavily trafficked get stronger and thicker. The mind shapes the brain. Neurons that wire together fire together. In other words, when you practice hope, love, or joy, your mind is actually, literally, rewiring itself. . . . Because you were made in the image of

God, you have the capacity for what might be called "directed mental force."[4]

Paul advised, "Whatever is true, whatever is noble, whatever is right, whatever is pure, whatever is lovely, whatever is admirable—if anything is excellent or praiseworthy—think about such things" (Philippians 4:8). As a counter-practice to a consumerist and sensual culture, we must daily think about noble and lovely things. The lifestyles of the rich and famous are not likely to offer us many positive examples. When you practice directed mental force to love God from your mind, a renewed mind results, along with a transformed character and a missional spirituality. You begin to see the world through his perspective and also think of ways to love others.

It's difficult, isn't it, to resist the relentless barrage of ideas and images popular culture hurls at us through television, movies, music and the Internet? Our culture programs us to love physical beauty, material possessions, sexuality, success and personal freedom apart from God. Hollywood and YouTube set the agenda for many people. Our thoughts and decisions reflect what we love and to what we are captive. Do you find it difficult to "take captive every thought to make it obedient to Christ" (2 Corinthians 10:5)? This requires mental discipline. What about "see to it that no one takes you captive through hollow and deceptive philosophy" (Colossians 2:8)? A missional spirituality means you will love God from all your mind as you then help others hear and understand God's grace in all its truth (Colossians 1:6). You will guide others to the truth so they are in turn not held "captive by hollow and deceptive philosophy" propagated by the world (Colossians 2:8).

To love God from your mind does not imply you become committed to reason, rationalism and academics.[5] Jonathan Edwards argued that we must cultivate vigorous and lively religious affections or inclinations of both heart and mind, the chief spring of our actions.[6] The fervent exercise of the heart toward God also includes the mind. Edwards wrote, "In the production of gracious affections, our minds are so enlightened that we obtain proper and spiritual views of divine things."[7] With that in mind, consider the significance of this text:

> This is what we speak, not in words taught us by human wisdom but in words taught by the Spirit, expressing spiritual truths in spiritual words. The man without the Spirit does not accept the things that come from the Spirit of God, for they are foolishness to him, and he cannot understand them, because they are spiritually discerned. The spiritual man makes judgments about all things, but he himself is not subject to any man's judgment: "For who has known the mind of the Lord that he may instruct him?" *But we have the mind of Christ.* (1 Corinthians 2:13-16, italics ours)

We have the mind of Christ? How is that possible? How do a twenty-year-old business major, a forty-three-year-old carpenter, a divorced Hispanic woman or an inner-city school teacher, as Christians, have the mind of Christ? Well, they know something of his mind because they know what the Spirit reveals in spiritual words taught by the Spirit in Scripture. To have the mind of Christ means to look at life from his worldview. George Barna suggests that Jesus' life shows at least four elements that worked together in his worldview: (1) he had the foundation of God's Word that was clear, reliable and accessible; (2) he maintained a laser-beam focus on God's will; (3) he evaluated all information and experiences through a filter that produced appropriate choices; (4) he acted in faith.[8] We are to think Christ's thoughts by the Spirit as spiritual persons and not as carnal persons without the Spirit. Paul taught, "The mind controlled by the Spirit is life and peace" (Romans 8:6). What about the mind *not* controlled by the Spirit? What are the results of that?

Christ-Mindedness

You've likely heard the accusation "he's so heavenly minded, he's no earthly good." The biblical perspective is that to be earthly good we *must* be heavenly minded. After a presentation of magnificent theology about the supremacy and sufficiency of Christ in Colossians 1–2, Paul turned his application to the Christian mind (Colossians 3:1-3). He concluded with present-tense habits of orientation: "Since, then, you have been raised with Christ, *set your hearts* on things above, where Christ is seated at the right hand of God. *Set your minds* on things above, not on earthly things. For you died, and your life is now hidden with Christ in God" (italics ours). According to Douglas Moo, "This refers not to a purely mental or intellectual process, but to a more fundamental orientation of the will . . . suggesting a habit of the mind."[9]

Then Paul said to put to death whatever belongs to the earthly nature—immorality, greed, anger, slander—and to put on holiness and love (Colossians 3:5-14). A habit of godly thoughts fosters godly living for the sake of others. You must think Christianly to develop your mind in the process of spiritual formation (Romans 12:1-2; 1 Corinthians 14:20; Philippians 4:8; 2 Peter 3:1). Sharp biblical thinking is imperative. The practice of a *missio* reading of Scripture coupled with a spiritual reading of Christian classics and theology will enrich you. But Jesus said we must love God from our mind and not simply love study or thinking about God. How can we practice this?

Christian and Missionary Alliance founder A. B. Simpson offered three questions that can help us cultivate a sanctification (sacredness) of our mind:

1. Is it separated? Have we learned to withdraw our attention and perception from all that is unholy and to refuse to see forbidden things? . . . The very first thing . . . is to separate it from all evil by absolutely ignoring evil and refusing any contact with it.

[This does not mean to withdraw from the world but to not let the evil in the world contaminate you; see Ephesians 4:22-24; 5:1-17.] . . . We should separate ourselves from thoughts as well as objects which are not purifying. . . .

2. And so, we apply our second test to the faculties of the understanding. Are they dedicated? Is our attention dedicated to God? Can we say, "My heart is fixed, my mind's stayed on Thee"? Are our thoughts dedicated to God? Is our intelligence devoted to know His Word and will? . . .

3. And finally, is our understanding and intellect filled with God, for He must possess us Himself and put in us His thought and mind as well as His spirit and grace? . . . The Holy Spirit is a quickening force to the consecrated intellect.[10]

To love God from your mind is a willed choice. It's to place him and his ways into your daily thought life. He and his Word become the filter for your thoughts. You begin to ask, "What do you want, Lord?" or to pray, "Please guide me today, Lord." You will think like him. To face life's challenges and Christian mission like Jesus, you bring Scripture to bear on your circumstances. Jesus cited Scripture regularly when he faced Satan and the Pharisees, and when he taught his disciples. God's will and Word occupied his thoughts.

To love God from your mind, he must occupy your thoughts. As you wake in the morning, plan your day, drive your car and go about your work, converse with him, think of him and thank him. "Pay absolute unmixed attention" to his presence and influence in your thoughts, just as you pay attention to your spouse, children and friends. As a fruit of love, you will daily muse on him.

The first fruit of love is the musing of the mind upon God. He who is in love, his thoughts are ever upon the object. He who loves God is ravished and transported with the contemplation of God. "When I awake, I am still with thee" (Psa 139:18). The thoughts are as travelers in the mind. David's thoughts kept heaven-road, "I am still with Thee." God is the treasure, and where the treasure is, there is the heart. By this we may test our love to God. What are our thoughts most upon? Can we say we are ravished with delight when we think on God? Have our thoughts got wings? Are they fled aloft? Do we contemplate Christ and glory? Oh, how far are they from being lovers of God, who scarcely ever think of God! "God is not in all his thoughts" (Psa 10:4).[11]

The Practice of Faith Thinking

On Monday afternoon, April 3, 1995, Roger and his wife, Gail, were babysitting the three little sons of their close friends Tom and Judy. On his way to work, Tom would drop off his sons Andrew, Jesse and Stephen for the day. Judy worked as a nurse at Kelowna General Hospital. Their firstborn son, Andrew, would turn six that month. Roger and Gail's youngest son, Micah, was already six. After Micah came home from school, he and Andrew would play together until Tom came to fetch Andrew and his younger brothers on his way home from work. Sometimes Micah's older brother, Joel, would also join them.

That day, Roger sat at his kitchen table as he prepared for a talk he was to give to recently arrived students from all over the world at a ministry school he was leading. Gail was preparing an early supper.

In the front yard of their home in Kelowna is a four-foot, rock retaining wall that overlooks a grass area alongside the street below. The boys invented a contest to see who could jump the farthest off that wall. After their son Joel jumped, Andrew went next but landed prostrate. Then Micah jumped. Andrew didn't get up. Because he lay motionless and started to breathe funny, Joel ran into the house to report it. Gail raced to the grass, scooped him up and carried him to the living room floor. Andrew was unconscious and not breathing. Panic set in. Gail phoned 911 while Roger performed CPR on him. Andrew had no pulse. His face was blue. They prayed.

The fire department and paramedics arrived and tried to revive him unsuccessfully. They rushed him to emergency. Five minutes later, Tom arrived and learned of the accident. All drove to the hospital as Judy, while on her shift there, was called to meet everyone in the waiting room. The emergency team got Andrew's heart to beat, but on his way to the operating room, he was pronounced dead.

As you can imagine, two couples stood stunned and grief-stricken. Andrew had had a freak accident. The autopsy revealed he likely fell headlong unconscious and immediately died of a neck and spinal injury. Years later, Tom and Judy learned that she and their son Stephen have a heart condition that can block consciousness. Now they suspect Andrew had the same condition, and he lost consciousness as he fell.

The book of Job and the lament psalms depict the agony of disorientation. In instances like this, theological questions can ransack your mind, left in its naked vulnerability as your whole being collapses under the weight of shock. This began a journey into a desert of colossal *faith thinking* for Roger. Theological reflection—what we call faith thinking—helps us love God from our minds and trust in his goodness and sovereignty when "our colored dawn turns to shades of gray."[12] Christian faith has to become living, not abstract.

During their dark night of the soul, Roger and Gail made desperate appeals: "Out of the depths I cry to you, O LORD; O Lord, hear my voice. . . . I wait for the LORD, my soul waits, and in his word I put my hope" (Psalm 130:1-2, 5). They chose to believe. They also asked, "Shall we accept good from God, and not accept trouble?" (Job 2:10), and said, "The Lord gave and the Lord has taken away; may the name of the Lord be praised" (Job 1:21). They chose to "give thanks to the Lord, for he is good; his love endures forever" (Psalm 118:1). They chose to believe that Jesus, the high priest who sympathized with their weaknesses, could be approached for mercy and grace in times of need (Hebrew 4:15-16).

Simone Weil said, "There are only two things that pierce the human heart. One is beauty. The other is affliction."[13] While afflicted, we must practice theological reflection because "more frequently than untested Christians expect, God removes the one source of joy and meaning that we were counting on to make our lives worth living, and replaces it with nothing. God puts us in a box where all we have is him. Tozer once compared a man complaining that all he had left was God to a fish bemoaning that all it had left was the ocean."[14]

Job is a case study in faith thinking. The book of Job is less about the problem of pain and why the innocent suffer and more about faith and God's faithfulness and whether God is worth worshiping even when someone loses all he has. Will we choose to love God even when it hurts? When an avalanche of grief presses the life out of you, you can still choose to love God from your mind through faith. Abraham Heschel observed, "Faith like Job's cannot be shaken because it is the result of having been shaken."[15]

One more point of theological reflection: "And we rejoice in the hope of the glory of God. Not only so, but we also rejoice in our sufferings, because we know that suffering produces perseverance; perseverance, character; and character, *hope*" (Romans 5:2-4, italics ours). Roger and Gail, Tom and Judy had to move on, return to work and persevere while God shaped their character, sustained by *hope*. Regularly Gail would look out their living room window at the hills around Kelowna and reflect on Psalm 121:1-3: "I lift up my eyes to the hills—where does my help come from? My help comes from the Lord, the Maker of heaven and earth. He will

not let your foot slip—he who watches over you will not slumber."
Brian Doerksen's worship song "Faithful One" and later on Matt
Redman's "Blessed Be Your Name" helped, as did Henri Nouwen's
The Inner Voice of Love.

To love the Lord your God from your mind requires the practice of faith thinking—the heart of theology.[16] Theology was not
meant to be theoretical and academic but practical. Theology must
be an *activity* of faith more than a *study* of faith. When you think
about God, you practice theology. The substance of eternal life is
to *know* God and Jesus Christ (John 17:3). As your knowledge of
God increases, your love for him also increases, and you thereby
come to know him more through *praxis* (Colossians 1:9-10).

Theological reflection and culture. In missional literature today,
there's a legitimate call to engage culture and popular media
through theological reflection. Media both shapes and expresses
popular culture with its smorgasbord of spiritualities and idolatries served through Hollywood. *Culture cultivates.* Movies like
Avatar and celebrities like Oprah Winfrey cultivate people's
imaginations as these icons also express deeper social and spiritual longings.

While Oprah is benevolent, her self-styled beliefs in God, spirituality and "living your best life" are a syncretism of the Bible and
various spiritualities drawn from such people as *New York Times*
bestselling author Eckhart Tolle, the Oprah's Book Club author of
A New Earth: Awakening to Your Life's Purpose.[17] His book became
the key textbook for Oprah and Eckhart's course "A New Earth."
He teaches that Jesus and Buddha are early but not yet mature
guides for enlightenment and awakening who pave the way for us
to experience Presence.

Other spiritual influences come from California Episcopal Reverend Ed Bacon, Reverend Michael Bernard Beckwith and Omega
Institute guru Elizabeth Lesser, author of *Seeker's Guide: Make
Your Life a Spiritual Adventure.* Lesser was an Oprah's Book Club

author and panelist for the "Spirituality 101" broadcast in January 2009. Here's her view of spirituality:

- Who Has Authority? You are your own best authority.
- What Is Spirituality? You listen within for your own definition of spirituality.
- What Is the Path to God? Many paths lead to spiritual freedom and peace.
- What Is Sacred? Everything is sacred—your body, mind, psyche, heart, and soul.
- What Is the Truth? The truth is like the horizon—forever ahead of you, changing.[18]

Oprah also aired several broadcasts that promoted the teaching from Rhonda Byrne's book *The Secret*, which sold fourteen million copies in forty languages with its accompanying movie.[19] The book and movie convincingly claim the Law of Attraction is "the most powerful law in the Universe," determining its complete order. Byrne says this is a "secret" delivered through all the ancient writings of Hinduism, Buddhism, Judaism, Christianity and Islam. What you think, you bring into your life. You reap what you sow. Your thoughts are seeds of creation. *The Secret* teaches that you are the creator who taps into the Mind of the Universe, which is ready to grant your wishes for health and wealth that you attract with attitude and gratitude, because your wish is a command. She writes, "The Creative Process used in *The Secret*, which was taken from the New Testament in the Bible, is an easy guideline for you to create what you want in three simple steps: ask (Matt 21:22; Mark 11:24); believe; receive."[20] Rhonda has a follow-up book, *The Power* (Atria Books, 2010).

Though Oprah Winfrey's show is over after twenty-five years, she now leads OWN (Oprah Winfrey Network) on cable TV and continues to be regarded as one of the most influential and wealthiest women on the planet. Her heart and care for people are obvious. The finale to her twenty-five-year series contained a moving challenge to live our call and ended with her declaration of, "To God be the glory." Many innocent and searching people accept what she promotes, including nondiscerning Christians, especially women. How would you practice theological reflection with the teachings above? How do you set your mind on things above and counteract alluring teaching offered by well-meaning spiritual gurus? Would you follow *The Secret* to achieve financial success?

However, not everything is misguided in popular culture. We can evaluate elements in popular culture as we practice theological reflection. This requires that we interpret culture by the tools (or texts) that culture makes available to us. Stanley Grenz remarked:

> Because these "world fashioning" tools carry transcendent significance—i.e. they claim to disclose the essence of reality—they are theological in character. In other words, cultural expressions speak about what a society believes to be ultimate, and in this sense, they are theological.[21]

Many movies and songs in popular culture contain spiritual elements consistent with Scripture or which Scripture addresses, such as longings, anxieties and evil in the human condition. All theology is done in particular contexts in which we seek biblical understanding of cultural struggles, hopes and values expressed through "texts" that we can "read," such as movies, music, TV, art, literature and advertising. God is at work in culture through common grace, or what Wesley called prevenient (or preceding) grace. We can love God from our minds more effectively as we read and interpret popular culture's texts and trends. *Christianity Today* movie critic Jeffrey Overstreet notes that some Christians are uncomfortable with this.

> This unsettles Christians who have come to believe that the only source of God's revelation is the Bible. But the Scrip-

tures relentlessly point us *outward*, teaching us how to hear God's voice in the natural world, in human events and in history: "The heavens declare the glory of God" (Ps 19:1). "I lift up my eyes to the hills—where does my help come from?" (Ps 121:1). "Go to the ant, you sluggard; consider its ways and be wise!" (Prov 6:6).[22]

Secular songwriters and moviemakers offer glimpses into the human condition or into social or spiritual issues and ask questions worth exploring. Consider Nickelback's song "If Today Was Your Last Day."[23] This song declares that life is a gift and not a given right, so we should leave our fears behind and take the path less traveled. It suggests we might be generous down to our last dime, forgive our enemies and contact friends we never see, mend broken hearts and shoot for the stars. It challenges us to consider a philosophy of life as a whole that asks, Would you live each moment like your last and leave the past, because every second counts and there's no way to rewind life? Yes, rock bands can press us to reflect theologically.

Of course, the book of Ecclesiastes argues that God at the center of your life is most important. But most of Nickelback's song carries timeless values whose consideration would benefit us all.

In the same way, when you make cultural references in your preaching, teaching and conversations, you help others practice theological reflection as you also build missional bridges to your community, as Paul did in Athens with the idol to an unknown god (Acts 17). The goal is to connect secular searches for spirituality with Christian truth and spirituality. This is a way to do theology in context to serve a missional purpose, as all people long to live life with purpose.

Theological imagination. We must recover a lively theological imagination that will incite rigorous faith thinking for a missional spirituality. Jesus taught in parables to illustrate his truths with concrete word pictures that stimulated his hearer's imaginations. Leonard Sweet wrote, "The Jesus method of communication was not the exegesis of words but the exegesis of images: 'the kingdom of heaven is like . . .' "[24] We all think in pictures, not in propositions. Albert Einstein wrote, "Logic will get you from A to B, but imagination will take you everywhere" and "Imagination is more important than knowledge. Knowledge is limited. Imagination encircles the world."

While the modern world was word based, we learned to cultivate an intellectual faith. Our postmodern culture is image based, with visual language through story, symbols, logos, conversation, metaphors and pictures shaping our lives. Paul's doxology captures the boundless potential of imagination: "Now to him who is able to do immeasurably more than all we ask or *imagine*, according to his power that is at work within us . . ." (Ephesians 3:20, italics ours).

According to Kenneth Bailey in his book *Jesus Through Middle Eastern Eyes*, Jesus was a *metaphorical* theologian. His primary method of teaching was through metaphor, simile, parable and dramatic action rather than through logic and reasoning. His method was that of a poet, not of a philosopher. In the Western tradition, theology is often constructed from ideas held together by logic that is often abstract. Paul used ideas *and* metaphors. The West has tended to expound his concepts but use his metaphors only as illustrations. Jesus taught subversive theology and spirituality through parables and images, primarily as a *metaphorical* rather than as a *conceptual* theologian.[25] A metaphor communicates in ways that rational arguments cannot. Pictures portray but do not replace abstract meaning. And an image is worth a thousand words.

Discover ways to lodge truth in the imagination. Paint word pictures of the God-life. As Jesus did through the parable of the prodigal son, let your theological imagination liberate God's lavish love from the principled abstraction of the elder brother to the messy concreteness of the younger brother. When we love a God like that, we love others like that. Or, as Jesus did through the parable of the good Samaritan, let your theological imagination liberate you to be a neighbor to marginalized outsiders. A missional spirituality is subversive, shaped by love for God and neighbor.

Theology and practice. Most of us can relate to how we love God from our hearts, the seat of our emotions and affections. But we must also love him from our minds if we expect proper practices. Defective theology produces defective practices. Alan Hirsch points out that wrong mental images of God produce defective character and actions, as pharisaic zeal without proper knowledge of God attests. Islamic jihadism and Europe's so-called Christendom, which produced the Crusades, the Inquisition, genocide, apartheid and anti-Semitism, also have sick and distorted theological roots or views of God. In *Untamed,* Hirsch and his wife, Debra, cite William Temple, who wrote, "If your conception of God is radically false, then the more devout you are, the worse it will be for you. You are opening your soul to be molded by something else."[26]

But the link between belief and practice is not solely based on right thoughts and theology; it's also right human *desire.* Using Jonah as an example, Amy Plantinga Pauw wrote,

> The problem is not that Jonah fails to believe the right things; he fails to *desire* the right things. As the Augustinian tradition insists, the link between belief and practice is forged by human desire and attitude. Both our cognitive and practical efforts arise out of our loves. Right beliefs are by themselves insufficient in shaping good practice. . . . This appropriate attitude is what Jonah lacks. His practice is deplorable because he resents the truth of his beliefs. He arguably has true insights in God's nature, but his beliefs are not productive or appropriate

attitudes towards God and neighbor. Jonah's spiritual short-comings are primarily affective, not epistemic.[27]

When innocent people suffer, our views of God are challenged. We believe God is good, loving and all-powerful. But when painful circumstances scream otherwise, the structure of our faith in him can collapse. We feel abandoned and alone; we feel injustice. During personal earthquakes, seemingly stable though untested Christians sometimes jettison their faith, turn on God and the church, and go it alone.

If we go with God, we must choose to love him from our hearts and then our minds before we negotiate treacherous paths of adversity. We cannot muster faith in the moment of pain if we have not made a choice to love him beforehand. It's difficult to start a diet and then resist food at a smorgasbord or pledge ourselves to purity and then resist the lure of pornography if we don't settle these issues privately in our hearts and then our minds beforehand. Theology and its practice are affective as much as they are intellectual.

There's a "paradox that when life is good we tend to have no questions, but when life is bad we have no answers."[28] Tragedy has a stark way of shaking people. If you've suffered, you can offer hope and comfort to those who experience grief and loss. When you choose to love God even when it hurts, you can also love others when they hurt. Adversity is a natural bridge for a missional spirituality to reach people.

The tragedy of Andrew's death at the Helland home touched many people. It enlarged the Hellands' compassion and capacity to identify with, comfort and love others who encounter personal tragedy—as 2 Corinthians 1:3-7 teaches. God the Father who lost his Son also suffers with broken people through broken people. Faith thinking shapes who we are and how we act missionally; our suffering shapes our spirituality. Comfort rooted in a nonmissional spirituality falls short in comforting those who suffer grief and loss.

Rigorous faith thinking is a practice of missional spirituality that includes using theological imagination to reflect on situations of life and ministry, nurtured in desires that arise out of our love for God. You might ask, "Where is Jesus in this situation? How does Scripture address this situation? How shall I respond to this situation Christianly? How do I let Jesus live through me to touch the lives of others around me who hurt?"

The Practice of Gratitude

As a child, did your mother scold you with "Be thankful!" or "Don't be so ungrateful!"? Gratitude is a universal virtue that all parents want to instill in their kids. Society values it too. A Google search on the word *gratitude* on June 3, 2011, netted 47,400,000 results. Gratitude is an *attitude*. It is basic to spirituality. It is also a theological practice. Notice how a lack of thanksgiving to God can result in futile thinking and a darkened heart: "For although they knew God, they neither glorified him as God nor gave thanks to him, but their thinking became futile and their foolish hearts were darkened" (Romans 1:21). We must glorify God and give thanks to him as a spiritual practice grounded in theology. Liturgical traditions reflect this with their regular practice and the centrality of the Eucharist (Communion) in their worship.[29]

The practice of gratitude is also basic to community life, to prayer and in all circumstances. Notice the tone of the following exhortations:

> Let the peace of Christ rule in your hearts, since as members of one body you were called to peace. And be thankful. . . .
> And whatever you do, whether in word or deed, do it all in the name of the Lord Jesus, giving thanks to God the Father through him. (Colossians 3:15, 17)

Devote yourselves to prayer, being watchful and thankful. (Colossians 4:2)

Be joyful always; pray continually; give thanks in all circumstances, for this is God's will for you in Christ Jesus. (1 Thessalonians 5:16-18)

People who practice gratitude exude the sacrament of God's presence to those around them. Their perspectives are filtered through a theological lens that acknowledges God's gifts and grace in the enchanted world around them. They view the world and all of life from a grateful vantage point, full of appreciation. Henri Nouwen wrote,

To be grateful for the good things that happen in our lives is easy, but to be grateful for all of our lives—the good as well as the bad, the moments of joy as well as the moments of sorrow, the successes as well as the failures, the rewards as well as the rejections—that requires hard spiritual work.[30]

Jesus said, "Therefore, I tell you, her many sins have been forgiven—for she loved much. But he who has been forgiven little loves little" (Luke 7:47). The more people realize the extent of their forgiveness (their canceled debt), the more they love as a response of gratitude (see Luke 7:41-43). The practice of gratitude shapes you into a grateful person, attractive to those around you for missional impact.

Note the missional dimension of the following: "He who sacrifices thank offerings honors me, and he prepares the way so that I may show him the salvation of God" (Psalm 50:23).[31] God shows salvation to those who offer sacrifices of thanksgiving.

Make gratitude a daily rule of life. It's easy to complain of an arthritic elbow until you meet a man at the local pool whose arm is cut off at the elbow. Daily, in an attitude of prayer, practice the discipline of gratitude. Be aware of God's gifts of family, friends,

home, food, work, health, rest, beauty in creation, opportunities
disguised as problems, answers to prayer, salvation and life itself.
May the following poem enlarge your sense of gratitude:

> For flowers that bloom about our feet,
> For tender grass so fresh, so sweet,
> For the song of bird and hum of bee,
> For all things fair we hear or see,
> Father in heaven, we thank Thee.
> For blue of stream and blue of sky,
> For pleasant shade of branches high,
> For fragrant air and cooling breeze,
> For beauty of the blooming trees,
> Father in heaven, we thank Thee.
> For this new morning with its light,
> For rest and shelter of the night,
> For health and food, for love and friends,
> For everything Thy goodness sense,
> Father in heaven, we thank Thee.[32]

The practice of gratitude emerges from a passionate intellect
that practices faith thinking endowed with Christ-mindedness.
The practice of gratitude is a concrete way to love God from your
mind. As we learn to love God from our minds, we must also learn
to love him from our strength.

Suggested Practices

1. Contemplate the truth that you have "the mind of Christ."
   Practice faith thinking and theological reflection in the situations of your life as they occur. Talk to the Lord as a friend, not
   as a religious person. Choose to love the Lord from your mind
   as you do your family.

2. Reread through A. B. Simpson's three points. Go through each

one slowly, and apply each to sanctifying your thought life and devoting it to God.

3. Daily practice gratitude. When you get up in the morning, name at least five things you are thankful for. As you come upon situations in your day-to-day life and work, choose to say thank you to God. In your prayer life, always include heartfelt thanksgiving and praise.

Discussion Starters

1. How can you strengthen your capacity for right-brained thinking and stimulate your theological imagination for God? Do you believe this is needed today? Why or why not?

2. Roger and Len state, "But the link between belief and practice is not solely based on right thoughts and theology; it's also right human *desire*." Reread the quote from Amy Plantinga Pauw, who suggests that the problem with Jonah was primarily affective— he failed to desire the right things—and that our cognitive and practical efforts arise out of our loves. Do you agree or not? How do our desires affect our love for God from our minds?

3. As you follow the narrative of Roger's story about Andrew and the following theological reflections, what is your response? How would you practice faith thinking and try to love God from your mind in a similar circumstance? How have you been shaken, and how did you feel? What is theological reflection?

8

From All Your Strength

In her book *God Never Blinks*, Regina Brett tells the story of Leslie Hudak, a high school English teacher who made it her job to help the "problem" teens who needed encouragement the most. She did not just teach and then go home. She cosigned car loans for students, helped pay their rent and gave her old car to one student who needed transportation to work. When one student wanted to try out for pole vaulting, Leslie watched videos on it and became his coach. She would show up at students' homes to thank them, host spaghetti dinners at her place, and deliver Easter baskets and Christmas gifts to needy teens.

To motivate the girls to quit smoking in their school restroom, Leslie decorated it with colorful wallpaper and fresh paint, and placed baskets that contained free hair spray, tampons, hand lotion and candy. It worked. She stocked the girls' refrigerators with food, taught them to do laundry and held their hands when they delivered their babies. She also attended their weddings.

One girl wanted to be a singer, so Leslie gave her money to help her record a CD. That student sang "Amazing Grace" at Leslie's funeral. At age fifty-eight, she died in an automobile accident on her way home from school. Thousands came to honor her at the memorial. Here was a high school teacher who truly served in missional "youth ministry." The lesson that author Regina Brett concludes from Leslie's life is this: "Don't Audit Life. Show Up and Make the Most of the Now."[1] In other words, love God from all your *strength*.

Let's return to our foundation. In chapter three we offered the key theological substance and structure for a missional spirituality: the Jesus Creed/*Shema* spirituality, captured in the Great Commandment. Jesus answered a scribe by quoting Deuteronomy 6:4-5 and Leviticus 19:18:

> "The most important one," answered Jesus, "is this: 'Hear, O Israel, the Lord our God, the Lord is one. Love the Lord your God with all your heart and with all your soul and with all your mind and with all your strength.' The second is this: 'Love your neighbor as yourself.' There is no commandment greater than these." (Mark 12:29-31)

In Mark 12:30, the Greek word for "strength" is *ischuos*. Its meaning includes physical capacities, ability, power and strength. The supreme command is to love God personally from one's affection, one's intellect, the entirety of one's being and energy. The source of one's strength is in the Lord: "Finally, be strong in the Lord and in his mighty power [*ischuos*]" (Ephesians 6:10). To love God from our strength means we put all the energy of who we are and what we have toward his will and work in the world. This requires that we learn to practice the stewardship of our treasure, talents and time in the Father's house.

The Practices of Treasure-Talents-Time

God needs suburban Christians who will take a sharp look at their environment, recognize the challenges of the suburban setting and stay there to do something about it. Some Christians live in suburbia because it is a fulfillment of their

personal dreams for comfort and prosperity. Others are there
only out of necessity and would move away at the drop of a hat.
But whatever we may feel, the call is the same: Seek the welfare
of the suburb while living in it.

ALBERT HSU, THE SUBURBAN CHRISTIAN

Two hundred years ago, 3 percent of the world's population lived
in cities. Today more than 50 percent of people worldwide live in
cities. In the West, urban reality exists in different forms, including sprawling slums and suburbs. So "seek the welfare of the suburb you live in." That's a paraphrase of God's call to Israel: "Seek
the peace and prosperity of the city to which I have carried you
into exile" (Jeremiah 29:7). Sometimes we focus more on the slums
than the suburbs.

What does it mean to steward our treasure-talents-time in the
city? First, it means we resist the relentless temptation of *more*.
Advertising companies, marketing everything from cars to cray-
ons and soup to nuts, intentionally feed the idol of consumerism.
A PBS TV program called "Affluenza" addressed the modern-day
plague of materialism. It noted that the average American shops
six hours per week yet spends only forty minutes playing with
her or his children, and by age twenty, we've seen one million
commercials.[2] It's enormously difficult to resist these appeals.
As James Smith noted,

> The church has clung to an intellectual view of the human
> person while Disney (and Hollister and Apple and VW, etc.)
> have appreciated that, in fact, our actions and behaviors are
> driven by something more affective. So they steer our desires
> in more affective ways, shaping our desires through stories
> and images and "icons" of the good life, while the church
> keeps pouring rather abstract ideas and beliefs into my head.
> It's not that beliefs and ideas are wrong. It's just that they're

not reaching the center-of-gravity of the human person. The church strategy is an insufficient counter-measure. If we're going to counter the formation of desire we absorb through secular liturgies, then Christian worship and education needs to be equally affective and holistic. Discipleship takes practice.[3]

In an intellectualist perspective, our actions are viewed as the outcome of rational thinking. The assumption is that if we order all our beliefs, our actions will follow from those beliefs. The problem is, our experience tends to confirm this doesn't work. We believe many things, and yet, like Paul, we still do what we don't want to do. We are primarily lovers, and the affective realm of our loves and desires of our heart are shaped by embodied practices. A missional spirituality begins at the heart level with an identity in Christ.

However, we can live out our identity in one of three ways: (1) I am what I do, (2) I am what people say about me, or (3) I am what I have. The typical temptations are toward seeking productivity, popularity or possessions. But if I must perform or produce, if I need popularity or approval, or if I connect my worth to what I have, it will be very difficult for me to thrive in the kingdom. In contrast, note a different missional practice: "No one claimed that any of his possessions was his own, but they shared everything they had. With great power the apostles continued to testify to the resurrection of the Lord" (Acts 4:32-33; see also 2:44-45).

Living as stewards of our treasure-talents-time requires that we relinquish the drive for acquisition and constant upgrades—like an obsession to own the latest Mac or Mercedes, buy a bigger condo, or go on another cruise. Some of us can afford to work less and give more time to serve in the community. As we get to know our neighbors and workmates, we become friends—present and available to them. As we connect, doors of opportunity open for us to offer care when they hurt. And new possibilities open, such as sharing resources, which can reduce our need to work long hours to acquire things we now can borrow.[4] As we come home to the Father's house, a place of extravagant provision, we learn to love God from all our strength—from our treasure, talents and time.

The Practice of Loving God from Our Treasure

Because our home is in the Father's house, our missional spirituality will never find expression or satisfaction in the world's home, where we spend its products only on ourselves. When we seek to love God from all our strength, first and foremost we realize that where we invest our *energies* and our *economics* are inseparably related.

Jesus taught a lot about money; 15 percent of his recorded words focus on this one subject.[5] Money is an indicator of our spiritual values: "Store up for yourselves treasures in heaven, where moth and rust do not destroy, and where thieves do not break in and steal. For where your treasure is, *there your heart will be* also" (Matthew 6:20-21, italics ours). Kingdom economics is an issue of the heart. Our heart will actually follow to the place where X marks the spot of our treasure. If you invest your hard-earned money into a certain stock, your heart is sure to pay close attention to that stock. Show us your monthly bank statement, and we'll show you your heart.

Where is your treasure? Consider these statistics: Of the 6.7 billion people on earth, almost 50 percent live on less than two dollars per day. Ninety-three percent of the world's population does not own a car. The average giving for American church members in 2005 was just 2.58 percent of their income, and only 2 percent of total giving to churches goes to missions and to assist the poor. If all American Christians gave 10 percent of their incomes, there would be an extra 168 billion dollars to fund missions and mercy work around the world.[6] This is not meant to guilt Christians into giving but to put economics into perspective.

Brian McLaren tells of an experience he had:

At 6:20 I walked out the front door, bundled in scarf and coat against the chill, thinking of my first meeting. As I opened the car door my heart froze. A man sat behind the wheel. I reacted instantly, defensively. Not knowing whether the man was dead or dangerous, I drew my fist back to strike him before he recovered from his surprise. He slowly turned to meet my angry, startled face.

"What are you doing in my car?" I blurted out, my fist still clenched.

"I'm not in your car, sir," the man slurred in a frightened, thick-tongued voice. "I'm not in your car, sir," he muttered again and again as he slowly maneuvered his body out of my car and teetered off across the front lawn.

My heart was still pounding as I drove past him on the street. I remembered my thoughts in the shower. I had been glad our house was tight and well insulated. There are worse things than sleeping too warm. I remembered how good it felt to shave and slip into freshly pressed clothes. Why should it be, I wondered, that I am so concerned about sleeping too warm when another human being equally loved by the Creator barely survives in a cold car outside my door?[7]

Stuff. We become so attached to it. We defend it, worry about it and work hard to get more of it. The energy we spend to protect our stuff or to maintain and keep it in pristine condition can both distract us from God's kingdom and blind us to needy people. The nicer our stuff, the less likely we are to share it. But if we learn to live in our weakness, maybe we can change our practice. It was of the Macedonians that Paul wrote, "Out of the most severe trial, their overflowing joy and their extreme poverty welled up in rich generosity" and "they gave as much as they were able, and even beyond their ability" (2 Corinthians 8:2-3). The key was, *"they gave themselves first to the Lord* and then to us in keeping with God's will" (8:5, italics ours).

What comes to mind when you think about your "stuff," your "treasure"? Maybe you are committed to environmental issues. Or perhaps you are involved with people who have lots of stuff and yet are anxious and stingy rather than happy. Or maybe you relate with people who have very little and are relentlessly in need. Jesus expects his followers to invest in kingdom work and earn a solid return on their spiritual investment (Matthew 25:14-30).

One Christian businessman we know met an overwhelming need for housing during Christmas 2008, making rooms available in a small hotel at less than cost for months. Another businessman provided affordable housing in a condominium he was financing by dedicating some extra units. The result was praise for God's goodness and surprise on the part of some locals who thought Christians were mostly concerned about the carpeting in their large buildings. This is a spiritual investment tied to a financial one.

One day Len needed a specialized brake tool for his Honda Accord, so he checked with his neighbor, who was also a Honda owner. Sure enough, Darren had the tool, and he promptly dropped what he was doing to go over and help Len finish his job. As Len recalled how vulnerable he felt expressing his need to Darren, he remembered Luke 10, the record of Jesus sending his disciples out with instructions to take no "purse, or bag, or sandals"—to be vulnerable and dependent on those they met.

We need a similar vulnerability on the public level, but money is a difficult thing to share in most communities. Sunday gatherings at Metro Community in Kelowna, British Columbia, where Len and Betty used to serve, include an open mic, which is rarely censored. Regularly, someone will share an immediate need for food or rent money, or of a car repair that is beyond his or her resources. The collective strength of communal love of God often becomes tangible. Though Metro is a small community (about twenty families with regular employment), it has immediately contributed as much as two thousand dollars at a time. Greed results in idolatry (Colossians 3:5) and generosity results in gratitude: "You will be made rich in every way so that you can be generous on every occasion, and through us your generosity will result in thanksgiving to God" (2 Corinthians 9:11).

The practice of loving God from our treasure, in generosity and gratitude, is a counter-practice to consumerism. It is the type of missional spirituality Paul praised when he wrote of the Corinthians, "because of the service by which you have proved yourselves, men will praise God for the obedience that accompanies your confession of the gospel of Christ, and for your generosity in sharing with them and with everyone else" (2 Corinthians 9:13).

Like Israel, "remember the LORD your God, for it is he who gives you the ability to produce wealth" (Deuteronomy 8:18). Randy Alcorn offers these practices to help us love God with our treasures:

1. I affirm God's full ownership of me (1 Cor 6:19-20) and everything entrusted to me (Psa 24:1). I recognize that my money and possessions are in fact His. I am His money manager.

2. I will set aside the firstfruits—starting with at least 10%—of all that I receive, treating it as holy and belonging exclusively to the Lord. I do this in obedience to Him (Mal 3:6-12). [Though tithing is not required in the New Testament, many find it a good principle for the sake of discipline and a regular structure.]

3. Out of the remaining treasures God entrusts to me, I will seek to make generous freewill gifts. I recognize that God

has entrusted wealth to me so I can be "generous on every occasion" (2 Cor 9:11).

4. I ask God to teach me to give sacrificially to His purposes, including helping the poor and reaching the lost. I commit myself to avoiding indebtedness so that I don't tie up His funds.

5. Recognizing that I cannot take earthly treasures from this world, I determine to lay them up as heavenly treasures—for Christ's glory and the eternal good of others and myself. Affirming that heaven, not earth, is my home and Christ is my Lord.[8]

The Practice of Loving God from Our Talents

Did you ever attend or participate in a talent show when you were in school? Were you surprised when a plain Jane got up and played a musical instrument like a virtuoso or recited from a Shakespearean play like an A-list movie star? We sat amazed when our ordinary schoolmates showed their talents as singers, dancers, magicians and comedians. In recent times, talent shows have become a successful genre of reality television, with such programs as *Britain's Got Talent, So You Think You Can Dance* and, of course, *American Idol.* Before shows like these launched them into international stardom, unknowns such as Kelly Clarkson and Susan Boyle lived in obscurity. Though few will become a star, every person on earth has God-given talents, abilities and skills—usually expressed outside the public eye. Each believer must steward her or his talents in a way that enriches others.

However, talents are more than the special abilities of musicians, actors, athletes and artists. God created us in his image, so our talents include our abilities, personalities, passions, knowledge and capacities. Some are good with numbers while others are good with words. Some have a passion for children while others have a passion for seniors. Some can teach while others can organize. In addition, believers have "treasure in jars of clay" as parts of the body of Christ; we are endowed with spiritual gifts to build up the body, with each member doing his or her part in love (Romans 8; 1 Corinthians 12). To love God from all our strength is to employ our possessions, our health and our talents in serving him and glorifying him. It is to refer all our actions to him, as our last end.

Paul wrote an oft-cited passage:

It was he who gave some to be apostles, some to be prophets, some to be evangelists, and some to be pastors and teachers, to prepare [equip] God's people for works of service, so that the body of Christ may be built up until we all reach unity in the faith and in the knowledge of the Son of God and become mature, attaining to the whole measure of the fullness of Christ. (Ephesians 4:11-13)

Is it possible to understand Ephesians 4 (and perhaps the entire epistle) as written to a *missional* movement? We tend to confine the application of this text to encouraging people to use their gifts in church programs as a form of volunteer work. But could it be that Paul is speaking of leaders equipping others for a *missional* spirituality, not just for church work? The purpose of equipping is that people will do works of service with a result: "that the body of Christ may be built up until we all reach unity in the faith and in the knowledge of the Son of God." What might that look like?

First, we nearly always frame ministry and its results in individual terms. However, the end Paul has in view is a mature body of Christ. Nouwen wrote,

A mosaic consists of thousands of little stones. Some are blue, some are green, some are yellow, some are gold. When we bring our faces close to the mosaic, we can admire the

beauty of each stone. But as we step back from it, we can see
that all these little stones reveal to us a beautiful picture,
telling a story none of these stones can tell by itself. That is
what our life in community is about. Each of us is like a little
stone, but together we reveal the face of God to the world.
Nobody can say: "I make God visible." But others who see us
together can say: "They make God visible."[9]

Like a mosaic, the body of Christ is diverse; it consists of varied
gifts in varied personalities. Only together do the various parts
compose a body. In William Cavanaugh's words, "We are God's
body language,"[10] a royal priesthood deployed into the world.

We tend to think of the stewardship of our talents in individual
terms, but we need to think in more communal terms. The needs
around us will always outstrip individual resources, and the more
we live on mission, the more we need the strength and resources
of the wider body. People at Metro helped a single mom who had
been evicted. They even helped her pack, which would have been
very difficult without them. One family took her dog, which had
no place in her new, cramped apartment. Someone else took up a
collection so she would have groceries. Still another accompanied
her to see her social worker to ask what kind of financial help she
might get. The result was a single mom who could scarcely believe
how much love she felt from God's people. This is an *embodied*
communal apologetic. Tim Morey summarizes it this way:

> An embodied apologetic will be communal. That is, the mes-
> sage of Christ will be more readily accepted when it is em-
> bodied not just in an individual but in a community of
> Christians who are committed to being shaped into the
> image of Christ, loving one another and serving their world.
> This is especially true as we are able to move beyond merely
> showing Christian community to others and actually allow-
> ing our non-Christian friends to participate in this commu-

nity. . . . In a postmodern world where experience is often the primary gauge for measuring truth, the experience of an individual's community confirms what a person believes to be true.[11]

Second, to love God from our talents means we look for opportunities to serve out of our capacities in our neighborhoods, workplaces and communities. It means we plot goodness and watch for opportunities to meet a need. It may mean we help a shut-in with yard work or help a single mother fix a car. It may mean we offer support or babysitting for a workmate going through a divorce. A spiritual gift or talent is only used when given away. We must give away our talents to people and in situations in which we can teach, help and administrate, and express mercy, hospitality and generosity. We might use our connections or networks to help someone find a good job, a reliable car or a place to live. When we make ourselves available, God opens doors for mission.

We must think in practical terms and ask, "What talents do I have to offer? What am I good at? What do I like to do? What need can I meet?" As we practice our love for God with our talents, we intentionally channel and use our physical energy and capacities as *servants* of God. Paul wrote, "Whatever you do, work at it with all your heart, as working for the Lord, not for men, since you know that you will receive an inheritance from the Lord as a reward. It is the Lord Christ you are serving" (Colossians 3:23-24).

The Practice of Loving God from Our Time

Be very careful, then, how you live—not as unwise but as wise, making the most of every opportunity, because the days are evil.

Ephesians 5:15-16

Time may be the ultimate treasure—once it's spent, we can't recover it. We can be busy through the practices of love for God from our treasure and talents and yet not love God through our time. Einstein said time is relative. We say, "Yes, relatively short!"

Time is both linear and cyclical. The clock and the calendar move forward second by second, day by day, from fall to winter to spring to summer. Each day of the week returns in a regular pattern. In Ecclesiastes 3, the writer portrays the endless cycle. But time also marches toward a goal—a *telos*—when Jesus will return and establish his eternal kingdom (Ephesians 1:10). The Latin word *regula* means rhythm, a regular pattern of life. Practice includes rhythms—a repeated pattern that forms the foundation of a way of life lived for God. A missional spirituality is more about investing in a way of life than investing in a system of belief.

Francis de Sales said, "Spiritual direction begins when people are helped to walk more slowly, talk more slowly and eat more slowly."[12] It's difficult to move more slowly when we measure our worth by what we achieve in a day, as if time management is sovereign over the Spirit. But the ability to live more slowly grounds other abilities, including the ability to see and hear. In the words of Rabbi Abraham Heschel, learn to make a "sanctuary in time."[13]

God is mindful of *kairos* time[14] and its strategic importance in his missional purposes: "Jesus went into Galilee, proclaiming the good news of God. 'The *time* has come,' he said. 'The kingdom of God is near. Repent and believe the good news!'" (Mark 1:14-15, italics ours) and "But when the *time* had fully come, God sent his Son, born of a woman, born under law, to redeem those under law, that we might receive the full rights of sons" (Galatians 4:4, italics ours).

The strength of rest and trust. The prophet Isaiah made a stunning statement about a missional spirituality: "This is what the Sovereign LORD, the Holy One of Israel, says: 'In repentance and rest is your salvation, in quietness and trust is your *strength*, but you would have none of it'" (Isaiah 30:15). The Hebrew word for "strength" is not *meod* as we saw in the *Shema* of Deuteronomy 6:5. That word translated as "strength" refers more to muchness or exceeding. The synonym *geburah,* also translated as "might" or "power," is the Hebrew word in Isaiah 30:15. The Septuagint translates *geburah* with the Greek word *ischus*—the same Greek word Mark used for loving God from all one's *strength* (Mark 12:33). In context, salvation and strength are parallel ideas. Israel decided to trust her military might rather than the Lord for salvation and strength.

As an alternative to relying on Egypt, Isaiah advocated a restful return to God (repentance) for deliverance (salvation) and a quiet trust for strength (power). An example we have of patterns of rest and trust is Sabbath—a subversive practice that challenges idols of power and consumption. "Sabbath" is a translation of the Hebrew word *shabbat,* which means "to cease."

The foundation for the practice of Sabbath is the seventh day of the week, when God rested from his work of creation and blessed the seventh day and made it holy (Genesis 2:2-3). That became the theological basis for Israel to set apart the seventh day (make it holy) as a day of rest from all work (Exodus 20:8-11). For Jews, Sabbath was from sundown Friday to sundown Saturday. Israel was to cease from work and to trust God to supply their needs from the land that he owned.

The manna-collecting episode in the wilderness demonstrates the key issue and how difficult it was for Israel to rest and trust God (Exodus 16). Even before Moses gave the Ten Commandments (Exodus 20), God began to mentor his people in the practice of faith as he commanded them to observe sacred rhythms. He sent manna in the desert and instructed them not to gather more than he allowed; when they did, it rotted. But on the sixth day, God instructed them to gather enough for two days, and the extra did not rot. On the seventh day God did not supply manna. There was provision only on the first six days. The lesson: God faithfully supplies all we need, as we trust him. Eugene Peterson comments on Genesis 1,

> The Hebrew evening/morning sequence conditions us to the rhythms of grace. We go to sleep, and God begins his work. As we sleep he develops his covenant. We wake and are called out to participate in God's creative action. We respond in faith, in work. But always grace is previous. Grace is primary. We experience this grace with our bodies before we appreciate it with our minds.[15]

The strength of practices is that they are embodied, and therefore they form us bodily. Similarly, sacred liturgies train our hearts through our bodies. Every liturgy constitutes a pedagogy that teaches us to be a certain kind of person.[16]

New Testament theology advances the rhythms of grace and Sabbath to a deeper level. Believers are complete in union with Christ and not bound to Sabbath days, as Paul affirmed for the Colossians, a church compromised by legalism and syncretism. He regarded religious festivals, new moon celebrations and Sabbath days as a shadow of things to come with the reality found in Christ (Colossians 2:16-17). In Hebrews 4 the core issue is not a mere observance of one Sabbath *day* per week (like not working on Sundays or taking a "day off" for God) but entry into a Sabbath *realm* where time, rest and faith relate to the larger *life of salvation*. The theological father of Pietism, Johann Arndt, wrote,

> In the forecourts of our God, the plants of the Lord grow green as cedars in Lebanon (Ps. 92:12). What are the forecourts of our God? They are the inner, spiritual feast days of the heart, the inner, spiritual Sabbath, and the growing Lebanon in the wilderness, in the solitariness of the spirit. Seek this and you will discover for yourself and will see God's wonder and pleasure.[17]

The rest in Canaan was a physical type or symbol that was to depict the life of *shalom* in the land of promise. God prepared a place of rest for his people to cease from their work, to enter into the seventh day where he rests. After he completed his work of creation, God rested (curiously, in Genesis, there is reference to an evening and morning on the first six days, but not on the seventh). However, the first generation of Israelites set the pattern of unbelief. The writer of Hebrews cites Psalm 95, written long after Exodus, to prove that Today is the continuous day during which we are called to enter Sabbath-rest by faith:

Now we who *have believed* enter that rest, just as God has said,

"So I declared on oath in my anger,
'They shall never enter my rest.'"

And yet his work has been finished since the creation of the world. For somewhere he has spoken about the seventh day in these words: "And on the seventh day God rested from all his work." . . .

It still remains that some will enter that rest, *and those who formerly had the gospel preached to them did not go in, because of their disobedience.* Therefore God again set a certain day, calling it Today, when a long time later he spoke through David, as was said before:

"*Today*, if you hear his voice,
do not harden your hearts."

For if Joshua had given them rest, God would not have spoken later about another day. There remains, then, a *Sabbath-rest for the people of God; for anyone who enters God's rest also rests from his own work, just as God did from his.* Let us, therefore, *make every effort* to enter that rest, so that no one will fall by following their example of disobedience.

For the word of God is living and active. (Hebrews 4:3-12, italics ours)

Belief and concerted effort are what activate entry into the Today of God's rest, the realm of salvation to which the gospel points. It's a realm for both unbelievers and believers to enter Today, with its ultimate fulfillment in the age to come, sustained by the living and active word of God. *We rest from our work, knowing that God's work always continues,* because his rest is not inactivity. God sustains his creation and is at work even on the Sabbath (Psalm 104; John 5:16-17). Our rest is not inactivity either, but rather one of freedom from toil and struggle.

As we make every effort to enter the Sabbath-rest as a way of life, we embrace an alternative approach to time. We enter *kairos* time, a sacred realm. Sabbath-rest seems a peculiar way to connect time and strength. This practice that connects the two is a spiritual paradox: we find strength in weakness. To enter Sabbath-rest is to enter a physical, intellectual and emotional life of faith bound to a love of God. Sabbath rest moves us beyond the dualism of spirit and body as it invites us to slow down enough to "pay absolute unmixed attention" to God and to stop our restless, self-reliant, unbelieving activities of human toil and struggle. The practice of Sabbath helps to shape in us a Sabbath heart. Mark Buchanan writes,

> A Sabbath heart is restful even in the midst of unrest and upheaval. It is attentive to the presence of God and others even in the welter of much coming and going. . . . A Sabbath heart sanctifies time. This is not a ritual. It's a perspective. . . . Unless we trust God's sovereignty, we won't dare risk Sabbath. And unless we receive time as abundance and gift, not as a ration and burden, we'll never develop a capacity to savor Sabbath.[18]

Jesus offered a true Sabbath-rest for weary, law-burdened people: "Come to me, all you who are weary and burdened, and I will give you rest. Take my yoke upon you and learn from me, for I am gentle and humble in heart, and you will find rest for your souls. For my yoke is easy and my burden is light" (Matthew 11:28-30). He offered a compelling invitation to discipleship, according to Craig Keener in *The IVP Bible Background Commentary:*

> When a man carried a yoke he would carry it on his shoulders (cf., e.g., Jer 27:2); Judaism applied this image of subjection to obedience. Jewish people spoke of carrying the yoke of God's law and the yoke of his kingdom, which one accepted by acknowledging that God was one and by keeping his commandments. Matthew intends Jesus' words about rest as a contrast with Pharisaic Sabbath rules in the following passage (12:1-14): the promise of "rest for your souls" comes from Jeremiah 6:16, where God promises to stay his wrath if the people turn to him instead of to the words of the false religious leaders (6:13-14, 20).[19]

The practice of loving God from our strength begs the questions: do we redeem our time because the days are evil? Do we steward our time so that we gain strength through Sabbath-rest and trust? Are we a people of faith, who, because of a missional spirituality, love God from all our strength as we invite burdened people to come home to the Father's house, a place of rest?

Suggested Practices

1. Read through Randy Alcorn's practices above to help you consider ways to love God more effectively from your treasure. Pray through and determine an intentional way to build them into your thoughts, weekly plans and actions.

2. Talk to a trusted family member or friend about your talents, or take a personality, skills and strengths inventory to evaluate what talents, abilities and capacities you have. Look for specific ways to

love God through the way you serve people using your talents.

3. Interview someone you know who seems to live a life that has
entered a Sabbath-rest, from the heart. Learn how she or he
practices it and what difference it makes in her or his life and
mission. Be open to others in your sphere of influence who are
yoked with burdens, and find ways you might tell your story
about Jesus, who invites them to find rest in him.

Discussion Starters

1. After reading this chapter, how would you describe what it
means to love the Lord your God from all your strength? What
are the implications for your life and a missional spirituality?
What does it mean to live an "embodied apologetic" commu-
nally as a church, and how can you practice loving God with
your talents? How do you understand Ephesians 4:11-13?

2. Gather some friends and watch "The Story of Stuff" ator rent *The Corporation*. Discuss their impact on you and why. Explore "Make Poverty History" atand "Make Affluence History" at, and discuss these approaches
to change.

3. Read Hebrews 4:3-12 in several different versions. Identify the
key verbs and summarize the key theological point. What does
it mean to "make every effort" to enter God's Sabbath-rest? How
do you understand the nature of *kairos* time and how to sanctify it?

9

Love Your Neighbor

The love of God and the love of neighbor are one thing and must not be divided. The true divine love cannot be better noted or proven than in the love of neighbor. . . . Faith demonstrates that love of God and man make a true Christian.

JOHANN ARNDT, TRUE CHRISTIANITY

In January 2009 a group of Denver pastors gathered to dream about how their churches could join to serve the community. They asked the mayor to come and talk about his dream for their city. They also asked him to identify the hindrances that would keep that dream from materializing. He came with a list of chronic issues and troubled groups of people: decaying housing, hunger and homelessness, at-risk kids and elderly shut-ins. Before he spoke he shared this: "It occurred to me that what our city really needs are good neighbors. The majority of the issues we face would be eliminated or drastically reduced if we could just become a community of people who are great neighbors."

The pastors were first stunned, then excited. The mayor, in effect, expressed that the city could be transformed if Christians would simply live out the second half of the Great Commandment in community service. Mark Butler, police chief of nearby Longmont, Colorado, says that "for 80 percent of the calls we receive, people do not need a uniformed officer; they need a neighbor."[1] James Bryan Smith got to the heart of this when he wrote,

> Spiritual formation and community service is the way piety and actions are united. Christ-in-me must be cultivated in personal exercises [practices], but that same Christ-in-me propels me to love others. . . . Our daily encounters with others are the arenas in which our relationship with God becomes incarnate.[2]

Smith's book offers numerous insights about how to love our neighbors and build community. But we have a challenge. In a 2003 blog, Todd Hunter remarked,

> True community, by definition, has a strong geographical component. True community requires routine, unplanned contact, like what you have at work, school, neighborhood, etc. Here is the second loss: while running to [church] meetings, and thinking of them as our Christianity, we ignore the authentic communities we are already in! We neglect the very places we could be working with God as ambassadors of the Kingdom.[3]

We return to the Jesus Creed in Mark 12:30-31—the theological structure and substance for a missional spirituality: "Love the Lord your God with all your heart and with all your soul and with all your mind and with all your strength.' The second is this: 'Love your neighbor as yourself.' There is no commandment greater than these." In chapters five through eight we discussed the practices that address the first commandment—toward our God. We now move to the practices that address the second commandment— toward our neighbor. What does it mean to love our neighbor as ourselves? The age-old question *Who is my neighbor?* seems to push the command to love our neighbor to a more distant level of impersonal abstraction. In his reply, however, Jesus brings it right back to the personal and concrete.

In Luke 10:25-28, the law expert quizzed Jesus about what he could do to inherit eternal life. Jesus replied, "What is written in the Law?" The law expert answered, "Love the Lord your God . . . and . . . your neighbor as yourself." After Jesus said, "Do this and you will live," the law expert sought to justify himself and then asked, "And who is my neighbor?" Jesus launched into his story of the good Samaritan (Luke 10:30-37), which could be retitled "The Bad Religious Leaders."

Kenneth Bailey, a resident in the Middle East for many years, reveals some of the less obvious meaning of Jesus' answer.[4] First, he says, Jesus tells a story that features a priest and a Levite. In the first century, many priests lived in Jericho, seventeen miles from Jerusalem. They traveled this road on their way to and from Jerusalem, as did the man who was attacked by robbers. The complications a priest and Levite would have faced as they consider whether they would help an unknown man of unknown origin would be legion. The wounded man may have appeared to be dead. In that case, to touch him would have rendered these religious leaders ceremonially unclean. This was not exactly a sin, but in the religious view of the day, the result would have been similar: separation from God.

Second, Bailey says, such stories, told in seven parts, were highly structured. To meet the expectation of the hearers of the story, the third person to come along *should* have been a Jewish layman. Instead, to the shock of the hearers, the hero of the story was a despised Samaritan. Moreover, the Samaritan even left enough money to cover the wounded man's food and lodging for one or two weeks and promises to return with more if necessary. Bailey concludes:

In this parable the Samaritan extends a costly demonstration of unexpected love to the wounded man. . . . The lawyer's question, "Who is my neighbor?" is not answered. Instead, Jesus reflects on the larger question, "To whom must I become a neighbor?" The answer being: Anyone in need. At great cost, the Samaritan became the neighbor to the wounded man. The neighbor is the *Samaritan*, not the wounded man.[5]

But there's the twist! Jesus asked, "Which of these three do you think *was a neighbor to the man* who fell into the hands of robbers?" Wait a minute! Is not the main question "Who is my neighbor?" The parable turned the question around to ask, "Am *I* a neighbor to those that come along my path in desperate need?" This parable is an illustration of the Golden Rule Jesus taught: "So in everything, do to others what you would have them do to you, for this sums up the Law and the Prophets" (Matthew 7:12). Furthermore, Jesus agreed with the lawyer that the one who shows mercy to a needy person is a neighbor (Luke 10:37).

Being a Neighbor

The Word became flesh and blood, and moved into the neighborhood.

JOHN 1:14 THE MESSAGE

Though the English word *neighborhood* does not match the Greek of John 1:14, Peterson offers a fresh application in his Bible paraphrase, *The Message.* In his theological reading, he extends the meaning of the incarnation: Jesus came to a particular place, people and culture. He lived as a Jew in a Jewish culture. He was not an abstract man but a real, down-to-earth man who mingled with people in their natural contexts. He spoke Aramaic, ate meals with people, attended weddings and worked as a carpenter. The literal translation of this verse is "he pitched his tent among us." Any desert dwellers among John's readers would understand the metaphor. Jesus camped with his people!

In a largely impersonal, isolated and fast-moving culture, many find it difficult to relate to people in their neighborhood. Sometimes we are like Charlie Brown, who bemoaned, "I love mankind; it's people I can't stand." We exist in multiple communities and are rarely rooted where we live. How can you be a neighbor when everyone on your street is on the move? Simon Carey Holt writes,

> God is revealed and encountered in place. . . . The radical liberation of our encounter with God is in its impact upon every aspect of life, from our daily work to the food we eat, from the places we choose to inhabit to the relationships that color our lives. God is a God of place. Our call to mission is a call to discern, embody and proclaim the presence of God *where we are*. It's a call to neighborhood.[6]

The Gospel of John begins with a theological reflection on the incarnation: Jesus was human, visible, physical and local. People saw and heard him. Yet, so often people become invisible to us: our workmates aren't neighbors; panhandlers aren't neighbors; and our *actual* neighbors are often anonymous to us. But what if we read *neighbor* back into neighborhoods? What if we developed a theology of *place*? Eugene Peterson wrote, "Everything that the Creator God does in forming us humans is done in place. . . . All living is local: this land, this neighborhood, these trees and streets and houses, this work, these people."[7]

Our fast pace and constant motion push us to withdraw from the people around us, as we do from expressionless pedestrians on a busy sidewalk. And we attempt to live on mission anywhere but in the neighborhoods where we reside. Our call to mission comes to us in a particular place—with Bill and Linda right next door. We have the greatest potential for impact among those with whom we can relate casually, because we have a natural reason for interaction: we live in the same place. The incarnation shows that we should begin where we are.

In addition, when we think of our neighborhoods, we must also think of our *networks*, places where we do life together in natural relationships: at work, at the kids' soccer and baseball games, in the schools, at pancake breakfasts, in community events, at Starbucks. The kingdom of God is a *people* and a *place* of community—with local opportunities to belong and to meet others.

To love our neighbor as ourselves and to be a neighbor to others means we will not just pass by that hurting person we see along our pathway and in our network. We must be ready to offer mercy with a good cup of coffee or a room to stay in or a free meal to enjoy or payment for a medication or next month's rent.

The challenges to missional living in suburbia are legion. Simon Carey Holt reminds us that suburbia has a utopian vision of life: "A community of like minded citizens escaping one place to reside together in tranquility and peace in another."[8] He points to the billboards along the highway, which offer the dream. The words "community," "security" and "home" are plastered over images of children riding their bikes, fathers rolling in the grass, airbrushed sunsets and candlelit dinners. We all long for community, but the community that marketing technicians offer is no "place." It's an empty abstraction.

And yet, Jesus became a man and moved into the neighborhood. How do we make a difference? How do we as the physical church body of Jesus become visible to people? How do we become "placed" and invite people to come home? Cavanaugh writes,

People are usually converted to a new way of living by getting to know people who live that way and thus being able to see themselves living that way too. This is the way God's revolution works. The church is meant to be that community of people who make salvation visible for the rest of the world. Salvation is not a property of isolated individuals, but is only made visible in mutual love.[9]

The Practice of Presence

A missional spirituality requires the practice of embodied *presence* through proximity. Jesus was not merely an ambassador from God. He was God in a human body. He was present and close, not detached and aloof. Jesus became one of us and lived among us. Consider Joan Osborne's song, "What If God Was One of Us?"

When we enter our neighborhoods and networks, we enter pubs, restaurants, supermarkets, dentist offices and schools where broken and needy people live, and we become Jesus for them. Lots of people feel like slobs and strangers on a bus trying to get home. When we engage in mission, we connect with people where they are and don't wait for them to come to us. Jesus still lives in our neighborhoods and relates to people in vast networks of relationships. A powerful way we can practice presence through proximity is in third places. We'll talk more about this below.

A counter-practice to presence is churches acting as *service providers* but not *stakeholders* in their communities. They offer religious goods and services to meet needs, especially of those people looking for a church. Often people drive across a city to attend Sunday services. They can seem like tourists more than pilgrims. Yet we have a natural reason to care about the neighborhoods in which we live. When we become stakeholders, we invest where we live and we see God at work there, even as Jesus did (John 5:17). To practice presence, we must look beyond the narrow range of middle-class values.

Robert Lupton tells a story that could come out of our own experience:

She's sixty-six, mildly retarded, dangerously overweight, twice a great-grandmother, and a devoted member of our church. She wants to sit beside me, and although the smell of stale sweat and excrement is often nauseating, she makes me feel a little special. Her internal plumbing doesn't work as well as it used to. She often hints that she would like to come home with us for a visit. Nothing would delight her more than to have a Sunday dinner with my family. But there is a conflict. It has to do with values I learned from childhood. We believe that good stewardship means taking care of our belongings, treating them with respect and getting long service from them. . . . To invite Mrs. Smith into our home means we will have filth and stench soil our couch. . . . My greatest fear is that she will want to sit in my new corduroy recliner.[10]

Why is it so hard to love those who are different from us? The attraction of the suburbs is that we can avoid our differences or hope they remain concealed behind closed doors and gated condo communities. But a missional spirituality climbs over gates and open doors to help those who are lonely, depressed and needy.

Todd Hunter writes of "the golden triangle of presence."[11] He notes that the practice of presence requires "multi-attention"; we simultaneously pay attention to God, self and others. The Spirit alerts us to what God is doing in the people and events around us and to the part we should play. As we have argued in previous chapters, other practices nurture our ability to pay attention to God, through union with Christ, *missio* reading and prayer, and humility. These rhythms deepen our connection with God, which in turn heightens our awareness of those around us. To love God *is* to love our neighbor. We invite them to their homecoming into the Father's house through the practice of refuge.

The Practice of Refuge

The ability of people to move to a new place tomorrow depends on the love and acceptance they feel today. . . . The only thing greater than our awareness of each other's sins is the awareness of God's love for us and God's desire to see us healed and made whole. The principal lesson of community is that God breaks in at the weak places.

JIM WALLIS, THE CALL TO CONVERSION

She was an alcoholic. She was also a chronic manipulator and had a personality disorder. Though brilliant, she couldn't keep a job. Finally she lost custody of her daughter. Though people spent time with this woman, they had to endure being cursed and hounded.

One Sunday morning, she jumped onto the stage during a worship service at Metro and tried to take over worship. This led to another psychiatric assessment. She was put back on anti-anxiety medication, and things started to change. Now she visits her daughter again and has worked for months full-time at a coffee shop. She is happy, grateful, loves to be with others, and is one of the most perceptive and gentle people you could know. Through grace, acceptance and support, the church community helped her to come home.

We are all wounded in some way, but few will disclose their wounds until they are sure it's safe. They need to know you will listen and handle them gently. Their story may be all they have. Fortunately some people at Metro were able to be a neighbor to the mentally ill woman and love her because, as John Ortberg remarks, "God is the God of the do-over; the Lord of the second chance."[12] Conventional wisdom says we need to be kind, because everyone we meet is fighting a hard battle.

Many groups try to build community around their strengths and special events. It seldom works. Community—real life together—is built around shared weakness. Until we know it is safe to be weak, we protect ourselves and hide behind competency and stability, and we quickly become lonely. But when we see people who are reliable and gentle, we eventually take small steps of trust and become vulnerable. If those small steps are respected, we risk larger ones. Finally we reveal our true selves, our deep wounds, and suddenly there is the possibility of healing. Henri Nouwen offers a compelling picture from Jean Vanier, the founder of L'Arche, which creates communities of people with disabilities and those who care for them:

> When Jean Vanier speaks about that intimate place, he often stretches out his arm and cups his hand as if it holds a small, wounded ird. He asks, "What will happen if I open my hand fully?" We answer, "The bird will try to flutter its wings, and it will fall and die." Then he asks again, "What will happen if I close my hand?" We say, "The bird will be crushed and die." Then he smiles and says, "An intimate place is like my cupped hand, neither totally open nor totally closed. It is the space where growth can take place."[13]

Offering a place of refuge requires sacrifice and inconvenience. Some people use distance to maintain control, but the result is not trust and openness. If we replace love with power, it only generates oppression and resistance. To love is to become vulnerable and to enter an intimate place together. Home is a place where we can laugh and cry and be ourselves without risk of judgment. When we invite others into this space, they flock to come home.

God established cities of refuge in the Old Testament. And Isaiah says of God himself, "You have been a refuge for the poor, a refuge for the needy in his distress, a shelter from the storm and a shade from the heat" (Isaiah 25:4). God cares about refugees, who are homeless. A missional spirituality is theological, but not intangible, and it becomes concrete through practices like hospitality. The practice of refuge creates safety and shade for others.

The Practice of Hospitality

The neighborhood serves as a bridge between the private world of my own home and the public world into which I move every day. It acts a bit like the old front porch used to do. Environmental psychologists have long agreed that essential to a healthy human experience of place is the reciprocal relationship between one's home and one's horizon of reach.

SIMON CAREY HOLT, GOD NEXT DOOR

Some time ago an ad in the local community league newsletter asking for a coach for a neighborhood soccer team caught the eye of Howard, a pastor. As he began to organize his team of children under five years old, he realized that they and their parents had already established many connections through a myriad of neighborhood associations. And he realized that he had *not* participated in the community life of his neighborhood. As he was welcomed through his new role as soccer coach, it was evident that children's activities at the Community Center brought families of diverse nationalities and cultures together in rich fellowship.

Weeks before he joined the soccer team, Howard received a flyer in his mailbox from a church in the neighborhood, welcoming him and his family to participate in one of its programs. Two thoughts came to mind as he read the invitation: (1) none of the neighbors he knew would be interested in such a program, and (2) as a resident of the neighborhood, he knew *none* of the people who sent the invitation. This well-meaning church knew little about the neighborhood and apparently did not value meeting those who lived there. It engaged in a practice of abstraction as it designed a program and hoped that people in the neighborhood would show up, rather than meeting people on their own turf.

It was obvious to Howard that the church's intention was, in the words of his neighbor, to "recruit" people to that church. Since the soccer parents are not likely to turn up at the church service on Sunday to be "recruited," the only way to share Christ's love with them is to go and be present among them.

Jesus sent his disciples with clear instructions on mission. In Luke 10 we read a strange caution: we go out as "lambs among wolves" yet we take no "purse or bag or sandals" (vv. 3-4). The road is dangerous, and we take nothing for the journey. The Jesus life is sometimes counterintuitive. We must radically depend on God and on the hospitality of neighbors (Luke 10:5-7). These instructions contain wisdom rarely embraced. Most churches we have visited over the decades are not strong in hospitality to strangers. Many claim to be friendly, but the question is, to whom? Churches may welcome visitors from the pulpit but by the time they get back to the lobby, they can feel more like strangers than when they first walked in. How often do we talk to strangers at church or invite neighbors into our homes?

People love barbecues, potlucks and meals together. There's something spiritual, missional and even sacramental about biblical hospitality. It is a missional and sacramental practice because it is rooted in the very character and presence of God himself, in his love for sojourners, strangers and aliens. Hospitality lives at the heart of the gospel and missional life.[14] Jesus declared, "Then the King will say to those on his right, 'Come, you who are blessed by my Father; take your inheritance, the kingdom prepared for you since the creation of the world. For I was hungry and you gave me something to eat, I was thirsty and you gave me something to drink, I was a stranger and you invited me in'" (Matthew 25:34-35). Consider the following texts:

When an alien [stranger, *ger*] lives with you in your land, do not mistreat him. The alien living with you must be treated as one of your native-born. *Love him as yourself,* for you were aliens *[ger]* in Egypt. I am the LORD your God. (Leviticus 19:33-34, italics ours)[15]

Share with God's people who are in need. Practice hospitality. (Romans 12:13)

Now the overseer must be above reproach, the husband of but one wife, temperate, self-controlled, respectable, hospitable, able to teach. (1 Timothy 3:2)

Offer hospitality to one another without grumbling. (1 Peter 4:9)

Christine Pohl describes hospitality this way:

Hospitality is the attitude and practice of providing the atmosphere and opportunities, however risky, in which strangers are free to become friends, and thereby feel accepted, included and loved. The relationship thus opens up the possibility for eventual communion among the host the stranger, and God. The stranger is any person or group not known to the host.[16]

In Scripture, hospitality included providing food, housing and treating a stranger as a guest. The Greek words for *hospitality* and *hospitable* literally mean "love of strangers." The English words *hospitality, hospital* and *host* come from the Latin *hospes,* whose root meaning means "guest" or "host," which implied a guest chamber or inn—thus the English words *hospice, hostel* and *hotel.* A hospital is literally a "shelter for strangers," though the word now means a place of medical care. And yet there is a theological connection between hospitality and healing.

Through hospitality, we move from "the community for me" to "me for the community." Home becomes a place where God's presence is mediated through hospitality. God is hospitable. Molly Marshall writes, "When we envision the church as an idealized family, we are not very capable of welcoming the stranger. Since intimacy often depends on social and economic similarities, church then becomes a place of retreat rather than true hospitality."[17] Hospitality is a tangible kingdom practice of a missional spirituality in our postmodern, fragmented culture.

> Our contemporary situation is surprisingly similar to the early Christian context in which the normative understandings and practices of hospitality were developed. We, like the early church, find ourselves in a fragmented and multicultural society that yearns for relationships, identity, and meaning. Disturbing levels of loneliness, alienation, and estrangement characterize our mobile and self-oriented society. People are hungry for welcome but most Christians have lost track of the heritage of hospitality.[18]

As a *diaspora* people, Filipinos understand what it feels like to be strangers and aliens in foreign countries. And yet they express joy in extending hospitality to others. The Mennonites, Greeks and Italians are similar. Talk about food, festivity and family— they know how to welcome others! Many cultures build natural bridges for household evangelism and mission.

Networks and Third Places

When we think of loving our neighbors as ourselves through the practice of hospitality, we do not instantly think of networks, but our children do. They are already immersed in Facebook culture. For some, the image of a church is that of a fortress. When the number of people in the fortress grows, it feels like success. Meanwhile, the territory outside the fortress lies unclaimed. Mike Breen writes,

> To establish new outposts, to claim territory and put it under

the full reign of God (his Kingdom), we *actually have to go into the territory!* We can't just stay holed up in the fortress. However, the metaphor starts to break down when you think about it only geographically. The BIG territory is NET-WORKS, not neighborhoods. Think about it: even within neighborhoods there are existing networks of relationships.[19]

Third places are those networks in which people meet to develop friendships, discuss issues and interact casually. According to Ray Oldenburgh, our first place is the home, our second place is work, but our third place is the sphere of community life. It may be a restaurant, bar or social club. But wherever a third place is, it must be free or inexpensive: food and drink are important but not critical ingredients. It must be accessible, a place people can comfortably walk to; regulars should frequent it; and it should be a safe and welcoming space.[20]

Tom is a friend who pastors in a neighborhood church. He used to spend about twelve hours a week locked away in his study as he prepared for his Sunday message. But for a couple of weeks one March, his study was being renovated, so he decided he would do his preparation at a Starbucks near his home. He packed his laptop, walked down the street, entered the café and ordered a latte.

On that first afternoon nothing happened. But on the second afternoon, a female barista asked him what he was working on. He told her he was a pastor who lived nearby and that he was preparing a sermon for Sunday morning. She had some idea of what a pastor does, but "sermon" stumped her. He talked a bit about faith, justice and God's kingdom, and after two minutes she excused herself to get back to work.

The next week Tom returned to Starbucks to prep again. The same barista came to chat and had pulled in her friend from behind the bar. The young ladies asked if they could sit down and then began to share their stories. The next week when he returned, three of the barista's friends were waiting to talk to him. Like Jesus with the woman at the well, he had unwittingly connected to a network. He had discovered the potential of the third place, and he realized he wouldn't do his sermon prep in his office anymore. Now he connects with people in his mission field and practices the art of listening, the heart of hospitality. Henri Nouwen wrote,

> Listening is much more than allowing another to talk while waiting for a chance to respond. Listening is paying full attention to others and welcoming them into our very beings. The beauty of listening is that, those who are listened to start feeling accepted, start taking their words more seriously and discovering their own true selves. Listening is a form of spiritual hospitality by which you invite strangers to become friends.[21]

As a secular business consultant, Peter Block offers interesting counsel on how to develop community and what he calls restorative justice in a fragmented culture where businesses, schools, social service organizations, churches and neighborhoods tend to operate in isolation from one another. For him, community is a structure of belonging, nurtured through conversation, in which the small group is the unit of transformation and in which hospitality and generosity are the ethos. The role of leaders is convening, and listening is the critical practice, coupled with asking questions. In his chapter titled "Bringing Hospitality into the World," he writes,

> We usually associate hospitality with a culture, a social practice, a more personal quality to be admired. In western culture, where individualism and security seem to be priorities, we need to be more thoughtful about how to bring the welcoming of strangers into our daily way of being together.[22]

In chapter three, we cited Tony Campolo, who said the kingdom of God is a party, an extension of hospitality. What are the essentials of a good party? Succulent food, tasty drinks, great music, good friends, engaging conversation and maybe some dancing. When Luke closed his account of the new community, he wrote, "There were no needy persons among them" (Acts 4:34).

God is not stingy or scarce. He is extravagant and abundant. When the kingdom of God comes, peace and justice reign and neighbors show mercy to neighbors: "Never again will they hunger; never again will they thirst" (Revelation 7:16). At the table we meet as equals in the warmth of God's hospitality, and we experience what it truly means to love our neighbor as our self.

Suggested Practices

1. Throw a neighborhood block party. Invite your neighbors to contribute and participate.

2. Find a way you can show love to your neighbor weekly.

3. Bless someone in your workplace or neighborhood with an unexpected gift, or help him or her in a tangible way.

4. "Pay absolute unmixed attention" to how God might open doors of opportunity to meet a need of someone who comes across your path.

5. Identify someone who has lived in your neighborhood for a long time. Enter a conversation with her or him to discover how she or he understands your neighborhood. If you are comfortable, ask the person how she or he thinks the neighborhood could be a richer, better place for people to live.

Discussion Starters

1. Download the e-book by C. Christopher Smith *Growing Deeper*

in our Church Communities: Fifty Ideas for Connection in a Disconnected Age from <http://erb.kingdomnow.org/free-ebook-growing-deeper-by-chris-smith/>. Gather some friends and experiment with his resources for connecting with neighbors in your community.

2. With some friends, watch *Lars and the Real Girl* or *Henry Poole Is Here* or *The Visitor*. Discuss what you saw and felt. What did you learn about hospitality, healing, giftedness, family and friendship? Ask the Lord if you could become a friend to someone who's outside your comfort zone. Consider volunteering with a church or agency that works with the poor or marginalized, in prison, in rehab, or in other situations.

3. Read and then talk about Howard's story in a group. If you were him, how would you feel? How would you feel if you were one of the people in the church who had sent out the invitations and then read Howard's story? What might you do differently?

10

The Gospel According to You

God has created each of us with a unique contribution to make to our world and our times. No other person has our same abilities, motivations, network of friends and relationships, perspectives, ideas, or experiences. When we, like misplaced puzzle pieces, fail to show up, the overall picture is diminished.

RICHARD STEARNS, THE HOLE IN OUR GOSPEL

Roger served two years, six months and twenty-one days in the U.S. Army. While on Christmas leave from boot camp, he surrendered his lost life to Christ after a recently converted high-school buddy shared the gospel with him while Roger was stoned on LSD. About eight months later he received orders for a twelve-month tour in Vietnam followed by orders for an eight-month stint in West Germany. He had little opportunity to grow as a new believer and yet felt compelled to be a witness to his military comrades.

The trouble was, he lived a double life—he continued to do drugs and drank with those same guys all the while feeling the joy of his newfound faith. This came to a head in the barracks one

Saturday night in West Germany when Roger tried to talk about Jesus to one of his buddies, who then hurled an unforgettable indictment at him: "Roger, get your story straight. You've got a beer in one hand and a Bible in the other hand." Like King David confronted by Nathan, Roger felt that God had sent him a word. He turned, went to his room and wept bitterly over his hypocrisy.

The gospel according to Roger marred the gospel according to Jesus. Our walk must match our talk. We all fail; none of us is perfect, but unbelievers are acutely sensitive to hypocrisy. Gandhi remarked about the church, "I like your Christ; I do not like your Christians. Your Christians are so unlike your Christ." Roger had not realized he was actually a missionary for Jesus in a soldier's uniform. The problem was, he confused his marching orders and worked for Uncle Sam rather than Jesus.

Being Missionaries in Our Communities

It's one thing to memorize the Jesus Creed. It's another to live it. Jim Wallis says, "The only way to propagate a message is to live it."[1] As missionaries we each need a consistent life message. A foundation of a missional spirituality is an understanding that the trinitarian God is a missionary God, a God on mission, with a church sent on his mission with him to *be* and *bear* the good news. The church is to be a missionary people with a living message.

Lesslie Newbigin wrote, "How is it possible that the gospel should be credible, that people should come to believe that the power which has the last word in human affairs is represented by a man hanging on a cross? I am suggesting that the only answer, the only hermeneutic of the gospel, is a congregation of men and women who believe it and live it."[2] A missionary people will live the gospel in their communities and workplaces with an incarnational missional spirituality. We suggest *a missional spirituality is an attentive and active engagement of embodied love for God and neighbor expressed from the inside out.*

What would it take to orient ourselves around the notion that we are missionaries sent on mission as salt and light within our communities, workplaces and networks to invite people home? What would it take to integrate mission as a nonnegotiable aspect of what it means to be a disciple? What would it take for churches to organize around mission, with leaders who equip people for local missionary work and missional spirituality? Missional living is about spirituality and discipleship before it's about church strategy or structure. A missional spirituality with an incarnational posture can help us navigate the troubled waters of liminality and also surpass temple spirituality.

What would it take to turn church members into local missionaries? An enormous obstacle to overcome is the paradigm of well-meaning pastors and parishioners who naturally think of church as a *place*: Christians "go" to church and invite the unchurched to "come to church." The building they assemble in is called a church. An organization like the Presbyterian Church is called a church.

But the church is a *people*. Conventional seminaries tend to train pastors for *church* work in preaching, leadership, counseling, theology, church history, hermeneutics and biblical languages. Parishioners often come to "get fed" at church by professionals and programs. In a survey of churches in the United States, researcher Thom Rainer found that 95 percent of the ministries in those churches were for members only, and many churches had *no* ministries for those outside the congregation.[3] Even the secular world expects churches to focus outside themselves. For a church to gain charitable status in Canada, it must demonstrate that it provides a direct benefit to society. If it provides a direct benefit to its members only, it really ceases to be a church and becomes a club.

Most pastors and people are not trained in how to be missionaries in their communities, the mission field. Jesus said, "The harvest is plentiful but the workers are few. Ask the Lord of the harvest, therefore, to send out workers into his harvest field" (Matthew 9:37-38). However, some hold to a refuge mentality that withdraws from culture because that is the world, outside the faith, inhabited by evil and forsaken by God. But "rather than seeing culture outside the faith as abandoned by God and operating outside his control, missional spiritual leaders see God actively at work in the world, on mission himself, redeeming people to himself."[4]

Hugh Halter and Matt Smay discuss the concepts of *modality* and *sodality*, coined by missiologist Ralph Winter. They argue for a church that both gathers and scatters as two arms that work in harmony. The *modalic* arm is the local, structured, gathered aspect of church life focused on the inside. The *sodalic* arm is the missional, spontaneous, scattered aspect of church life focused on the outside. The ancient Celts talked about the rhythms of spiritual life as inward in love and outward in mission. This fits with the very nature of God. The church moves inward and outward in love, and a weakness in this rhythm results in weak churches.

For a variety of reasons, and in particular because of the settled

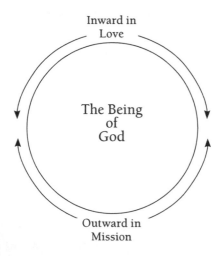

Figure 10.1.

nature of the church in Christendom, most seminaries and churches organize around and focus on the modalic aspect. This is our strong hand. However, a mature church will be equally sodalic. The Great Commission says to "go" (sodalic) and "make disciples" (modalic). Christianity as a movement must have a centrifugal force like a tornado that pushes out from a central vortex where both the modalic and sodalic exist together.[5]

> Most churches have at their center a modalic leader. By nature, a modalic leader tends to not push out from the center, but actually tries to attract toward the center. That's why we often call the typical church "attractional." From the central command, these leaders work at getting everyone and everything to center around church. But a movement is "commandeered" much differently. As the central command pushes outward from the center, it creates a natural "sucking" response. . . . It's a known statistic that the churches that give away, that take risks, that send out, and that sacrificially push their people out, create vacuums that God fills with even more. . . . It doesn't matter whether you begin sodalically and morph modalically, or begin modalically and morph to the sodalic side. The critical issue is that both forces *work together from the center and push out.*[6]

Church leaders must think in missional ways, push out from the center and begin to measure more than the ABCs (attendance, baptisms, cash), because "the current scorecard rewards church activity and can be filled in without any reference to the church's impact beyond itself, and promotes the internally focused, program-based, church-based side of the ledger."[7] Furthermore, "loving God and loving our neighbors cannot be fulfilled at church. Being salt and light cannot be experienced in a faith huddle."[8] Rather, we must see our identity and function as disciples of Jesus who are missionaries in our communities and workplaces.

As God blessed Abraham to be a blessing, as his spiritual off-spring, we too are blessed to be a blessing (Galatians 3–4).

This means that when we *gather* in worship services and small groups, our purpose is to worship God, connect with others and be equipped in missional spirituality so that when we *scatter* we go as missionaries of Jesus. Churches become kingdom base camps and outposts for disciples to gather and from which they are deployed on mission. The main event is not Sunday services and programs, but what happens the rest of the week when God's people serve on mission.

Exegeting Culture

We spend most of our time in our community and living in our culture. Christians listen to secular music, attend movies, watch television on big-screen TVs and use the Internet as much as non-Christians. We go to McDonald's and Starbucks, and we enroll our children in music lessons and soccer as much as non-Christians. We become enthralled with *American Idol*, the World Cup, Face-book and certain music groups as much as non-Christians. We work in all sectors of the workplace and suffer job dissatisfaction, depression and divorce as much as non-Christians.

Common experiences and networks of relationships bind people together. Evangelicals value exegesis (interpretation) of Scripture. However, an effective missional spirituality also exegetes (interprets) culture. As helpful as the Christian subculture can be, it is not enough to restrict ourselves to James Dobson, Hillsong and Beth Moore. It's not enough to simply wag our heads about Britney Spears or denounce sexuality and violence in movies.

Like the "men of Issachar, who understood the times and knew what Israel should do" (1 Chronicles 12:32), "the first responsibility of a leader is to define reality," according to Max DePree.[9] Christians need to define reality and "interpret the signs of the times" (Matthew 16:1-3). We need to exegete popular culture and cultivate a missional spirituality that engages and interprets it theologically. Of course, we all seem to know that the movie *Avatar* and show hosts like Oprah Winfrey communicate syncretistic, New Age messages, but what are the messages, how are they depicted and why? What are the values, beliefs, concerns and anxieties in our culture that they reveal? What can we learn from them? How do we interpret their messages from the perspective of Christian theology?

Americans continue to show interest in spirituality and rarely talk about God. For example, Benjamin Zeller notes how the final episode of the TV series *LOST* offered flirtations with religion that followed an intriguing bricolage that mirrored contemporary developments in American religion. The writers combined a hodgepodge of Christianity, Buddhism, Hinduism, Taoism, Egyptian religions and New Age spirituality shorn of their historical and theological contexts. The show's writers even offered a vision of the afterlife. The *LOST* survivors met in the afterlife in an interfaith chapel replete with sacred objects and symbols from a variety of world religions. Rather than focus on a single religion or spirituality, the writers created a postmodern patchwork.[10]

What motivates Lady Gaga's lyrics, appearance and view of spirituality? As a pop culture phenomenon—not unlike Taylor Swift, who has colossal popularity with very different messages so far—Lady Gaga is a commentary on popular culture's spiritual, sexual and social values. How do we help our youth exegete her from the standpoint of Christian theology? On February 13, 2011, Anderson Cooper interviewed her on *60 Minutes*.[11] She offers an intriguing glimpse into a person whose views on sexuality, spirituality and social justice emerge from her own pain and rejection she suffered in her growing-up years, especially in a Catholic school. Media both *shapes* and *expresses* popular culture through shared meaning.

It's not possible to read Scripture and then do theology without involving the context of culture in the theological task. Culture is a *lived worldview*. The products of culture are cultural *texts*, which are human actions that communicate meaning and require interpretation. For example, multilevel marketing, Ponzi schemes and white-collar crime grabbed headlines in the first decade of the twenty-first century. Greed motivates these. Theologically interpreted, greed is idolatry. Another trend is social networking, including Facebook, MySpace, Twitter and blogs. Community in Christ alone will satisfy the human longing to belong. We must involve ourselves in and read these texts of culture. Mark Driscoll writes,

> I am encouraging Christians on Reformission to involve themselves in their local cultures not merely for the purpose of entertainment but primarily for the purpose of education. As a missionary, you will need to watch television shows and movies, listen to music, read books, peruse magazines, attend events, join organizations, surf websites, and befriend people that you might not like to better understand people that Jesus loves.[12]

Kevin Vanhoozer states, "The church is to *be* a community of interpreters."[13] Effective missionaries interpret the culture. They don't expect people from the host culture to come to their turf to learn their language, values and customs. They cross borders and learn the language, customs, values and trends of the culture. Here are a few trends that we see as examples to interpret theologically:

1. Fixation on fitness, diet, alternative therapies, beauty, youthfulness

2. Home improvement and extreme makeovers

3. Environment and justice issues, health care, retirement

4. Reality TV and audience participation

5. Fascination with celebrities

6. Increasing action, violence, sexual immorality, vulgarity in movies and TV

7. Marriage and family identity confusion, breakdown, common-law, blending, gay tolerance, avatar and online relationships, chats, eHarmony, etc.

8. Interest in spirituality, self-improvement, talk shows

9. Consumerism, convenience, experience, extreme sports and entertainment

10. Alternative forms of Christian church life detached from the institutional

As we exegete the meaning behind texts and trends, we use the filters of Scripture and Christian theology to read them theologically. Vanhoozer states, "The believing community 'reads' the world in light of the Word of God. In other words, the church interprets the world and the surrounding culture through the lens of the biblical text."[14] Yet you can exegete culture and still be formed by its values, untransformed because you are being exposed only to appealing, abstract informational sermons. Unless you actually engage culture as a missionary, nothing will change. James Smith makes the point that the values and practices of the mall and the marketplace shape our imaginations about the "good life." If culture shapes your heart and what you desire and love, how will the church offer countermeasures? Both the market and the mall do not primarily aim at your head but at your heart and feelings.[15]

In *How Christianity Changed the World*, Alvin J. Schmidt documents enormous amounts of missional spirituality in stories of ordinary people who accomplished extraordinary things for God as they exegeted their culture and loved their neighbors. People transformed by Christ became a shaping force that inspired some of the highest achievements in Western civilization outside church walls. Did you know that Christians were behind the early formations of the YMCA and YWCA, hospitals, mental institutions, the Red Cross, braille, colleges and universities, the abolition of slavery in England and the United States, women's rights and the rights of the unborn, and social welfare?[16]

God @ Work

What do Kelowna, the Walt Disney Company and God at work have in common? The answer is one of the fastest-growing virtual websites for children ages six to fourteen, offered by Club Penguin, a web-based company tucked away in this resort city of 110,000. Since its launch in October 2005, Club Penguin has handled millions of users and is perhaps an Internet entry point for many kids. The site features animated penguins that inhabit a snow-covered virtual world, conversations with other users, group activities and the creation of virtual homes with currency earned inside the game.

One of the three cofounders of Club Penguin, President Dave Krysko, considers himself a kingdom entrepreneur. He and his partners wanted to offer an immersive online entertainment journey for children that parents could trust was safe, morally pure, creative and high quality, without any third-party advertising. Club Penguin uses "culture watchers" and real-time moderators who keep abreast of the ever-changing language and objectionable nuances in our culture to monitor and censor what occurs on the live chats among the kids around the world.

Dave has a casual yet charming demeanor and humility, and he expresses love for God. He and his two partners had a vision to see positive values permeate Club Penguin and penetrate the homes of children. They believed strongly that people would respond positively to the values they held. As they were about to sell the website to Disney, they stipulated certain conditions to ensure their values would be upheld. This included an unheard-of condition that 10 percent of all profits go to a foundation for impoverished children. The founders are also proud of their Coins for Change program, in which kids help Club Penguin give one million dollars to three or four groups every Christmas. The kids online donate their own money and show where they want the money to go.

From the inception of Club Penguin, scriptural obedience, prayer, a vision for positive impact, generosity and the love of God have sustained Dave in this venture. Many of the young-adult employees are solid local Christians, but that is not a requirement for employment. What Club Penguin requires is that all employees work by the values of the company. Dave also devotes time to other kingdom ventures, such as an online live-streaming worship café to bring music and worship to the world.[17] By the way, Dave's Ukrainian last name, Krysko, is derived from Krystos, meaning "bearer of Christ." He has been a Christ bearer through a missional spirituality that partners with God at work.

People spend significant amounts of time each week in the workplace. The paradigm for many Christians, however, is to serve God on Sunday at church and then enter the real world at work on Monday. What would it take to foster the identity of Christians as missionaries in their work as businesspeople, bankers, carpenters, schoolteachers and waitresses? Who can best reach police officers, secretaries, computer techies and supermarket cashiers? Is it not those who work in those sectors?

God at work is central to missional spirituality. In fact some key biblical characters practiced a missional spirituality and held secular jobs where God was active at work: Joseph was a prime minister, Amos was a fig farmer, Nehemiah was a wine taster,

Luke was a doctor, Lydia was a merchant, and Philemon was a businessman and slave owner.

Paul mentions numerous lay leaders with significant ministries in the church and community (see, for example, Romans 16 and Colossians 4). However, it's important to keep in mind that there's a biblical place for some people to leave secular jobs to commit themselves to full-time ministry as a vocation. For example, Moses left shepherding, Paul left tent making, and Jesus left carpentry. Nevertheless, as Os Hillman puts it in his aptly titled book *The 9 to 5 Window*,

> We have wrongly equated "ministry" to what takes place inside the four walls of the local church. We have failed to affirm that the work the worker at IBM, the clerk at Wal-Mart, the nurse at the hospital or the sixth-grade teacher at the elementary school does five days a week is as important as any ministry she or he does within the four walls of a local church. In fact, surveys reveal that more than 90 percent of church members do not feel they are being equipped by the church to apply their biblical faith in their daily work life. As a result, they are ineffective for Christ at their places of employment.[18]

A missional spirituality should inform our career choices and our journey of *vocation*. We must listen to the "call," the voice of vocation, and how God places us in the world to make a difference. We must discern God's purpose and design for our lives and how he made us to love him and others with our passion, personality and gifts. What each of us do flows from who we are in the world, where self and service meet at the crossroads of mission and ministry in the workplace. This isn't about finding the right job or employment in a lucrative occupation. It's about identity and function.

Missional spirituality enjoys a home-field advantage when you have natural bridges to embody God's love to people in your field of work. Builders reach other builders, artists and musicians reach other artists and musicians, those in law enforcement reach others in law enforcement, and so on. All vocations are sacred and sacramental when you serve according to your "call" from God. If he calls you to the fields of medicine, education or technology, don't sell the farm to grab a call in the field of pastoring, Bible translation or worship. Some are called to fields in the church while most are called to fields in the community. As Frederick Buechner said, "The place God calls you to is the place where your deep gladness and the world's great hunger meet." *All* service offered as a response to your call or vocation from God to meet human need is *ministry*.

People don't have to go out into the world and do missions and ministry. They are already out there, where they can love their neighbor at work where God is at work too (John 5:17-19). In a sense, a "God at Work" movement has been underway. In 2001, *Fortune* magazine's cover story was "God and Business" and the October 31, 2004, *New York Times Magazine's* cover story was "With God at Our Desks." Similar stories have appeared in the *London Times, Boston Globe, Atlanta Journal* and *Los Angeles Times*, and on *CBS Morning News*, the BBC and CNN, just to name a few. On March 31, 2005, CNBC aired a one-hour story on faith at work.[19]

Jesus knew God was in the workplace.

Jesus' ministry focused on the marketplace, where people spent most of their time. Of his 132 public appearances all but 10 of them were in the marketplace, and 45 of his 52 parables had a workplace context. Of the 40 divine encounters and miracles listed in the book of Acts, 39 occurred in the workplace.[20]

Paul's epistles presume as much, if not more, Christian activity in the public sectors of life—where commerce and work occurred and where diverse people, both believer and unbeliever,

mixed—as in the private gatherings of Christians. A great text
on a missional spirituality emerges in Paul's final appeal to the
Colossians:

> Devote yourselves to prayer, being watchful and thankful.
> And pray for us, too, that God may open a door for our mes-
> sage, so that we may proclaim the mystery of Christ, for
> which I am in chains. Pray that I may proclaim it clearly, as
> I should. Be wise in the way you act toward outsiders; make
> the most of every opportunity. Let your conversation be al-
> ways full of grace, seasoned with salt, so that you may know
> how to answer everyone. (Colossians 4:2-6)

So, what are the possibilities if you practiced this passage before you went to work and while at work? What could happen
if you devoted yourself to prayer, being watchful and thankful
to God for the doors of opportunity he opens for you to share
your story of faith with coworkers who ask about the hope that
lies within you? How would your approach to work change as
you lived wisely and engaged in seasoned conversation with
people? Do you see yourself as salt and light, a living temple
of God, a royal priest, as a blessing to your coworkers and
customers?

You might buy a box of donuts and a plate of fruit for coffee
break. You might leave a birthday card with a ten-dollar Starbucks
gift card for a coworker. You might offer to help coworkers when
they move or when they need some help with errands or need a
ride to the airport. Perhaps a coworker is going through a divorce,
so you invite him or her to a DivorceCare discussion group at your
church or in a home. Perhaps your church offers a vacation Bible
school or has a dynamic youth group or you have a very fun small
group. It's fine to invite people to church functions, because these
too can be missional.

Missional Spirituality as Sacramental

Now think a moment about the following questions: When you are in union with Jesus, what are the implications of this reality when you are at work, as you build relationships in your networks and naturally exegete culture as a local missionary? When you cultivate the practices of a missional spirituality as a *lifestyle* and not merely at selected devotional times, what are the implications? As you orient your life to love God and neighbor as yourself and live the gospel according to you, what are the implications?

Theologically, you mediate God's presence and his rule as a royal priest to people. You restore enchantment and incarnation rather than disenchantment and *excarnation*. You embody the tangible kingdom for people through holy deeds, allowing them to experience God's presence and grace through you. Your missional spirituality becomes *sacramental;* godly action confers God's grace and reveals his glory. For example, "Let your light shine before men, that they may see your good deeds and praise your Father in heaven" (Matthew 5:16). As a royal priesthood, "live such good lives among the pagans that, though they accuse you of doing wrong, they may see your good deeds and glorify God on the day he visits us" (1 Peter 2:12).

Seventeenth-century spiritual writer Thomas Traherne, who influenced C. S. Lewis, wrote of how the world is full of God's glory—the Father's palace—and how ordinary people are temples or habitations of his glory. Keith Meyer writes, "Traherne wrote, 'so eye the Lord and become a mirror, home and temple of God,' which I try to practice so others might get a good eyeful of their Father in me and see God. Formation that is only about theology, practices or even spiritualities, and not people, is without the Father's heart."[21] We are sacramental people, glory bearers of God. Practicing our faith in winsome ways is a living witness to nonbelievers. This is missional action.

It's amazing what a simple thank-you card with a plate of muffins can do to bless a school teacher—or patiently listening to and praying for someone who has recently lost a loved one to cancer, or mowing your neighbor's lawn or shoveling the snow in her driveway. As a salt-and-light missionary, you penetrate your world and bring God into the nonreligious spheres where most people live. The result: "The person acted on and the person acting find God in a new way."[22] You experience the God-life in missional action. You capture the sense of Jesus' missional spirituality in action: "You know what has happened throughout Judea, beginning in Galilee after the baptism that John preached—how God anointed Jesus of Nazareth with the Holy Spirit and power, and how *he went around doing good and healing* all who were under the power of the devil, *because God was with him*" (Acts 10:37-38, italics ours). Our ministries of good works and healing become sacramental when God anoints us with the Holy Spirit and is with us.

†

David Hansen remarked, "People meet Jesus in our lives because when we follow Jesus, we are parables of Jesus Christ to the people we meet."[23] Our desire is that the gospel according to Jesus will be a duplicate copy in your life with the gospel according to you. Thanks for reading our book. We hope you will engage in the daily practices to love God from all your heart, soul, mind and strength, and love your neighbor as yourself as you embody and express a missional spirituality from the inside out. Our prayer is that "you [will] show that you are a letter from Christ, the result of our ministry, written not with ink but with the Spirit of the living God, not on tablets of stone but on tablets of human hearts" (2 Corinthians 3:3).

Welcome home!

Suggested Practices

1. Set aside the first day of your workweek to read and pray through

Colossians 4:2-6. Be attentive to doors of opportunity to share your faith and to enter into spiritual conversations with people in your neighborhood, networks and work.

2. Begin to operate more like a missionary than a member of a church. What are the challenges? What does it require? Develop some actions and attitudes of a missionary.

3. Consider placing Jesus as your board chairman, as your silent business partner or as your boss at work, and develop the worldview that you ultimately work for him and he leads the way as you pray and consult him in every situation.

Discussion Starters

1. When you reflect on being a missionary in your community and workplace, what comes to mind? How does it make you feel? What does it take for a missionary to succeed in a culture of unreached people groups? How would you apply that to you? Study Paul's practices in Acts 17:16-34. What are ways to exegete and engage culture from this text?

2. Have you ever thought of the notion of godly deeds having a sacramental effect? What does this mean? Do you agree or disagree? How do you understand Matthew 5:16 and 1 Peter 2:12? Compare a few different translations and a good commentary or two. Discuss the missional application to you and your church or small group.

3. Analyze the definition of a missional spirituality used throughout this book: "a missional spirituality is an attentive and active engagement of embodied love for God and neighbor expressed from the inside out." A missional spirituality both forms and feeds mission. How do you understand *form* and *feed*? What are the implications of each word?

Afterword

The Chronicles of Narnia movie *Voyage of the Dawn Treader* offers analogies for a missional spirituality. The central characters, Edmund and Lucy, desire yet another adventure and are thrust back to the enchanted land of Narnia. With Eustace, their obnoxious and secularist cousin, in tow, Edmund and Lucy rejoin King Caspian, the talking mouse Reepicheep and the crew of the ship, the *Dawn Treader*. Sailing on a vast ocean, it's caught in the middle of nowhere—in liminality—as it embarks on a perilous quest to the farthest edge of the Eastern Seas.

On a sworn mission to find the seven lost lords of Narnia, the children and Caspian face a raging storm, slave traders, sea serpents, dragons and invisible foes to reach lands where magicians cast spells and dreams come true. They long for peace in Narnia and to be truly at home, but they must rely on Aslan the Lion to help them face their personal and group fears and trials.

Along the way, the children encounter the temptation of their heart's desires: Lucy, the beauty of her older sister, Susan; Edmond, power; and Eustace, treasure. As they battle external foes, they must battle internal foes and surrender them to Aslan and rely on him for the *subversive* strength to defeat evil. Although Edmund and Lucy are high king and queen of Narnia, it's only when they surrender themselves that they rule.

At the end of their quest, despite Lucy's longing to stay, Aslan insists that she and Edmund must leave, and never return to Narnia. Reepicheep floats on into Aslan's heaven, but the others recognize their destinies are back home. In the end, Aslan tells Edmund and Lucy, "I shall be watching you always. In your world, I have another name. You must learn to know me by it. That was the very reason you were brought to Narnia; that by knowing me here for a little, you may know me better there."[1] They discover that they can "come home" outside of Narnia because Aslan promises to be with them. Through obedience, surrender, friendship and steadfastness, the children experience transformation while on mission.

We face the oceans of liminality in our own lives as we seek to navigate the uncharted waters of a changing culture and church. The foes we face while on mission are spiritual and cultural. They are external and internal. In a world of homelessness, we must "come home" to the Father's house and extend the invitation to others who need peace in their personal Narnias. It's an enchanted spirituality, sustained by surrender and subversion, where, in imitation of Jesus, our food is to do the will of him who sent us and to finish his work (John 4:34).

We are transformed for mission while on mission, as we venture from the confines of temple spirituality and a Christendom paradigm, and overcome the challenges of disenchantment, excarnation, consumerism, entitlement, extraction, mutant pietism and programism. Earl Creps said that we seek "to be transformed into a missional person, 'so that everyone may see our progress,' and my best practice must be me."[2]

The theological foundations of the Trinity, the incarnation, the priesthood of all believers and the Jesus Creed/*Shema* provide a glorious home for a missional people. The Jesus Creed expresses the substance and structure for a missional spirituality: "Hear, O

Roger, Len and readers, the Lord our God, the Lord is one. Love the Lord your God with all your heart and with all your soul and with all your mind and with all your strength. And love your neighbor as yourself." In this way, a missional spirituality is an attentive and active engagement of embodied love for God and neighbor expressed from the inside out. This is the heart of discipleship, an inward and an outward journey, an invitation for people to come home.

The early church in the book of Acts and what we label classic Pietism serve as potent examples of a missional spirituality in action. The river of renewal through the German Lutheran Pietists and on through the Moravians, Methodists, and the Christian and Missionary Alliance offer inspiring lessons for a renewal of Pietist missional spirituality for today's church.

Forming and feeding a missional spirituality requires specific practices that align with loving God from our heart, soul, mind and strength, and our neighbor as our self. Rather than attempt them all at once, perhaps pick one practice on which to focus for a season. You may want to focus on the practices of *missio* reading and prayer, enchantment, faith thinking, Sabbath, or hospitality. Practices provide sacred space in which the Spirit can move as you learn to live in Christ as he lives in you by faith. You may also want to develop a missional small group and go through the suggested practices and discussion starters. You may even want to watch *Voyage of the Dawn Treader* with a group and discuss it.

Finally, as you seek to "pay absolute unmixed attention" to God at work in the daily rounds of your life, you will develop an embodied, incarnational perspective and connect spirituality to everyday mission. You will exegete and engage your culture as you seek to be a missionary in your community and workplace, living according to your vocation. Your life will be the main message people read with "the gospel according to you" personalized and in relationship. Remember Aslan's parting words to Edmund and

Lucy, who were also on mission: "I shall be watching you always. In your world, I have another name. You must learn to know me by it. That was the very reason you were brought to Narnia; that by knowing me here for a little, you may know me better there."[3] We journey together in obedience, surrender, friendship and steadfastness.

May Luci Shaw's words encourage you to face the mystery of the unknown:

> The cliff edge of our anxiety about the future may indicate that God is calling us to a new and different level of faith. When we walk, praying for guidance, to the edge of all the light we have and breathlessly take the first step into the foggy mystery of the unknown, we must believe that one of two things will happen: either God will provide us with something rock-solid to land on and stand on, or he will teach us how to fly.[4]

Appendix 1

Equipping for a Missional Spirituality in the Church and Academy

As you have lived, so have you believed.

SØREN KIERKEGAARD,
IN AN INTRODUCTION TO KIERKEGAARD

A group of Alberta pastors were invited to meet for a monthly Missional Training Forum to be equipped in missional spirituality. One pastor responded,

Our problem is not lack of missional but of leadership development and training (discipleship). We want to bring Jesus to the world around us, but most of our people are so spiritually young, they don't have a clue how. They don't yet understand what a passionate relationship with Jesus looks like, so how are they going to influence the community around us? Unless we help them become mature in God's Word, they will become like our community, tossed back and forth by the waves, and blown here and there by every wind of teach-

ing and by the craftiness of people in their deceitful schem-
ing. I see it all the time in the life choices of our people. *They
try to live in the world and in the Kingdom of God, not experiencing life to the fullest in either.* I see a need in our church to
develop spiritual leaders that can lead our church into the
future.[1]

This young pastor expresses the dire need to equip people in a
missional spirituality. But how do we equip people to love God
and neighbor? Our focus should not be on making worship services so attractive that people will return or on learning more
leadership skills so we can run the church better. A weakness of
evangelical ecclesiology is an emphasis on *personal* discipleship
over *corporate* life and mission. We must equip obedient disciples
and disciple makers who do mission together corporately. Following are some suggestions on how to do that.

Equipping Content in the Church

All effective teaching and equipping involves relevant content. As
we continue to teach and preach the whole counsel of God, let us
offer some equipping content for a missional spirituality. This
content is not comprehensive, but it's a good start.

1. *Teach people the Jesus Creed in Mark 12:28-34.* The Jesus
Creed is what we call *Shema* spirituality, the primary substance
and structure for a missional spirituality. We must teach people
what it means to love God from all their heart, soul, mind and
strength, and their neighbor as themselves. This is the meta-theme
for all of life and love. With this in view, we must equip people to
evaluate their "loves" in light of the shaping forces of a consumer
culture. Spirituality is relational and missional to the extent that
we express and embody love for God and neighbor from the inside
out. We must also teach the *practices* of *Shema* spirituality.

2. *Teach people Christology: The doctrine of Jesus Christ.* The

resurrected Lord Jesus Christ is central to all Christian theology, spirituality, mission and practices. We must teach and preach Christ the living Word and help people understand the practical implications of the Trinity and the incarnation. We must equip people in the practice of union with Christ (John 15) and teach them to obey Jesus, not just to study Scripture. We must teach people what the *telos* of human life is, with practices that will help them live in Christ and live a life of virtue. A good place to start is with the Gospels and the book of Colossians.

3. *Teach people ecclesiology: The doctrine of the Christian church.* Ecclesiology naturally flows from Christology, as Jesus Christ is the head of his body, the church universal and local. We must teach people that the church is a living temple of Christian *people*, not a *place* or an institution. As disciples, they are to express and embody Jesus through the medium of their lives as a royal priesthood in their communities. We must equip them to be and make disciples and to see spiritual formation as integrally related to this process—and connected to mission, because the church is a missionary people.

4. *Teach people missiology: The doctrine of Christian mission.* Missiology naturally flows from ecclesiology, as the church is gathered, shaped and led by Jesus Christ on mission. As the Father sent the Son, energized by the Spirit, so the Son sends the church, also energized by the Spirit. God through the Son is on mission to seek and save lost people and to destroy the works of the devil. He forms his church to participate with him on that mission. We must equip people to be incarnational missionaries in their communities and workplaces who know how to exegete and engage culture and *live* the gospel in deed and word.

Equipping Contexts in the Church

To equip effectively, we should not assume that if we just lecture good content, people will apply all that truth. We must teach, model and practice truth in the context of relationships, in a learning community, forged in *praxis*, not in abstraction. To teach is to help people learn. If people do not learn, a teacher has not taught. While we acknowledge the complexities of the teaching-learning context, let us offer the following:

1. *Model it.* We affirm that *example* is the best teacher. We cannot lead what we do not live. Discipleship is best taught and caught as the student observes and imitates the teacher. Leaders must model a missional spirituality so people have a concrete example of what it's like. Leaders should teach solid content that they demonstrate with their lives. This is not a call to perfection but to consistency and integrity. In addition, the mental model or paradigm that a leader carries in his or her mind brings focus to actions. What is the *telos* in that mental model that will focus the equipping?

2. *Mentor it.* Many words are used to describe equipping in relationship: coaching, discipling, spiritual direction, mentoring. To mentor is to impart wisdom. Pastors and church leaders must be mentors and spiritual guides who offer direction. Leadership and spirituality are intertwined. Leaders must mentor people in a missional spirituality—the heart of discipleship. A classroom context with good content is inadequate apart from mentoring relationships. Teachers must help people "pay absolute unmixed attention" to God in the ordinary junctures of their lives beyond church gatherings, beyond the confines of what we call temple spirituality.[2] One mentoring tool is to help people develop an individual and corporate "rule of life."[3]

3. *Mobilize it.* Church pastors and leaders tend to spend enormous amounts of time on the mobilization of church services, programs and structures, driven by a Christendom mental model. Imagine what could happen if, as in the classic Pietist movement, pastors and leaders spent time on the mobilization of a missional spirituality. Here are some contexts in which this can occur:

Through membership. Most churches run membership classes to orient new people to the history, vision, beliefs, programs and expectations of their particular church. What could happen if membership classes oriented newcomers to missional spirituality as the core of what it means to be a member of that church? The class could help new people explore discipleship pathways on which they would implement practices of a missional spirituality. To become a member could mean they affirm, "I am a disciple of Jesus and an ambassador for his kingdom,[4] and I surrender my sense of entitlement as I 'come and die' to myself for the sake of others." Membership could be more about entering into covenant relationships as a "new society" with others, with a call to discipleship and mission in the context of mentored Christian living.[5]

Through small groups. What could happen if small groups became places of discipleship, where equipping and mentoring in missional spirituality occurred as the curriculum? What if Bible studies became expository conversations about biblical obedience and missional actions in the community that emerged from the text? What if small-group leaders were trained and commissioned to serve in spiritual direction?[6]

Through gatherings. What could happen if church worship gatherings were designed to cultivate a missional spirituality? What would it take to repurpose worship gatherings to exalt God and equip and edify the saints for ministry and mission, as a gathering place from which to scatter a priesthood back into the game in the world? What would it take to reorient the spiritual routines of worship gatherings—attendance, prelude, doxology, Scripture reading, sermons, liturgy, offering, Communion, benediction—so they become launching pads to life and mission?[7]

Through church boards. Many church boards concentrate on matters that do not deal with mission, discipleship and spiritual formation. They tend to get bogged down with lengthy agendas in micromanagement rather than in spiritual governance and leadership. What could happen if church boards became communities of spiritual leaders that focused more on direction and discernment, and on monitoring a missional spirituality?[8] What if board members functioned more as mentors and spiritual directors?

Through retreats. Family retreats, men's and women's retreats, youth retreats, and leadership retreats are wonderful contexts for exploring the meaning and implications of a missional spirituality. With good planning, the setting can build community, open up godly conversations and enrich the practice of classic spiritual disciplines. Retreats can offer rich contexts for spiritual reading and theological reflection, prayer, spiritual direction, worship, Communion, and fellowship to help renew a vision for mission. Different discipleship training schools like Youth With a Mission and Capernwray use a retreat setting and format over a longer timeframe to cultivate spirituality and mission.

Through departments. What could happen if all church departments became unified around a common vision, a common set of teachings and a common set of practices that cultivated a missional spirituality? What could happen if all the leaders of all departments—children's, youth, young adults, worship, small groups, Christian education, men's, women's, counseling, care-giving, preaching, prayer, ushers and hospitality—moved out of their silos and collaborated together as a missional spirituality team?

Through practices. We cannot believe our way, preach our way or teach our way into a missional spirituality if we don't practice it. Too many studies, sermons and seminars stay in people's heads and notebooks, with good theory and great inspiration disconnected and abstracted from real-life practice. Love for God and neighbor must be tangible not theoretical. People must commit to practices that will embody the Jesus Creed and train them in godliness.

Through conversations. Informal and formal conversations can help equip and mobilize a missional spirituality in a community. Genuine listening can slow us down enough for true conversations to occur, and thus true learning. We must create contexts in which open and honest dialogue takes place. In these transitional times, the temptation is to rush ahead and "fix" things. Conversations can connect us to one another and to the wider networks that provide learning and collaboration. They can reduce the anxious sense that we are in this alone and allow us to be truly present with each other and with our neighbors.[9] Spiritual conversations can help nurture community when fostered by a generous and hospitable ethos in which people have a shared sense of belonging and contribution. It is possible that the essence of transformation is *linguistic*, governed by the power of language, context and possibility, through shifts in our speaking and listening.[10]

4. Measure it. What we measure indicates our values and focus. So, what do many pastors and church leaders measure? Attendance, baptisms and cash (the ABCs). These quantitative measures normally reveal only a numerical increase or decrease without a context by which to interpret them. But what if people are away on vacation when the counting happens, new believers are dunked but not discipled and key givers have lost their jobs? All of these people could still love God and neighbor a lot.

What would it take to develop *qualitative* measures to reveal the extent to which people love God and neighbor? Did not Paul have a qualitative idea of the extent to which the Colossians and Thessalonians practiced faith, hope and love (Colossians 1:4-6; 1 Thessalonians 1:3)? What would it take to develop ways to measure missional spirituality in our personal and corporate lives—for example, the extent to which people practice union with Christ, gratitude, prayer, Scripture reading, hospitality and missional activity in their community and workplace? What *telos* do we have in mind that we use as the goal or standard for our measuring? What we focus on and give leadership to tends to grow.[11]

Equipping for a Missional Spirituality in the Academy

*It takes most men five years to recover from a college
education, and to learn that poetry is as vital to thinking
as knowledge.*

BROOKS ATKINSON, ONCE AROUND THE SUN

A denominational executive discussed the need to bring theological training back into local contexts. It wasn't simply that his denomination's Bible college was so far away or that the costs of both study and accommodation were so high, though both were true. Factors that subvert discipleship in the local church, such as disenchantment, excarnation, abstraction, extraction and temple spirituality, were also alive and well in the academic context.[12]

Moreover, much Bible college and seminary support comes from conservative and pragmatic constituencies, not necessarily ones who recognize a need for change, such as developing better delivery mechanisms available through Internet technology. The need within seminaries, no less than in churches, is for a fundamental shift in paradigms and practices: from equipping managers to equipping spiritual directors and leaders, from maintenance to mission, from church at the center to a kingdom frame.

Evangelical seminaries and summits seem fascinated with modernist American business models and CEO styles of leadership with a *telos* of vision casting, public speaking, team building and organizational efficiency. A syncretism of such secular models is often not theologically informed. The New Testament avoids letting the surrounding culture define the nature and function of church leadership.[13] Servant, slave and shepherd are prevalent New Testament metaphors that focus on character and the care of people with the roles of pastors, elders and deacons (see Mark 10:41-45; Luke 22:14-38; Acts 20:17-38; 1 Thessalonians 2; 1 Timothy 3:1-13; 1 Peter 5:1-4).

As we interviewed seminary professors in the United States and Canada who also wrestle with these issues, it quickly became evident that the academy faces the same challenges as churches face.[14] Like the foot and handprints of yesteryear's celebrities set in the cement sidewalk of Grauman's Chinese Theatre in Hollywood, paradigms get set in cement. Temple spirituality seems to prevail: the goal of many theological schools is still to produce "professionals" for a Christendom church model quickly growing obsolete.[15] This is similar to Swiss watchmakers who continued to believe in and improve their mechanical watches while losing substantial market share in the new world of crystal technology and watches as fashion accessories. Moreover, those under thirty-five continue to lose interest in questions posed by the previous generation. The anxiety generated by such challenges tends to push us simply to improve what we have always done. In addition, academic institutions are often led by academics rather than by organizational leaders. What occurs in the academy affects the church. A need is to equip for a missional spirituality anchored in *theological reflection.*

Dr. Phil Zylla of McMaster Divinity School holds that all ecclesial doctoral degrees should make doctors for the church, not doctors for the academy. Gerald Hiestand argues that pastors, not professors, should set the theological agenda of the church—as its theologians. The pastoral vocation should be a theological vocation. He notes that historically the church's most influential theologians were *church*men—pastors, priests and bishops.

> Not only has theology left the church, but the church has left theology. To be sure, many academic theologians view themselves as self-consciously serving the theological needs of the church. But on the whole, academic discourse has lost its way, becoming preoccupied with questions—especially questions regarding its right to exist—that minimize its ecclesial relevance.[16]

In 2009, the Wheaton Theology Conference sought to gain perspective on the disciplines and practices of spiritual formation as it considered its theological foundations. A collection of excellent essays emerged, which resulted in the book *Life in the Spirit.*[17] An essay by Linda Cannell offers four factors that, taken together, threaten the seminary and the church:

1. the rise of institutions

2. the rise of academic theology and academic rationalism

3. the rise of professionalism in higher education

4. how the church and academy have understood and fostered the desire to know God[18]

Cannell summarizes the developments that have shaped theological education. The first three constitute a powerful array of forces that should not be new to our readers. But the fourth is particularly interesting:

> Discussions of the loss of a suitable understanding of theology in relation to theological schooling, or the loss of what it means to know God, typically reference Edward Farley's *Theologia.* He positions the meaning of *theologia* within three major historical periods: From the patristic era through most of the medieval period *theologia* was understood as the knowledge of God—that is, a divine illumination of the intellect. From the twelfth to seventeenth centuries, *theologia* became a cognitively oriented "state and disposition of the soul which has the character of knowledge." Finally, from the Enlightenment to the present, *theologia* is seen as "the practical know-how necessary to ministerial work."[19]

Cannell notes that the loss of earlier understandings has made theological education the "grasping of the methods and contents of a plurality of regions of scholarship." Properly understood, "*theologia* cannot be taught, but it can be the unifying principle for theological study and the orienting philosophy of the curriculum."[20]

But if *theologia* cannot be taught, where do we begin? Henri Nouwen offered a timeless reflection in his book on Christian leadership, *In the Name of Jesus*. He described the leader of the future as the praying leader, the vulnerable leader and the trusting leader. He also intimated what Gordon Cosby identified explicitly: "Our culture promotes a constant filling up, but our disciplines will draw us toward a greater emptiness, so that we can be better prepared for obedience and, ultimately, for finding our place in God's plan finding true relevance."[21] Theological reflection could evolve into a grasp for control when what we need is to embrace our powerlessness. Nouwen's trusting leader is a surrendered/powerless/subversive leader.

Commenting from John 21:18, Nouwen wrote that a mature leader follows where he or she does not want to go. The Christian leader of the future, the missional leader, is radically poor, taking nothing for the journey and dependent on Christ (Mark 6:8; Luke 10:4).

For Nouwen, the discipline for discernment of where we are being led is *theological reflection*.

> Just as prayer keeps us connected with the first love, and confession and forgiveness keep our ministry communal and mutual, so strenuous theological reflection will allow us to discern where God is leading. . . . Real theological thinking, which is thinking with the mind of Christ, is hard to find in the practice of ministry. Without solid theological reflection, future leaders will be little more than pseudo-psychologists, pseudo-sociologists, and pseudo-social workers. . . . Thinking about the future of Christian leadership, I am convinced that it needs to be a theological leadership.[22]

In *The Younger Evangelicals,* Robert Webber writes that the new evangelical leadership "is not shaped by being right, nor is it driven by meeting needs. Instead, it arises out of (1) a missiological understanding of the church, (2) theological reflection, (3) spiritual formation, and (4) cultural awareness." These four areas represent a circle of leadership with action at the center.[23] Connecting theological reflection explicitly with the *missio Dei* and missional spirituality, he writes,

> Theological reflection is inextricably linked with the *Missio Dei.* . . . The practice of ministry is already theology— theology in action. When one enters the circle of leadership through theology, one is driven to missiological reflection, to spiritual formation, to cultural awareness. One can enter the circle through spiritual formation. Spirituality is no longer exclusively identified with spiritual habits of prayer, Scripture reading, and attendance at church, or with an ethical list of do's and don'ts. Rather, spirituality is informed by the *Missio Dei* and the theological reflection of the church, emphasizing the holistic message of becoming truly human.[24]

Tyndale Seminary president Gary Nelson reaches a similar conclusion. In *Borderland Churches,* Gary exhorts leaders to face the challenges of living in a new pastoral landscape.

> When a clergy leader feels irrelevant outside the walls of the church, such a leader will have more at stake in what happens inside. . . . Seminaries and Bible colleges emphasize the academic and intellectual content framed in the Christendom model of pastoral formation. Many seminaries fail to nurture the spiritual, social, and relational intelligence required to lead effective congregational life.[25]

Nelson suggests four roles necessary for the task: a leader today is to be an "apprentice-pastor-theologian-missionary." On the theologian role, he writes, "The role of theology has been suppressed in the last decades because of our love for the pragmatic and technique oriented leadership and managerial missiology. . . . A deep theological and biblical reflective frame must be formed in the pastor's life."[26] These roles become core to what we call the practice of a missional spirituality. Fortunately, a number of seminaries and denominations are beginning to focus more on missional church leadership, spiritual formation and mentoring.[27] With the preceding in mind we offer three areas in equipping for a missional spirituality in the academy.[28]

1. Equip for theological reflection and integration. The core question and *telos* of theological education in the academy must be this: how do we equip leaders who will also equip others in what it means to love God from all one's heart, soul, mind and strength, and to love one's neighbor as oneself? This framework empowers all theology, spirituality and mission. It's inadequate merely to offer courses in systematic theology and ethics that are stand-alone studies abstracted from the practice of theology for spirituality and mission.[29]

Also, equipping in spiritual direction and the care of souls from a theological framework (not just pastoral counseling) is imperative.[30] Students will learn to lead in the new world through *praxis* with an integration and collaboration between teachers who offer courses and field experience in biblical, theological, historical and practical studies, and who are themselves grounded in missional communities. It is not enough for a pastor to know or have a theology but to also *practice* theology. Students and teachers will also benefit greatly if they develop and practice a "rule of life."[31]

2. Equip for mission and disciple making. It seems peculiar that many seminaries and Bible colleges do not require mission and disciple making as core courses in their degree program or at least as a unifying theme around which programs are arranged. Courses such as evangelism, world missions, mentoring and team building are often offered, but being disciples and making disciples on mission with Jesus is a prominent theme in the New Testament, particularly in the Gospels and Acts. Alan Hirsch writes, "You can't be a disciple without being a missionary: no mission, no discipleship."[32] Equipping for a missional spirituality in the academy requires that leaders are taught not only how to exegete Scripture but also how to exegete culture, how to be engaged incarnationally in their communities and how to make disciples. Their *telos* is to present everyone mature in Christ (Colossians 1:28).

3. Equip for spirituality and subversion. The academy will equip surrendered/powerless/subversive leaders in important competencies. However, a leader can't become competent to accomplish the tasks of church ministry without the foundation of spirituality —for example, the practices of union with Christ, obedience and humility with a surrendered life led by the Spirit. Spirituality and virtue are first, then leadership.[33] Leaders sometimes lead competently but not spiritually because of fear, control, performance and ambition. Perhaps they lead devoid of the knowledge that they are beloved.[34] They have not "come home."

How do we equip leaders to be self-emptied, broken, "nothing leaders" who resist the temptation to be powerful?[35] Nouwen wrote, "Power offers an easy substitute for the hard task of love."[36] We must shift the paradigm of equipping professionals to that of equipping servants and slaves (Mark 10:41-45). We must equip leaders in how to get out of their boxes of self-deception and blaming others as they discover their true motives for their actions and attitudes.[37] In this vein, the final suggestion we offer is that we equip people for a subversive missional spirituality. Eugene Peterson wrote,

> Most major religious figures have been subversive—they have tried to change in small and major ways the prevailing

framework of life. Religion is sometimes described as the institutionalization of a revolution; when the institution overpowers the revolution, what is needed to get back on track is subversion. Spirituality is always in danger of self-absorption, of becoming so intrigued with matters of soul that God is treated as a mere accessory to my experience. This requires much vigilance. Spiritual theology is, among other things, the exercise of this vigilance.[38]

Is not all theology spiritual theology? If so, will it be a subversive spirituality that thrives in sacred contemplation and sacramental action, from love of God to love of people, with often-hidden yet potent influences? The academy cultivates the mind. It should also cultivate the heart, the driving force of our affections, with love as the core desire.

David Bosch suggests we need a paradigm shift in a theology of mission: "To participate in mission is to participate in the movement of God's love toward people, since God is a fountain of sending love."[39] This becomes a core curriculum, perhaps the *theologia*, for discipleship and mission.

This shift will require an active partnership between churches, seminaries and Bible colleges, with corresponding resolve, prayer, conversation and curriculum revision. Together we must learn how to dwell in Christ, which will require the regular homecoming of God's people and a sustained willingness to be sent. The church and academy must together equip God's people theologically for a missional spirituality, to embody God's love from the inside out.

Appendix 2

Missional Spirituality in Action:
Gateway Community Church

What follows is missional spirituality in action as described by
Pastor John Klassen of Gateway Community Church, in Hinton,
Alberta—a community of ten thousand near the town of Jasper.
He and his wife, Shirley, have pastored this Baptist congregation
of 150 for eleven years.

✝

I see Gateway shaped by a missional spirituality because we are
not about a particular program, denomination or project, such as
mission trips or youth ministry. At the heart of our church is a
gathering of people who are concerned with the bigger purpose of
bringing God's kingdom to the larger community outside our
walls. Our foundation is built on Scripture, prayer, the Spirit and
relationships. Without those, nothing we do would be effective.

For a church to be missional, leaders must practice it. Jesus
didn't give his disciples directives and then sit back in the syna-

gogue and wait for them to come back to his office with their reports. He got to know the culture by getting immersed in it, so he was well aware of the needs, the mindsets and the lifestyles of the people he was reaching. We deliberately get involved in "nonreligious" activities outside church. For example, I joined Hinton Search and Rescue and the Rotary Club. I meet a variety of people in our community weekly. I build relationships, and when there is a crisis in their life, they have someone to call, and they do.

My wife, Shirley, deliberately chose to work outside the home, and that keeps her from being overinvolved in church life. Being a part of the regular workforce gives us many contacts that we would never have if we were only involved in "church-sanctioned" activities. Lately, even her boss has shown interest in her Christian "spirituality." Our church members are also involved in many community activities, such as sports teams, hiking groups, theater and dance. We seek to enlarge our circle of friends and the people we can influence.

As a church we also get involved in serving our community in nonreligious functions—for example, working in the local Share Shop, a secondhand clothing store, or serving at the Food Bank. This is a wonderful opportunity to meet people in our community who never think that attending church would be something they would want to do, because they wouldn't fit in. During the weeks when we volunteer at the Share Shop, we pray on Monday nights for the workers and the customers, and that we would represent Jesus well to the people who come in.

Our church is close to the school, and often students will stop by to play video games or air hockey and foosball in the youth room. On occasion our associate will set up his action games and a group of them will play far into the night. The junior youth group and the senior youth groups are 80 percent nonchurched kids, 20 percent churched kids. Those are just a few of the ways we try to be visible in the community and build relationships with people in their own territory. We also represent our church in various ways such as a biweekly singing service at the Good Samaritan Hospital and Pine Valley Senior's Lodge.

Our Alpha groups are open to people of all faiths or no faith. Working at Bingo for the Rotary Club has brought a young woman to our Alpha group this fall. She saw the ad in the paper, and because she knew me from Bingo, she phoned to ask if she would be able to attend. We offer the Alpha marriage course in one of the local restaurants. Our care groups integrate people of different faith backgrounds.

Seven years ago we started to place an advertising flier in the Welcome Wagon package. Along with that, we would get a report every month with names and addresses of new residents that have been given a Welcome Wagon package. We have a group of women who make up small baskets of goodies and then call everyone on the Welcome Wagon list to see if they can bring them a basket and welcome them to the community. That puts a face to the church, and they can answer any questions the people may have about specific programs. Also, if they should choose to check us out, there are at least two familiar faces in the crowd.

We not only welcome others to our worship services, we deliberately choose to invite nonchurched people individually to participate in our programs. For example, the Christmas Cantata is open to anyone who enjoys singing and acting. For our Christmas Cantata performances we invite the community and we pack out the sanctuary for four nights, reaching about seven hundred people with a Christmas message. This gives us an opportunity to interact with them personally during the dessert and coffee time after each performance.

To be missional is a long-term commitment; it's always deliberately choosing to be inclusive. In some instances it has taken years before seeing any results. We only want to model our ministry after Jesus. He went to the people, visited in their homes, attended their parties and drank their wine. When people experience us in their environment, our church becomes more incarnational. To be effective we must learn to function like crosscultural missionaries rather than be a gathering place where people come to receive religious goods and services. A missional church is comprised of a missional people whose spiritual lives shape their sense of mission. That is our passion and purpose here at our church.

Notes

Preface

[1]If you can find copies, read Elizabeth O'Connor's *Call to Commitment* (New York: Harper & Row, 1963) and *Journey Inward, Journey Outward* (New York: Harper & Row, 1968). Though her context was the Church of the Saviour, Washington, D.C., in the fifties and sixites, these books contain valuable insights for today's missional spirituality.

[2]Richard J. Foster, *The Freedom of Simplicity* (San Francisco: Harper & Row, 1981), p. 13.

Chapter 1: Exploring a Missional Spirituality

[1]For the origin of the term *liminality* and its implications, see Victor Turner, *The Ritual Process* (New York: Cornell University Press, 1969); for an application of its context in missional *communitas,* see Alan Hirsch, *The Forgotten Ways* (Grand Rapids: Brazos Press, 2006), pp. 220-31.

[2]William Knoke, *Bold New World: The Essential Road Map to the Twenty-First Century* (New York: Kodansha America, 1996)

[3]T. S. Eliot, "East Coker III," in *Four Quartets* (San Diego: Harcourt Brace Jovanovich, 1971), p. 22.

[4]Walter Brueggemann, *Spirituality of the Psalms* (Minneapolis: Fortress, 2002), p. 14.

[5]Dr. Peter Davids, who works in counseling with his wife, Judy, remarked, "While one cannot establish direct cause and effect, there's a statistical relationship between significant loss and the occurrence of cancer."

[6]Rosemarie Jarski, *Words from the Wise* (New York: Skyhorse Publishing, 2007), p. 201.

[7]See Ronald Heifetz et al., *The Practice of Adaptive Leadership* (Boston: Harvard Business Press, 2009).

[8]Vinoth Ramachandra opens his book with a discussion of terrorism. *Subverting Global Myths* (Downers Grove, Ill.: InterVarsity Press, 2008), pp. 17-56.

[9]Bill Easum remarks, "Experiential spirituality is transforming the public's view on many things such as health care, education, home schooling, and our search for new forms of community. An examination of any good bookstore reveals that there are almost as many references to spirituality in the business section as there are in the religious section." *Leadership on the Other Side* (Nashville: Abingdon, 2000), p. 116.

[10]Alan Roxburgh, "Derivatives with a Twist" <www.roxburghmissionalnet.com/index
.php?option=com_content&view=article&id=116:derivaties-with-twist&catid
=44:culture&Itemid=89>.

[11]Hans Küng, The Church (Garden City, N.Y.: Image Books, 1976), p. 176.

[12]William Hendriksen, The Gospel of Luke, New Testament Commentary (Grand Rapids: Baker, 1978), p. 185.

[13]Ibid., pp. 185-86.

[14]Leonard Sweet, So Beautiful (Colorado Springs: David C. Cook, 2009), p. 88.

[15]Clotaire Rapaille, The Culture Code (New York: Broadway Books, 2007), p. 96.

[16]Tim Keller, The Prodigal God (New York: Dutton, 2008), pp. 95, 97.

[17]Reggie McNeal, The Present Future (San Francisco: Jossey-Bass, 2003), p. 27.

[18]Perhaps Brian McLaren overstates the case for global crises in his book Everything
Must Change (Nashville: Thomas Nelson, 2009). The globe has been in crisis after
crisis since Genesis 3. Jesus changes everything global and local, and it began with
an anonymous Samaritan woman who thirsted for the water of life. Her community
of Sychar came in droves to hear him for themselves. When the gospel transforms
us, we become missionaries who build gospel bridges that we cross to our communities.

[19]Gary Nelson, Borderland Churches (St. Louis: Chalice Press, 2008), pp. 2, 13.

[20]N. T. Wright, Surprised by Hope (New York: HarperOne, 2008), p. 170.

[21]Reggie McNeal, Missional Renaissance (San Francisco: Jossey-Bass, 2009), p. xiv.

[22]Brad Brisco, "Transitioning from Traditional to Missional," Missional Church
Network <http://missionalchurchnetwork.com/index.php?s=start+with+spiritual+
formation>.

[23]See Alan Hirsch and Lance Ford, Right Here, Right Now (Grand Rapids: Baker,
2011).

[24]Jeffrey P. Greenman, "Spiritual Formation in Theological Perspective," in Life in the
Spirit: Spiritual Formation in Theological Perspective, ed. Jeffrey P. Greenman and
George Kalantzis (Downers Grove, Ill.: InterVarsity Press, 2010), p. 24, italics
ours.

[25]Bill Hull, The Complete Book of Discipleship (Colorado Springs: NavPress, 2006), p.
35.

[26]Eugene Peterson, Leap Over a Wall (San Francisco: HarperCollins, 1997), p. 4.

[27]See Tony Jones, The Sacred Way: Spiritual Practices for Everyday Life (Grand Rapids:
Zondervan, 2005), p. 26.

[28]See Dallas Willard, The Spirit of the Disciplines (San Francisco: Harper & Row,
1988), p. 158.

[29]Winston Churchill, October 28, 1943, to the House of Commons (meeting in the
House of Lords). From "We Shape Our Buildings," April 29, 2005, The Pacific Slope
<http://thepacificslope.blogspot.com/2005/04/we-shape-our-buildings.html>.

[30]Hugh Halter and Matt Smay, AND: The Gathered and Scattered Church (Grand Rapids: Zondervan, 2010), p. 169.

[31]Walter Brueggemann, Cadences of Home (Louisville: John Knox Press, 1997), p. 108.

Brueggemann writes, "While we may find wilderness-exile models less congenial, there is no biblical evidence that the God of the Bible cringes at the prospect of this community being one of wilderness and exile. Indeed this God resisted the temple in any case (cf. 2 Sam. 7:4-7). In the end, it is God and not the Babylonians who terminated the temple project. In the face of that possible eventuality in our own time and circumstances, the ways for the survival of an alternative imagination in an alternative community call for new strategies."

[32]See John Piper, *Brothers, We Are Not Professionals: A Plea to Pastors for Radical Ministry* (Nashville: Broadman and Holman, 2002).

[33]Dallas Willard, "How Do We Assess Spiritual Growth?" *Leadership*, Spring 2010, p. 29.

[34]See Keith Meyer, *Whole Life Transformation: Becoming the Change Your Church Needs* (Downers Grove, Ill.: InterVarsity Press, 2010).

[35]M. Robert Mulholland Jr., *Invitation to a Journey: A Road Map for Spiritual Formation* (Downers Grove, Ill.: InterVarsity Press, 1993), p. 12, emphasis added.

[36]Dallas Willard, *Renovation of the Heart* (Colorado Springs: NavPress, 2002), p. 183.

[37]Earl Creps, *Off-Road Disciplines: Spiritual Adventures of Missional Leaders* (San Francisco: Jossey-Bass, 2006), p. 3.

Chapter 2: Challenges for a Missional Spirituality

[1]John Patrick Diggens, "The Godless Delusion," *New York Times Sunday Book Review* (review of Charles Taylor's *The Secular Age*), December 16, 2007 <www.nytimes.com/2007/12/16/books/review/Diggins-t.html?pagewanted=2&_r=>.

[2]George G. Hunter III, *How to Reach Secular People* (Nashville: Abingdon, 1992), p. 22.

[3]George G. Hunter III says, "The breakup of Christendom continued with the Protestant Reformation, led by Luther and Calvin. The Reformation removed Church influence from western life by dividing the Church and by turning the Church's attention away from the management of society and inward toward renewal, reorganization, and theological matters. The Renaissance and the Reformation provided the one-two punch that got secularization rolling." Ibid., p. 27.

[4]Charles Taylor, *A Secular Age* (Cambridge, Mass.: Harvard University Press, 2007), p. 26.

[5]Roger Helland, "Earth Crammed with Heaven: Engaging Culture and Experiencing God" (DMin diss., Trinity Western University, 2007), pp. 3-4.

[6]For a detailed documentation of this view, see Conrad Oswalt, *Secular Steeples: Popular Culture and the Religious Imagination* (Harrisburg, Penn.: Trinity Press International, 2001); Peter Berger, *The Sacred Canopy: Elements of a Sociological Theory of Religion* (New York: Anchor, 1967), pp. 105-71; Francis A. Schaeffer, *Escape from Reason* (Downers Grove, Ill.: InterVarsity Press, 2006).

[7]Oswalt, *Secular Steeples*, p. 15, summarizing Berger, *The Sacred Canopy*, pp. 110-18, 123.

[8]Malcolm Muggeridge, *Jesus Rediscovered* (New York: Doubleday, 1969), p. 31.

[9]To get an idea of what we mean here, at least from the perspective of one observer of a Christian concert extravaganza known as Creation '99, read Rick Levin, "Christa-palooza: 20,000 Christians Convene at the Gorge: God Doesn't Show," August 19-25, 1999, *The Stranger* <www.thestranger.com/seattle/christapalooza/Content?oid =1766>. Please note: this site contains some graphic content.

[10]Taylor, *A Secular Age*, p. 554.

[11]Reggie McNeal, *The Present Future* (San Francisco: Jossey-Bass, 2003), p. 83.

[12]Doug Pagitt, *Reimagining Spiritual Formation* (Grand Rapids: Zondervan, 2003), p. 23.

[13]Ibid., p. 22.

[14]Reason is a human mental faculty, also called rationality, which generates conclu-sions from assumptions or premises. The concept of "reason" is closely related to the concepts of language and logic. Reason is often contrasted with authority, intu-ition, emotion, mysticism, superstition and faith, and is thought by rationalists to be more reliable than these in discovering what is true or what is best.

[15]Shane Hipps, *The Hidden Power of Electronic Culture: How Media Shapes Faith, the Gospel, and Church* (Grand Rapids: Zondervan, 2005), p. 51.

[16]We are indebted for some of the ideas in this paragraph to Shane Hipps, *Hidden Power*, and M. Rex Miller, *The Millennial Matrix* (San Francisco: Jossey-Bass, 2004).

[17]See Roger Helland, "Here's to Your Health," *Journal of the American Society for Church Growth* 16 (Winter 2005): 15-29.

[18]Skye Jethani, *The Divine Commodity: Discovering a Faith Beyond Consumer Christian-ity* (Grand Rapids: Zondervan, 2009), p. 12.

[19]William T. Cavanaugh, *Being Consumed* (Grand Rapids: Eerdmans, 2008), p. 9.

[20]Paul Krassner, "Celebrities: Aren't They Something?" *Los Angeles Times Magazine*, June 13, 1999, as quoted in Dick Staub, *The Culturally Savvy Christian* (San Fran-cisco: Jossey-Bass, 2007), p. 10.

[21]See <www.google.com/hostednews/afp/article/ALeqM5hLiHcxoI881MwIl5nD2I5c nRaJZg>.

[22]"The Big Gamble," *60 Minutes*, January 9, 2011.

[23]Eddie Gibbs, *LeadershipNext* (Downers Grove, Ill.: InterVarsity Press, 2005), p. 12.

[24]Alan and Debra Hirsch, *Untamed: Reactivating a Missional Form of Discipleship* (Grand Rapids: Baker, 2010), p. 110; See also Jethani, *Divine Commodity*.

[25]Bill Easum, *Leadership on the Other Side* (Nashville: Abingdon, 2000), p. 153.

[26]Ibid., p. 152.

[27]Charles Ludwig, *Francis Asbury: God's Circuit Rider* (Milford, Mich.: Mott Media, 1984), p. 1.

[28]Reggie McNeal, *The Present Future* (San Francisco: Jossey-Bass, 2003), p. 27.

[29]See "Reveal," Willow <www.revealnow.com/about.asp>.

[30]"Willow Creek Repents?" *Out of Ur*, Christianity Today, October 18, 2007 <www .outofur.com/ar chives/2007/10/willow_creek_re.html>.

[31]See ibid.

[32]Ibid.

³³See "Barna Studies the Research, Offers a Year-in-Review Perspective," 2009, Barna Group <www.barna.org/barna-update/article/12-faithspirituality/325-barna-studies-the-research-offers-a-year-in-review-perspective>, emphasis added.

³⁴Reggie McNeal, *Missional Renaissance* (San Francisco: Jossey-Bass, 2009), p. 45, emphasis in original.

Chapter 3: Theological Foundations

¹Karl Barth, *Dogmatics in Outline* (San Francisco: Harper Perennial, 1959), p. 7.

²Jeffrey P. Greenman and George Kalantzis, eds., *Life in the Spirit: Spiritual Formation in Theological Perspective* (Downers Grove, Ill.: InterVarsity Press, 2010), p. 35.

³See George G. Hunter III, *The Celtic Way of Evangelism* (Nashville: Abingdon, 2000).

⁴Cited by Eric Swanson and Rick Rusaw, *The Externally Focused Quest: Becoming the Best Church for the Community* (San Francisco: Jossey-Bass, 2010), p. 55.

⁵Ibid., p. 56.

⁶Lesslie Newbigin, *The Open Secret*, rev. ed. (Grand Rapids: Eerdmans, 1978, 1995), p. 70.

⁷Robert E. Webber, *The Divine Embrace* (Grand Rapids: Baker, 2006), p. 160.

⁸William P. Young, *The Shack* (Newbury Park, Calif.: Windblown Media, 2007).

⁹Stephen Seamands, *Ministry in the Image of God* (Downers Grove, Ill.: InterVarsity Press, 2005), p. 163, emphasis in original.

¹⁰See Roger Helland, "The Hypostatic Union: How Did Jesus Function?" *Evangelical Quarterly* 65, no. 4 (October 1993): 311-27. See also the ancient concept of *imitatio Christi*.

¹¹Jesus was a *Galilean* Jew. Legrand points out that this mattered a lot in terms of the prevailing Jewish culture in Palestine and to Jesus' contemporaries (Matthew 26:69; Mark 14:70; John 7:41, 52; cf. 1:46). See Lucien Legrand, *The Bible on Culture* (Maryknoll, N.Y.: Orbis, 200), pp. 97-112.

¹²Stephen Bevans, *Models of Contextual Theology* (Maryknoll, N.Y.: Orbis, 1992), p. 8.

¹³Webber, *Divine Embrace*, p. 173.

¹⁴James K. A. Smith, *Who's Afraid of Postmodernism?* (Grand Rapids: Baker, 2006), pp. 104-5.

¹⁵Alan Hirsch, *The Forgotten Ways* (Grand Rapids: Brazos Press, 2006), p. 135, emphasis in original. Also on this theme, see Hugh Halter and Matt Smay, *The Tangible Kingdom* (San Francisco: Jossey-Bass, 2008).

¹⁶*My Fair Lady*, Los Angeles: Warner Brothers, 1964 <www.imdb.com/title/tt0058385 /quotes>.

¹⁷Used by permission.

¹⁸Alan Roxburgh, "Missional Leadership: Equipping God's People for Mission," in *Missional Church*, ed. Darrell Guder (Grand Rapids: Eerdmans, 1998), p. 195, italics ours.

¹⁹According to Baptist scholar Stanley J. Grenz, the representative or Presbyterian model took its pattern from the parliamentary system of political government that

arose in sixteenth-century England. The democratic congregational model took its pattern from the town hall meeting in a local community. As he also suggests, this model is difficult to maintain in practice, especially when majority voting procedures contain factions who battle for control, or when apathy evidenced by declining participation sabotages a strong representation of people, or when churches become larger and more complex. *Theology for the Community of God* (Grand Rapids: Eerdmans, 1994, 2000), pp. 552-57. Stanley J. Grenz writes, "In addition, democratic congregationalism has also been open to misunderstanding. Often the 'democratic' aspect is interpreted in the sense of rule by majority. Actually, however, this principle has reference to the active role of all in the corporate search for the will of Christ for the church. True democratic congregationalism is the discerning of the will of Christ by the entire body under the guidance of its leaders, and not the rule by a select few nor by the voting majority at meagerly attended church meetings." *The Baptist Congregation* (Vancouver, B.C.: Regent College Publishing, 2002), p. 57.
[20]See David W. Bennett, *Metaphors of Ministry* (Eugene, Ore.: Wipf & Stock, 1993), p. 104.
[21]Wayne Grudem, *1 Peter*, Tyndale New Testament Commentaries (Downers Grove, Ill.: InterVarsity Press, 1988), p. 97.
[22]N. T. Wright, *After You Believe* (San Francisco: HarperOne, 2010), p. 86.
[23]Ibid., pp. 219-55.
[24]The Lausanne 2004 Forum Summary Affirmations say, " 'We affirm the priesthood of all believers and call on the church to equip, encourage and empower women, men and youth to fulfill their calling as witnesses and co-laborers in the world wide task of evangelization.' We are challenged to be what the church was always meant to be: people of flesh and blood carrying the reality of the gospel within them through their being and action. We therefore strongly believe that the priesthood of all believers will be the basic structure for the local church and for mission in the future" (*The Local Church in Mission: Becoming a Missional Congregation in the Twenty-First Century Global Context and the Opportunities Offered Through Tentmaking Ministry*, Lausanne Occasional Paper No. 39, from the 2004 Forum for World Evangelization hosted by the Lausanne Committee for World Evangelization in Pattaya, Thailand, Sept. 29-Oct. 5, 2004; see <www.lausanne.org/documents /2004forum/LOP39_IG10.pdf>).
[25]Wright, *After You Believe*, pp. 83-84, emphasis in original.
[26]Alan Hirsch, "Three Over-Looked Leadership Roles," *Leadership Journal*, May 2008 <www.christianitytoday.com/le/buildingleaders/ministrystaff/7.32.html>.
[27]See Len Hjalmarson, "Laity," in *An Emerging Dictionary for the Gospel and Culture* (Eugene, Ore.: Wipf & Stock, 2010), pp. 89-90. Also see Hans Küng, *The Church* (Garden City, N.Y.: Image Books, 1976), pp. 465-94.
[28]Unfortunately, to let go of control and actually practice the priesthood of all believers is an issue for numerous church leaders. For a lively and very practical discussion on how to let go of control and lead through the wormhole to the other side, see Bill Easum, *Leadership on the Other Side* (Nashville: Abingdon, 2000).

[29]Metro Community in Kelowna, B.C., ordains people who serve daily at a coffee bar, and will probably also ordain overseers who serve in the community garden. See Elizabeth O'Connor, *Call to Commitment* (New York: Harper & Row, 1963), pp. 101-7.

[30]Scot McKnight, *The Jesus Creed: Loving God, Loving Others* (Brewster, Mass.: Paraclete Press, 2004).

[31]Duane L. Christensen, *Deuteronomy 1–4*, Word Biblical Commentary, vol. 6a (Dallas: Word, 1991), emphasis in original.

[32]The Greek word for "mind" (psyche) in Mark 12:30 does not occur in Deuteronomy 6:5 as there is no word for "mind" in Hebrew; it is usually subsumed in the Hebrew word for "heart."

[33]Alan and Debra Hirsch, *Untamed: Reactivating a Missional Form of Discipleship* (Grand Rapids: Baker, 2010), p. 28.

[34]Moshe Weinfeld, *Deuteronomy 1–11*, Anchor Bible, vol. 5 (New York: Doubleday, 1991), p. 339.

[35]John Piper, *What Jesus Demands from the World* (Wheaton, Ill.: Crossway, 2006), p. 80.

[36]We are indebted to Dr. Dan Block for the direction of the exegetical insights in this section and the notion of loving God from the inside out, presented in a doctoral course he taught at Trinity Western University in Langley, British Columbia, October 2005, called "DMN 916: Leadership and Spirituality in the Old Testament."

[37]The parallel passage in Matthew 22:37 includes heart, soul and mind and omits the word *strength*. Some manuscripts of the Septuagint (Greek translation of the Old Testament) of Deuteronomy 6:4 use the word *mind* instead of *strength*. In Matthew, the Greek preposition *en* is also used and not *ek* as in Mark, and *ek* is also used in the Septuagint translation of Deuteronomy 6:4. The preposition *en* can denote either place, "in" or "with," but its root meaning is "within." See H. E. Dana and Julius Mantey, *A Manual Grammar of the Greek New Testament* (Toronto: Macmillan, 1955), p. 105. We would argue that the *place* of the heart, soul and mind, is more consistent with Mark and the Septuagint for an overall sense for New Testament theology rather than the heart, soul and mind being the *instruments* with which people love God, contrary to John Piper, who gives *ek* an instrumental usage the same as *en*, op. cit., pp. 80-81, fn. 2. James R. Edwards concurs with our exegetical position in *The Gospel According to Mark*, The Pillar New Testament Commentary (Grand Rapids: Eerdmans, 2002), p. 371.

[38]William L. Lane, *The Gospel of Mark*, The New International Commentary on the New Testament (Grand Rapids: Eerdmans, 1974), p. 433.

[39]Walter Wessel, *Mark*, The Expositor's Bible Commentary, vol. 8, ed. Frank E. Gaebelein (Grand Rapids: Zondervan 1984), p. 737, citing Mitton, *Gospel of Mark*, p. 99.

[40]Quoted by David Dark, *The Sacredness of Questioning Everything* (Grand Rapids: Zondervan, 2009), p. 9.

[41]Craig A. Evans, *Mark 8:27–16:20*, Word Biblical Commentary (Nashville: Thomas Nelson, 2001), p. 267.

[42]Edwards, *Gospel According to Mark*, p. 373.

[43]Tony Campolo, *The Kingdom of God Is a Party* (Nashville: Thomas Nelson, 1992).

[44]Ibid., p. 27.

Chapter 4: Missional Spirituality in Action

[1]A church leader made these comments in a church planters catalyst meeting in Calgary, Alberta.

[2]For stories of missional spirituality in action read Acts 4:23-35; 5:12-16; 9:31; 11:19-30; 14:21-28; 20:17-38; 28:17-31.

[3]For fuller treatments, see Roger Helland, *The Revived Church* (Kent, U.K.: Sovereign World, 1999); Ray S. Anderson, *Ministry on the Fireline: A Practical Theology for an Empowered Church* (Downers Grove, Ill.: InterVarsity Press, 1993).

[4]Eusebius *Ecclesiastical History* 3.37, cited by Ramsay MacMullen, *Christianizing the Roman Empire* A.D. *100-400* (New Haven: Yale University Press, 1984), p. 25.

[5]Within three centuries, Christianity included approximately 10 percent of the population of the Roman Empire of sixty million and had displaced other religions of the Empire. MacMullen estimates there were five million Christians by A.D. 300. Rodney Stark suggests a 40-percent growth per decade from A.D. 40 with six million Christians by A.D. 300, maxing out at approximately thirty-three million Christians by A.D. 350. Rodney Stark, *The Rise of Christianity* (Princeton, N.J.: Princeton University Press, 1996), pp. 1-10. MacMullen argues that mass conversions first came through the power of miracles and later through the social advantage of becoming a Christian. As such, he diminishes the importance of Christian love and piety and the testimony of martyrs but increases the importance of the miraculous. He also argues that when Christianity became the Roman state religion under Constantine and thus the start of Christendom in A.D. 313, it strongly diluted both the spiritual and supernatural nature of the church (as well as the missional).

[6]See Steve Addison, *Movements That Change the World* (Smyrna, Del.: Missional Press, 2009), pp. 71-84.

[7]For example, the Celts, Benedictines, Franciscans, Jesuits, Anglicans, Reformed, Anabaptists and Baptists and other missional movements. The ones we offer in this chapter are only a sample of those significantly influenced by classic Pietism. For further study see, Bradley P. Holt, *Thirsty for God: A Brief History of Christian Spirituality* (Minneapolis: Fortress, 2005).

[8]To that end, Spener stridently recommended John Arndt's book *True Christianity* and referenced Luther's recommendation of John Tauler's sermons (*Pia Desideria*, trans. and ed. Theodore G. Tappert [Philadelphia: Fortress, 1964], pp. 110-21). Tauler, a Dominican friar and mystic who encouraged love of God and neighbor, virtue, imitation of Christ, and union with Christ, also influenced John Arndt. Arndt's book is full of rich biblical, theological and practical challenges and insights for a missional spirituality.

[9]By the way, a number of Pietist leaders and such notables as John Wesley and A. B. Simpson and other evangelicals were and continue to be influenced by the spiritual

teaching of Catholic mystical writers such as Madame Guyon and Teresa of Ávila, whose teachings were transmitted by people such as Henry Scougal in *The Life of God in the Soul of Man* and Thomas à Kempis in *The Imitation of Christ.*

[10]Johann Arndt, *True Christianity*, trans. Peter Erb (New York: Paulist Press, 1979), pp. 23, 60.

[11]Dale W. Brown, *Understanding Pietism*, rev. ed. (Nappanee, Ind.: Evangel Publishing House, 1996), p. 86.

[12]Stanley M. Burgess and Gary B. McGee, *Dictionary of Pentecostal and Charismatic Movements* (Grand Rapids: Zondervan, 1988), pp. 279-81, and Allen C. Guelzo, "Pietism," in *Routledge Encyclopedia of Philosophy* (New York: Routledge, 1998): 7:392-95.

[13]"The golden decade of 1732-1742 stands unparalleled in Christian history in so far as missionary expansion is concerned. More than 70 Moravian missionaries, from a community of not more than 600 inhabitants, had answered the call by 1742." From "The Rich Young Ruler Who Said Yes," January 1, 1982, Christianity Today Library <www.ctlibrary.com/ch/1982/issue1/107.html>.

[14]According to D. Bruce Hindmarsh, "Scougal's spiritual teaching was received and naturalized as evangelical Methodist spirituality. . . . His text transmitted the ideals of pure love and entire resignation to God as expressed in the Catholic continental tradition of Fenelon, Mme Guyon and Molinos, and these ideals in turn were taproots of evangelical spirituality." "Seeking True Religion: Early Evangelical Devotion and Catholic Spirituality," in *Life in the Spirit: Spiritual Formation in Theological Perspective*, ed. Jeffrey P. Greenman and George Kalantzis (Downers Grove, Ill.: InterVarsity Press, 2010), p. 124.

[15]R. G. Tuttle Jr., "The Wesleyan Tradition," in *Evangelical Dictionary of Theology*, ed. Walter A. Elwell (Grand Rapids: Baker, 1984), p. 1167.

[16]Albert C. Outler, ed., *John Wesley* (New York: Oxford University Press, 1964), p. 7.

[17]Addison, *Movements That Change the World*, pp. 57-58.

[18]They were not ordained in the Anglican Church, but they were appointed, that is, ordained, by Wesley.

[19]Howard A. Snyder, *The Radical Wesley: Patterns of Church Renewal* (Grand Rapids: Francis Asbury Press/Zondervan, 1980), p. 3.

[20]"John Wesley: Did You Know?" October 1, 1983, ChristianHistory.net <www.christianitytoday.com/ch/1983/issue2/204.html>.

[21]J. Wesley Bready, *England: Before and After Wesley* (New York: Harper, 1938), p. 327.

[22]Heath, *Mystic Way*, p. 33.

[23]Holt, *Thirsty for God*, p. 140.

[24]A. E. Thompson, *A. B. Simpson: His Life and Work*, rev. ed. (Camp Hill, Penn.: Christian Publications, 1960), p. 9.

[25]Burgess and McGee, *Dictionary of Pentecostal and Charismatic Movements*, p. 406.

[26]Ibid., p. 164.

[27]Ibid.

[28]David F. Hartzfeld and Charles Nienkirchen, eds., *The Birth of a Vision: Essays on the Ministry and Thought of Albert B. Simpson* (Camp Hill, Penn.: Horizon House Publishers, 1986), p. 129.

[29]For example, 1 Thessalonians 5:2-24; Titus 2:11-13; 1 John 2:28; 3:2-3.

[30]Hartzfeld and Nienkirchen, *Birth of a Vision*, pp. 102-14, 186.

[31]The Alliance <www.roanoke-alliance.org/id4.html>.

[32]A. B. Simpson, "Aggressive Christianity," as cited in Kenneth L. Draper, comp., *Readings in Alliance History and Thought* (n.p.: n.p., 2001), p. 85.

[33]Thompson, *A. B. Simpson*, pp. 147, 182, 157, 175-77.

[34]Ibid., p. 126.

[35]A. B. Simpson, *The Fourfold Gospel* (Camp Hill, Penn.: Christian Publications, 1984), p. 79.

[36]Gordon T. Smith, "Conversion and Sanctification in the Christian & Missionary Alliance," in Kenneth L. Draper, *Readings in Alliance History and Thought* (n.p.: n.p., 2001), p. 157 n. 33.

[37]Ibid., p. 156. Italics his. See "Guidelines for Praying the Vision Prayer," Christian and Missionary Alliance in Canada <http://cmalliance.ca/visionprayerc611.php>.

[38]For an example of missional spirituality in action from a local church perspective see appendix two.

Chapter 5: Your Heart and Soul 1

[1]Craig R. Dykstra, *Growing in the Life of Faith: Education and Christian Practices* (Louisville, Ky.: Geneva Press, 1999), p. 66.

[2]Tim Morey, *Embodying Our Faith* (Downers Grove, Ill.: InterVarsity Press, 2009), p. 111; in footnote 20, he shows his indebtedness for the first part of his description to Dallas Willard, *The Spirit of the Disciplines* (San Francisco: HarperCollins, 1991), p. 156.

[3]For the discussion of *praxis* we are indebted to Ray S. Anderson, *The Shape of Practical Theology* (Downers Grove, Ill.: InterVarsity Press, 2001), pp. 47-49. His center of practical theology is what he calls "Christopraxis."

[4]Evelyn Underhill, *The Spiritual Life* (Harrisburg, Penn.: Morehouse Publishing, 1937), pp. 32-33.

[5]Eric Swanson and Rick Rusaw, *The Externally Focused Quest* (San Francisco: Jossey-Bass, 2010), pp. 65-66.

[6]Annie Dillard, *The Writing Life* (San Francisco: Harper Perennial, 1990).

[7]Roger Helland, *The Journey: Walking with God* (Kent, U.K.: Sovereign World, 2000), p. 66.

[8]Dallas Willard, *Renovation of the Heart* (Colorado Springs: NavPress, 2002), p. 37.

[9]Jonathan Edwards, *A Treatise on Religious Affections* (Grand Rapids: Baker, 1982), p. 14.

[10]For a fuller treatment see Roger Helland, "Union with Christ: Key to Fruitful Discipleship," in *Centered: Thoughts on Evangelical Spiritual Formation* 1, no. 6 (2009): 21-24; also James Fowler, "Union with Christ," 2003, Christ in You Ministries

<www.christinyou.net/pages/unionwithchrist.html>.

[11]Henri J. M. Nouwen, *Lifesigns* (New York: Image Books/Doubleday, 1990), p. 23.

[12]Stephen Seamands, *Ministry in the Image of God* (Downers Grove, Ill.: InterVarsity Press, 2005), p. 29.

[13]Nouwen, *Lifesigns*, p. 75.

[14]Photos of Doug and his story are available on the Teen Challenge website <www .teenchallenge.ca/abtc/doug>. Italics ours.

[15]Nouwen, *Lifesigns*, p. 85.

[16]Richard Foster, *Celebration of Discipline*, rev. ed. (San Francisco: Harper & Row, 1988), pp. 110-25.

[17]Willard, *Renovation of the Heart*, p. 88.

[18]John Calvin, *Institutes of the Christian Religion*, ed. John T. McNeill (Philadelphia: Westminster Press, 1960), 1.4.2.

[19]Dietrich Bonhoeffer, *The Cost of Discipleship*, rev. ed. (New York: Macmillan, 1963), p. 69.

[20]A. J. Jacobs, *The Year of Living Biblically: One Man's Quest to Follow the Bible as Literally as Possible* (New York: Simon & Schuster, 2007).

[21]See *Living Oprah* <www.livingoprah.com/>.

[22]Willard, *Renovation of the Heart*, p. 87.

[23]Andrew Murray, *Humility* (Ft. Washington, Penn.: Christian Literature Crusade, 1993), p. 78.

[24]Calvin *Institutes of the Christian Religion* 2.2.1.

[25]Alan E. Nelson, *Spirituality and Leadership* (Colorado Springs: NavPress, 2002), p. 107.

[26]Jonathan Edwards, "Some Thoughts Concerning the Revival of Religion in New England," in *The Works of Jonathan Edwards*, 2 vols. (Carlisle, Penn.: The Banner of Truth Trust, 1992), p. 401.

[27]Bill Hybels, *Descending into Greatness* (Grand Rapids: Zondervan, 1993), p. 17.

[28]Jim Collins, *Good to Great: Why Some Companies Make the Leap and Others Don't* (New York: HarperBusiness, 2001).

[29]Peter Mayer, "Fall," on the CD *Million Year Mind* (Blue Boat Records, 2001), used by permission.

[30]Murray, *Humility*, p. 23.

[31]See Roger Helland, "Nothing Leadership," *Ministry*, November 2006, pp. 12-14.

[32]"The Rule of Benedict" (sixth century) offers twelve practical steps to humility. See <www.osb.org/rb/text/toc.Html#toc>.

[33]Gordon T. Smith, *Beginning Well* (Downers Grove, Ill.: InterVarsity Press, 2001), p. 132.

[34]Gary L. Thomas, *The Glorious Pursuit* (Colorado Springs: NavPress, 1998), p. 49.

[35]William Law, *A Serious Call to a Devout and Holy Life* (Grand Rapids: Baker, 1977), pp. 201-2.

Chapter 6: Your Heart and Soul 2

[1]Earl Creps, *Off-Road Disciplines: Spiritual Adventures of Missional Leaders* (San Fran-

cisco: Jossey-Bass, 2006), p. xv.

[2]See Dallas Willard, "Spiritual Formation as a Natural Part of Salvation," in *Life in the Spirit: Spiritual Formation in Theological Perspective*, ed. Jeffrey P. Greenman and George Kalantzis (Downers Grove, Ill.: InterVarsity Press, 2010), pp. 45-60.

[3]Christopher J. H. Wright, *The Mission of God: Unlocking the Bible's Grand Narrative* (Downers Grove, Ill.: InterVarsity Press, 2006), pp. 23, 49, 51.

[4]Robert E. Webber, *The Divine Embrace: Recovering the Passionate Spiritual Life* (Grand Rapids: Baker, 2006), p. 210.

[5]Stanley J. Grenz, *Theology for the Community of God* (Grand Rapids: Eerdmans, 1994), p. 379.

[6]Mark Buchanan, *Your God Is Too Safe* (Sisters, Ore.: Multnomah, 2001), p. 218.

[7]Richard Foster, *Celebration of Discipline* (San Francisco: Harper & Row, 1988), p. 34.

[8]Alan Hirsch with Darryn Altclass, *The Forgotten Ways Handbook: A Practical Guide for Developing Missional Churches* (Grand Rapids: Brazos Press, 2009).

[9]Eugene Peterson, *Eat This Book* (Grand Rapids: Eerdmans, 2009), p. 91.

[10]Evelyn Underhill, *The Spiritual Life* (Harrisburg, Penn.: Morehouse Publishing, 1937), pp. 97-98.

[11]John Wesley, *The Works of John Wesley*, 3rd ed., vol. 14 (Kansas City: Beacon Hill Press, 1979), pp. 252ff. For a detailed exposition of Wesley's proposal, see M. Robert Mulholland Jr., *Shaped by the Word: The Power of Scripture in Spiritual Formation*, rev. ed. (Nashville: Upper Room Books, 1985, 2000), pp. 123-70.

[12]In Old Testament theology, sacrifice for sin was preparation for worship, not worship per se, and there were no sacrifices available to deal with deliberate sins. Vance Havner, as quoted on *The Quotable Christian* <www.pietyhilldesign.com/gcq /quotepages/worship.html>.

[13]See David Fitch, *The Great Giveaway* (Grand Rapids: Baker, 2005), p. 96.

[14]Stanley Grenz and John R. Franke, *Beyond Foundationalism* (Louisville, Ky.: Westminster John Knox, 2001), p. 121.

[15]A few years ago, Brian McLaren pondered the state of contemporary Christian music and concluded that much of it was overly sentimental, individualistic and focused on an experience of God without a response of sacrificial service and missional engagement. He wrote an open letter to worship songwriters; also see John Mortensen's "An Unauthorized Postscript" to his open letter, both at <www.brian mclaren.net/archives/resources/letters/>.

[16]George Barna, "Worship in the Third Millennium," in *Experiencing God in Worship*, ed. Michael D. Warden (Loveland, Colo.: Group Publishing, 2000), pp. 13-30.

[17]Sally Morgenthaler, *Worship Evangelism: Inviting Unbelievers into the Presence of God* (Grand Rapids: Zondervan, 1995).

[18]Gerrit Gustafson, "Worship Evangelism," *Psalmist*, February-March 1999, p. 31.

[19]Jim Wallis, *Agenda for Biblical People* (New York: HarperCollins, 1984), p. 110.

[20]James K. A. Smith, *Desiring the Kingdom* (Grand Rapids: Baker, 2009).

[21]Ibid., p. 25.

[22]Ibid., pp. 32-33, italics ours.

[23]Elizabeth Barrett Browning, "Aurora Leigh: A Poem," 1.2.812-26, University of Pennsylvania Libraries <http://digital.library.upenn.edu/women/barrett/aurora /aurora.html#7>.

[24]Simone Weil, *Gravity and Grace* (London: Routledge and Kegan Paul, 1972), p. 106.

[25]Abraham Joshua Heschel, *God in Search of Man* (New York: The Noonday Press, 1955), p. 33.

[26]Ibid., pp. 39-40.

[27]Bishop Kallistos Ware, *The Orthodox Way*, rev. ed. (Crestwood, N.Y.: St. Vladimir's Seminary Press, 1995), p. 119.

[28]Ken Gire, *Windows of the Soul* (Grand Rapids: Zondervan, 1996), p. 17. The author shows how we can experience God in new ways through "the discipline of awareness" that become windows of the soul: vocation, stories, art, wilderness, poetry, movies, memory, dreams, writing, Scripture, humanity, tears, depression, nature.

[29]For the lyrics, see "God Gave Me Everything" <www.lyricsmode.com/lyrics/m /mick_jagger/god _ gave_me_ everything.html>.

[30]Elizabeth A. Dreyer, *Earth Crammed with Heaven* (New York: Paulist Press, 1994), p. 6.

[31]Jonathan Edwards, *The Nature of True Virtue* (Goodyear, Ariz.: Diggory Press, 2007), pp. 5, 22.

[32]Ibid., p. 7, emphasis added.

[33]See Alasdair MacIntyre, *After Virtue*, 3rd ed. (Notre Dame: University of Notre Dame Press, 2007), pp. 184-203.

[34]N. T. Wright develops these themes in *After You Believe* (San Francisco: HarperOne, 2010).

[35]Aristotle and subsequent moral philosophers believed that virtue was the goal for a fruitful human being. For him, virtue was particularly developed in the context of the social interactions for the *polis*, city-state, through training. He used the word *arete* and taught that there are four principal, or cardinal virtues, from which all virtues are "hinged" that can be traced back to Plato: prudence (wisdom), temperance (self-control, moderation), courage and justice. Later, Christian theologians added the theological virtues of faith, hope and love.

[36]"Greek Philosophy" <www.nwlink.com/~donclark/hrd/history/greek.html>.

[37]Leonard Sweet makes this observation in *Postmodern Pilgrims* (Nashville: Broadman & Holman, 2000), p. 119, and cites *The Barna Report*, January-March 1999, n. 23.

[38]Eugene H. Peterson, *The Contemplative Pastor* (Grand Rapids: Eerdmans, 1989), p. 64.

Chapter 7: Your Mind Matters

[1]Paul J. Achtemeier, ed., "Mind," in *Harper's Bible Dictionary* (San Francisco: Harper & Row, 1985), p. 637. However, there is no word for "mind" in Hebrew as there is in Greek and English. "Mind" is subsumed in the word *heart*.

[2]"The Thoughts of the Emperor Marcus Aurelius Antoninus," *Wikisource* <http://en.wikisource.org/wiki/The_Thoughts_Of_The_Emperor_Marcus_Aurelius_Antoninus>.

[3]Leonard Sweet, *Post-Modern Pilgrims* (Nashville: Broadman & Holman, 2000), p. 100.

[4]John Ortberg, *The Me I Want to Be* (Grand Rapids: Zondervan, 2010), pp. 97-98.

[5]For example, J. P. Moreland, *Love Your God with All Your Mind: The Role of Reason in the Life of the Soul* (Colorado Springs: NavPress, 1997).

[6]Jonathan Edwards, *A Treatise of Religious Affections* (Grand Rapids: Baker, 1982), pp. 12-18.

[7]Ibid., p. 192.

[8]George Barna, *Think Like Jesus* (Brentwood, Tenn.: Integrity Publishers, 2003), p. 6.

[9]Douglas J. Moo, *The Letters to the Colossians and to Philemon*, The Pillar New Testament Commentaries (Grand Rapids: Eerdmans, 2008), p. 248.

[10]A. B. Simpson, *Wholly Sanctified* (Harrisburg, Penn.: Christian Publications, 1925), pp. 56-62.

[11]Thomas Watson, *All Things for Good* (1663; repr., Carlisle, Penn.: Banner of Truth Trust, 1986), p. 74.

[12]David Ruis, "Whom Have I but You" (Mercy/Vineyard Publishing, 1996).

[13]Quoted in Roger Helland, *The Journey: Walking with God* (Kent, U.K.: Sovereign World, 2000), p. 87.

[14]Larry Crabb, *The Safest Place on Earth* (Nashville: Word, 1999), pp. 12-13.

[15]Quoted in Helland, *The Journey*, p. 97. See chapter four for a fuller treatment of the trial of pain and loss.

[16]The compartmentalized and the self-maximized approach to life, common to many people, is a major challenge for pastors who must teach their people to integrate *faith* into all segments of their life as a *way of life*. See Christian Scharen, *Faith as a Way of Life* (Grand Rapids: Eerdmans, 2008).

[17]Eckhart Tolle, *A New Earth: Awakening to Your Life's Purpose* (New York: Penguin, 2008).

[18]Elizabeth Lesser, "Excerpt from *The Seeker's Guide*," June 9, 2008, Oprah <www.oprah.com/oprahsbookclub/Read-an-Excerpt-from-The-Seekers-Guide-by-Elizabeth-Lesser/2>.

[19]Rhonda Byrne, *The Secret* (New York: Beyond Words Publishing, 2006), pp. 47ff. See also <www.thesecret.tv/>.

[20]Ibid., pp. 47-69.

[21]Stanley J. Grenz, "What Does Hollywood Have to Do with Wheaton? The Place of (Pop) Culture in Theological Reflection," *Journal of the Evangelical Theological Society* 43, no. 2 (June 2000): 305.

[22]Jeffrey Overstreet, *Through a Screen Darkly: Looking Closer at Beauty, Truth and Evil in the Movies* (Ventura, Calif.: Regal, 2007), p. 56, emphasis added.

[23]"If Today Was Your Last Day" lyrics <www.elyrics.net/read/n/nickelback-lyrics/if-

today-was-your-last-day-lyrics.html>.

[24]Leonard Sweet, *Postmodern Pilgrims* (Nashville: Broadman & Holman, 2000), p. 95.

[25]Kenneth E. Bailey, *Jesus Through Middle Eastern Eyes* (Downers Grove, Ill.: InterVarsity Press, 2008), pp. 279-81. See Eugene Peterson, "The Subversive Pastor," in *The Contemplative Pastor* (Grand Rapids: Eerdmans, 1989), pp. 27-37.

[26]Alan and Debra Hirsch, *Untamed: Reactivating a Missional Form of Discipleship* (Grand Rapids: Baker, 2010), p. 55. For their preceding discussion about defective views of God, see pp. 61-62.

[27]Amy Plantinga Pauw, "Attending to the Gaps Between Beliefs and Practices," in *Practicing Theology*, ed. Miroslav Volf and Dorothy C. Bass (Grand Rapids: Eerdmans, 2002), pp. 45-46.

[28]Mike Mason, *The Gospel According to Job* (Wheaton, Ill.: Crossway, 1994), p. 141.

[29]The word *Eucharist* is taken from the Greek *eucharistia*, which means "thanksgiving."

[30]Henri Nouwen, *Bread for the Journey* (New York: HarperCollins, 1997).

[31]In the Old Testament, a thank offering was a voluntary act of worship offered in gratitude for deliverance from sickness, trouble, death, or a blessing received.

[32]Although this poem or parts of it are often attributed to Ralph Waldo Emerson, it does not appear in any of his published works. The true author is unknown.

Chapter 8: From All Your Strength

[1]Regina Brett, *God Never Blinks: 50 Lessons for Life's Little Detours* (New York: Grand Central Publishing, 2010), pp. 188-89.

[2]Randy Alcorn, *The Treasure Principle* (Colorado Springs: Multnomah, 2001), p. 52.

[3]Mike Dagle interview, February 2010, Woodward Theological Society <http://woodwardtheologicalsociety.org/interviews/2010/02/james-ka-smith-desiring-kingdom>.

[4]The growing community garden movement is an interesting variation here. See Christine Sine, "Is This a Move of God?" April 30, 2010, *Godspace* <http://godspace.wordpress.com/2010/04/30/is-this-a-move-of-god/>.

[5]Randy Alcorn, *Money, Possessions and Eternity* (Carol Stream, Ill.: Tyndale House, 2003), p. 4.

[6]Richard Stearns, *The Hole in Our Gospel* (Nashville: Thomas Nelson, 2010), pp. 215-17.

[7]Brian McLaren, *Everything Must Change* (Nashville: Thomas Nelson, 2007), pp. 17-18.

[8]Alcorn, *The Treasure Principle*, pp. 90-91.

[9]Henri Nouwen, quoted in the *Nouwen Society Newsletter*, May 2010 <http://Henri Nouwen.org>.

[10]William Cavanaugh, "The Church as God's Body Language," *Zadok Perspectives*, Spring 2006, p. 149.

[11]Tim Morey, *Embodying Our Faith* (Downers Grove, Ill.: InterVarsity Press, 2009), pp. 52-53.

[12]Quoted in Rowan Williams, "Urbanization, the Christian Church and the Human Project," in *Spirituality and the City*, ed. Andrew Walker (London: SPCK, 2005), p. 17.

[13]Cited by Mark Buchanan, *The Rest of God* (Nashville: W Publishing Group, 2006), p. 18.

[14]In Greek, there are two terms for "time." One denotes chronological time (minutes, hours, days). The other, *kairos*, denotes a season, an opportunity, an age.

[15]Eugene Peterson, *Working the Angles* (Grand Rapids: Eerdmans, 1987), pp. 66-72.

[16]Dorothy C. Bass, ed., *Practicing Our Faith* (San Francisco: Jossey-Bass, 1997), p. 25.

[17]Johann Arndt, *True Christianity*, trans. Peter Erb (New York: Paulist Press, 1979), p. 120.

[18]Buchanan, *The Rest of God*, pp. 4, 33, 62.

[19]Craig S. Keener, *The IVP Bible Background Commentary: New Testament* (Downers Grove, Ill.: InterVarsity Press, 1993), Mt 11:29.

Chapter 9: Love Your Neighbor

[1]Peter Block, *Community: The Structure of Belonging* (San Francisco: Berrett-Koehler Publishers, 2008), p. 132.

[2]James Bryan Smith, *The Good and Beautiful Community* (Downers Grove, Ill.: InterVarsity Press, 2010), pp. 16, 19.

[3]March 2003 <www.toddhunter.org>. Unfortunately, this blog no longer exists.

[4]Kenneth E. Bailey, *Jesus Through Middle Eastern Eyes* (Downers Grove, Ill.: InterVarsity Press, 2008), pp. 284-98.

[5]Ibid., p. 296.

[6]Simon Carey Holt, *God Next Door* (Melbourne: Acorn Books, 2005), p. 63, emphasis added.

[7]Eugene Peterson, *Christ Plays in Ten Thousand Places* (Grand Rapids: Eerdmans, 2005), p. 72.

[8]Simon Carey Holt, "A Mortgage, A Motor-Mower and a Mission" (Tinsley Annual Lecture, Morling College, New South Wales, May 2009), p. 8.

[9]William Cavanaugh, "The Church as God's Body Language," *Zadok Perspectives*, Spring 2006, p. 8.

[10]Robert Lupton, *Theirs Is the Kingdom* (New York: HarperCollins, 1989), p. 9.

[11]Todd Hunter, *Christianity Beyond Belief* (Downers Grove, Ill.: InterVarsity Press, 2009), p. 105.

[12]John Ortberg, *Love Beyond Reason* (Grand Rapids: Zondervan, 1998), pp. 15, 74.

[13]Henri Nouwen, *Lifesigns* (New York: HarperCollins, 1983), p. 22.

[14]See Len Hjalmarson, "Hospitality," in *An Emerging Dictionary of Gospel and Culture* (Eugene, Ore.: Wipf & Stock, 2010), pp. 75-77.

[15]The Hebrew term *ger* is "anyone outside the kin group or solidarity unit and, therefore, *defenceless*." Philip J. King and Lawrence E. Stager, *Life in Biblical Israel* (Louis-

ville, Ky.: Westminster John Knox, 2001), p. 137. The notion of being a *ger* was to be Israel's fundamental identity in covenant relationship with Yahweh in the land.

[16]Fred Bernhard and Steve Clapp, *Widening the Welcome of Your Church* (Elgin, Ill.: Brethren Press, 2004), p. 22.

[17]Molly Marshall, *What It Means to Be Human* (Macon, Ga.: Smyth & Helwys, 2005), p. 34.

[18]Christine D. Pohl, *Making Room: Recovering Hospitality as a Christian Tradition* (Grand Rapids: Eerdmans, 1999), p. 33.

[19]Mike Breen, "Claiming New Territory," May 11, 2010, italics in original <http://mikebreen.wordpress.com/2010/05/11/claiming-new-territory/>.

[20]Ray Oldenburgh, *The Great Good Place* (New York: Paragon House, 1989).

[21]"Listening as Spiritual Hospitality," March 11, 2008, *Learning to Pray* <http://learningtopray.blogspot.com/2008/03/listening-as-spiritual-hospitality.html>.

[22]Peter Block, *Community: The Structure of Belonging* (San Francisco: Berrett-Koheler, 2008), p. 145.

[23]Tony Campolo, *The Kingdom of God Is a Party* (Nashville: Thomas Nelson, 1992), p. 26.

Chapter 10: The Gospel According to You

[1]Jim Wallis, *The Call to Conversion* (San Francisco: Harper & Row, 1981), p. 116.

[2]Lesslie Newbigin, *The Gospel in a Pluralist Society* (Grand Rapids: Eerdmans, 1989), p. 227.

[3]Thom S. Rainer, "Seven Sins of Dying Churches," *Outreach Magazine*, January-February 2006, p. 16.

[4]Reggie McNeal, *A Work of Heart* (San Francisco: Jossey-Bass, 2000), p. 91.

[5]Hugh Halter and Matt Smay, *AND: The Gathered and Scattered Church* (Grand Rapids: Zondervan, 2010), pp. 124-40.

[6]Ibid., italics theirs.

[7]Reggie McNeal, *Missional Renaissance: Changing the Scorecard for the Church* (San Francisco: Jossey-Bass, 2009), p. xvii. He offers numerous suggestions for measuring and rewarding the missional work of the church.

[8]Ibid., p. 93.

[9]Max DePree, *Leadership Is an Art* (New York: Doubleday, 1989, 2004), p. 11.

[10]Benjamin E. Zeller, "The Bricolage Religion of LOST and American Religious Culture," *Sightings*, July 22, 2010, posted on The Martin Marty Center <http://divinity.uchicago.edu/martycenter/publications/sightings/archive_2010/0722.shtml>. *LOST* was a TV series about the survivors of an airplane crash on a mysterious tropical island that wove together stories of the survivors' pasts and presents. It also slowly introduced the inhabitants of the island and what fans of the show call the island's "mythos"—the supernatural features of this sacred space.

[11]See the full Lady Gaga interview available on multiple Internet sites and on YouTube.

[12]Mark Driscoll, *The Radical Reformission* (Grand Rapids: Zondervan, 2004), p. 103.

[13]Kevin J. Vanhoozer, Charles A. Anderson and Michael J. Sleasman, eds., *Everyday Theology: How to Read Cultural Texts and Interpret Trends* (Grand Rapids: Baker, 2007), p. 55, emphasis in original.

[14]Kevin J. Vanhoozer, "The World Well Staged? Theology, Culture, and Hermeneutics," in *God and Culture: Essays in Honor of Carl F. H. Henry*, ed. D. A. Carson and John D. Woodbridge (Grand Rapids: Eerdmans, 1993), p. 29.

[15]James K. A. Smith, *Desiring the Kingdom* (Grand Rapids: Baker, 2009), pp. 18-35.

[16]Alvin J. Schmidt, *How Christianity Changed the World* (Grand Rapids: Zondervan, 2004).

[17]See Streaming Café <www.streamingcafe.net/>.

[18]Os Hillman, *The 9 to 5 Window: How Faith Can Transform the Workplace* (Ventura, Calif.: Regal, 2005), p. 13.

[19]Ibid., p. 81.

[20]Ibid., p. 23.

[21]Keith Meyer, *Whole Life Transformation: Becoming the Change Your Church Needs* (Downers Grove, Ill.: InterVarsity Press, 2010), p. 117. See Thomas Traherne, *Waking Up in Heaven* (Spencerville, Md.: Hesed Press, 2002).

[22]Michael Frost and Alan Hirsch, *The Shaping of Things to Come* (Peabody, Mass.: Hendrickson Publishers, 2003), p. 137.

[23]David Hansen, *The Art of Pastoring* (Downers Grove, Ill.: InterVarsity Press, 1994), p. 11.

Afterword

[1]See IMDb, "Quotes for Aslan" <www.imdb.com/character/ch0004976/quotes>.

[2]Earl Creps, *Off-Road Disciplines: Spiritual Adventures of Missional Leaders* (San Francisco: Jossey-Bass, 2006), p. 3.

[3]IMDb, "Quotes for Aslan."

[4]Luci Shaw, *The Crime of Living Cautiously* (Downers Grove, Ill.: InterVarsity Press, 2005), p. 137.

Appendix 1: Equipping for a Missional Spirituality in the Church and Academy

[1]Used by permission. Italics ours.

[2]See Keith R. Anderson and Randy D. Reese, *Spiritual Mentoring* (Downers Grove, Ill.: InterVarsity Press, 1999); Howard Rice, *The Pastor as Spiritual Guide* (Nashville: Upper Room, 1998).

[3]See Kevin Meyer, *Whole Life Transformation: Becoming the Change Your Church Needs* (Downers Grove, Ill.: InterVarsity Press, 2010), pp. 161-83; Marjorie Thompson, *Soul Feast* (Philadelphia: Westminster Press, 2005), pp. 137-45; Wil Derkse, *The Rule of Benedict for Beginners* (Collegeville, Minn.: Liturgical Press, 2003).

[4]See Phil Wagler, *Kingdom Culture: Growing the Missional Church* (Winnipeg: Word Alive Press, 2009).

[5]See Elizabeth O'Connor, *Call to Commitment* (New York: Harper & Row, 1963), pp. 23-38; Hugh Halter and Matt Smay, *The Tangible Kingdom* (San Francisco: Jossey-

Bass, 2008); Dietrich Bonhoeffer, *Life Together* (San Francisco: HarperSanFrancisco, 1954).

[6]See Heather Webb, *Small Group Leadership as Spiritual Direction* (Grand Rapids: Zondervan, 2005); M. Scott Boren, *Missional Small Groups* (Grand Rapids: Baker, 2010).

[7]See Todd Hunter, *Giving Church Another Chance* (Downers Grove, Ill.: InterVarsity Press, 2010).

[8]See Charles M. Olsen, *Transforming Church Boards into Communities of Spiritual Leaders* (Herndon, Va.: Alban Institute, 1995). We suggest that board meetings should be moved from boardrooms and churches to homes or third places in the community.

[9]Finnish sociologist Niklass Luhmann comments that community is a network of conversations, and organizational theorists have been paying attention to conversation as the fuel of learning communities. See Len Hjalmarson, "Conversation," in *An Emerging Dictionary for the Gospel and Culture* (Eugene, Ore.: Wipf & Stock, 2010), pp. 27-28.

[10]See Peter Block's citing of Werner Erhard's insights, *Community: The Structure of Belonging* (San Francisco: Berrett-Koheler, 2009), pp. 14-16.

[11]For suggestions on ways to change the scorecard, see Reggie McNeal, *Missional Renaissance* (San Francisco: Jossey-Bass, 2009), and Earl Creps, *Off-Road Disciplines: Spiritual Adventures of Missional Leaders* (San Francisco: Jossey-Bass, 2006), pp. 87-97.

[12]The father of liberal theology, German professor Friedrich Schleiermacher, sought to make theology a respectable university discipline in the late nineteenth century. We still live with his influence. For insightful and well-documented discussions of the history and current challenges of theological education with a vision for more leadership, spiritual and missional orientations, see Linda Cannell, *Theological Education Matters* (Newburgh, Ind.: EDCOT Press, 2007), and Robert Banks, *Reenvisioning Theological Education* (Grand Rapids: Eerdmans, 1999). Also see Keith Drury, "The Trouble with Seminaries," March 11, 2008, *Drury Writing* <www .drurywriting.com/keith/trouble.with.seminaries.htm>.

[13]For alternatives, see David Fitch, *The Great Giveaway* (Grand Rapids: Baker, 2005), pp. 71-94.

[14]Our interview was with David Fitch at Northern Seminary and Kenton Anderson at ACTS Seminaries. Northern Seminary now offers a Doctor of Ministry degree in missional church leadership. See <www.seminary.edu/future-students/academic-programs/doctoral/dmin-missional-leadership/>.

[15]See John Piper, *Brothers, We Are Not Professionals: A Plea to Pastors for Radical Ministry* (Nashville: Broadman and Holman Publishers, 2002).

[16]Gerald Hiestand, "The Pastor as Wider Theologian," First Things <www.firstthings .com/onthesquare/2011/01/the-pastor-as-wider-theologian-or-whatrsquos-wrong-with-theology-today>.

[17]Jeffrey P. Greenman and George Kalantzis, eds., *Life in the Spirit* (Downers Grove,

Ill.: InterVarsity Press, 2010).

[18]Ibid., pp. 29-49.

[19]Ibid., p. 237. See Edward Farley, *Theologia: The Fragmentation and Unity of Theological Education* (Philadelphia: Fortress, 1983).

[20]Ibid.

[21]Jeff Bailey, interview with Gordon Cosby in "The Journey Inward, Outward and Forward" *Cutting Edge Magazine*, Fall 2001, p. 10.

[22]Henri Nouwen, *In the Name of Jesus* (New York: Crossroad, 1989), pp. 65-66, 69.

[23]Robert E. Webber, *The Younger Evangelicals* (Grand Rapids: Baker, 2002), p. 240.

[24]Ibid., pp. 241-42.

[25]Gary V. Nelson, *Borderland Churches* (St. Louis: Chalice Press, 2008), pp. 65, 68.

[26]Ibid., p. 84.

[27]For a thorough proposal, see Robert Banks, *Reenvisioning Theological Education: Exploring a Missional Alternative to Current Models* (Grand Rapids: Eerdmans, 1999).

[28]Unfortunately the academy has its fair share of astute professors, scholars and instructors who are not effective teachers though they are effective researchers, writers and thinkers. To teach and equip effectively requires gifts and skills that create learning environments not confined to the presentation of abstract information.

[29]See Helmut Thielicke, *An Exercise for Young Theologians* (Grand Rapids: Eerdmans, 1980).

[30]For example, Gary Moon and David Benner, eds., *Spiritual Direction and the Care of Souls* (Downers Grove, Ill.: InterVarsity Press, 2006); Henri Nouwen, *Spiritual Direction* (San Francisco: HarperSanFrancisco, 2006); Eugene Peterson, *The Contemplative Pastor* (Grand Rapids: Eerdmans, 1989).

[31]For assistance and examples, see Marjorie J. Thompson, *Soul Feast* (Louisville, Ky.: Westminster John Knox Press, 2005), pp. 137-45; Keith Meyer, *Whole Life Transformation*, pp. 161-83; Derkse, *The Rule of Benedict for Beginners*.

[32]Alan and Debra Hirsch, *Untamed: Reactivating a Missional Form of Discipleship* (Grand Rapids: Baker, 2010), p. 29.

[33]See Alan E. Nelson, *Spirituality and Leadership* (Colorado Springs: NavPress, 2002).

[34]See Henri Nouwen, *Life of the Beloved* (New York: Crossroad, 1992). Also see Matthew 3:16-17; Luke 3:21-22; John 15:9.

[35]See Roger Helland, "Nothing Leadership," *Ministry*, November 2006, pp. 12-14.

[36]Nouwen, *In the Name of Jesus*, p. 59.

[37]The Arbinger Institute, *Leadership and Self-Deception* (San Francisco: Berrett-Koehler Publishers, 2010).

[38]Eugene Peterson, *Subversive Spirituality* (Grand Rapids: Eerdmans, 1997), p. 15.

[39]David J. Bosch, *Transforming Mission: Paradigm Shifts in Theology of Mission* (Maryknoll, N.Y.: Orbis, 1997), p. 390.

About the Authors

Roger Helland (Th.M., Dallas Theological Seminary; D.Min., Trinity Western University) is district executive coach of the Baptist General Conference in Alberta, Canada. Roger has also served as a pastor, church consultant, and Bible college and seminary instructor. He is the author of numerous articles and three  books: *The Journey*, *The Revived Church* and *Let the River Flow*. He has been a leader in the Vineyard, Mennonite Brethren, Christian and Missionary Alliance, and Baptist traditions. His mission is to help establish and empower missional, disciple-making leaders and churches.

Len Hjalmarson (M.Div., Mennonite Brethren Biblical Seminary; D.Min., Trinity Western University) is lead pastor at Aylmer Evangelical Mennonite Mission Church in Aylmer, Ontario, Canada, and serves as missional navigator for the Ontario region of the EMMC. Len is a found-  ing member of the Resonate network and sits on the board of Cultivate in Ontario. He is the author of numerous articles and is the author or editor of several books, including *An Emerging Dictionary for the Gospel and Culture*, *The Missional Church Fieldbook*, *Fresh and Refresh* and *Voices of the Virtual World*. He also blogs on <http://nextreformation.com>.

To contact Roger or Len, visit their website and blog at <http://missionalspirituality.com/>.